BLOOM'S

HOW TO WRITE ABOUT

James Joyce

KIM ALLEN GLEED

Introduction by Harold Bloom

BLOOM'S
LITERARY CRITICISM
An imprint of Infobase Publishing

Bloom's How to Write about James Joyce

Copyright © 2011 by Infobase Publishing
Introduction © 2011 by Harold Bloom

Bloom's Literary Criticism
An imprint of Infobase Publishing
132 West 31st Street
New York, NY 10001

Library of Congress Cataloging-in-Publication Data
Gleed, Kim Allen.
   Bloom's how to write about James Joyce / Kim Allen Gleed ; introduction by Harold Bloom.
      p. cm. — (Bloom's how to write about literature)
   Includes bibliographical references and index.
   ISBN 978-1-60413-715-6 (hardcover)
   1. Joyce, James, 1882–1941—Criticism and interpretation. 2. Criticism—Authorship. 3. Report writing. I. Bloom, Harold. II. Title. III. Title: How to write about James Joyce.
   PR6019.O9Z534 2010
   823'.912—dc22
                        2010017119

Bloom's Literary Criticism books are available at special discounts when purchased in bulk quantities for businesses, associations, institutions, or sales promotions. Please call our Special Sales Department in New York at (212)967-8800 or (800)322-8755.

You can find Bloom's Literary Criticism on the World Wide Web at http://www.chelseahouse.com

Text design by Annie O'Donnell
Cover design by Ben Peterson
Composition by IBT Global, Troy, NY
Cover printed by Art Print Company, Taylor, PA
Book printed and bound by Maple Press, York, PA
Date printed: October 2010
Printed in the United States of America

10 9 8 7 6 5 4 3 2 1

All links and Web addresses were checked and verified to be correct at the time of publication. Because of the dynamic nature of the Web, some addresses and links may have changed since publication and may no longer be valid.

CONTENTS

SERIES
INTRODUCTION

BLOOM's How to Write about Literature series is designed to inspire students to write fine essays on great writers and their works. Each volume in the series begins with an introduction by Harold Bloom, meditating on the challenges and rewards of writing about the volume's subject author. The first chapter then provides detailed instructions on how to write a good essay, including how to find a thesis; how to develop an outline; how to write a good introduction, body text, and conclusions; how to cite sources; and more. The second chapter provides a brief overview of the issues involved in writing about the subject author and then a number of suggestions for paper topics, with accompanying strategies for addressing each topic. Succeeding chapters cover the author's major works.

The paper topics suggested in this book are open ended, and the brief strategies provided are designed to give students a push forward on the writing process rather than a road map to success. The aim of the book is to pose questions, not answer them. Many different kinds of papers could result from each topic. As always, the success of each paper will depend completely on the writer's skill and imagination.

HOW TO WRITE ABOUT JAMES JOYCE: INTRODUCTION

by Harold Bloom

A MONG WESTERN writers of prose fiction in the 20th century, only James Joyce could dispute the foremost place with Marcel Proust, author of the huge and beautiful *In Search of Lost Time*. Not even *Ulysses*, magnificent epic, would suffice to justify the comparison. But Joyce's masterpiece is his final work, *Finnegans Wake*. The two masters therefore are commensurate.

Unfortunately the *Wake*, because of its merely initial difficulties, seems doomed only to have relatively few devoted readers. Essentially the central concern in writing about Joyce has to be what William Blake would have called the Giant Form of the protagonist of *Ulysses*: Poldy Bloom. To avoid a confusion between Blooms, I will refer to him as Poldy in what follows.

Joyce considered the Odysseus (Ulysses) of Homer's *Odyssey* as the most complete character in the world's literature. Homer tells the whole truth, which demands completeness. Poldy is an unusual Dubliner, Irish Catholic on his mother's side, Hungarian Jew on his father's. Though Joyce struggles to achieve Shakespearean detachment toward Poldy, I rejoice that he did not succeed. Poldy and Dublin are the chief characters in *Ulysses,* and Poldy is infinitely more sympathetic.

I advise anyone writing about *Ulysses* to study how Poldy gets away from Joyce, rather in the way Falstaff, Hamlet, and Cleopatra run out of their plays and inhabit the total literary universe. Not even Poldy is as inexhaustible to meditation as Falstaff is, but then we cannot ask Joyce to be Shakespeare (though he desired just that). Loving Dante more than Shakespeare, Joyce nevertheless answered the one-book-on-a-desert-island question by saying, "I would have to take the Englishman because he is *richer.*"

Writing about Poldy, you need to explore his psychic wealth, his flor-abundance of intricate feeling, and his spontaneous and incessant intellectual curiosity. Gradually you will become aware that Poldy *is* James Joyce, perhaps at least partly against Joyce's wishes. Many of Joyce's attempts to distance himself (and us) from Poldy by perspectivism do not work (at least for me). Irony, which dissolves meaning, cannot affect Poldy. Why?

Literary critics who have taken an ironic stance toward Falstaff seem to me in danger of sinking without trace. So formidable is Falstaff's wit, so glorious is his language, that carpers always lose. With Poldy, it is different. More like Shakespeare's Bottom, Poldy radiates good will and affectionate concern. Surrounded by Dubliners much given to hatred, Joyce's hero returns love and forgiveness.

And yet, Joyce has loaded the deck against Poldy: a cuckold, a sado-masochist, and a hopeless optimist. But how powerfully Poldy's depth of emotional sympathy reaches us. He is a sufferer who refuses to suffer, a representative of the human impulse to survive, and not at the expense of others.

HOW TO WRITE
A GOOD ESSAY

By Laurie A. Sterling and Kim Allen Gleed

WHILE THERE are many ways to write about literature, most assignments for high school and college English classes call for analytical papers. In these assignments, you are presenting your interpretation of a text to your reader. Your objective is to interpret the text's meaning in order to enhance your reader's understanding and enjoyment of the work. Without exception, strong papers about the meaning of a literary work are built on a careful, close reading of the text or texts. Careful, analytical reading should always be the first step in your writing process. This volume provides models of such close, analytical reading, and these should help you develop your own skills as a reader and as a writer.

As the examples throughout this book demonstrate, attentive reading entails thinking about and evaluating the formal (textual) aspects of the author's works: theme, character, form, and language. In addition, when writing about a work, many readers choose to move beyond the text itself to consider the work's cultural context. In these instances, writers might explore the historical circumstances of the time period in which the work was written. Alternatively, they might examine the philosophies and ideas that a work addresses. Even in cases where writers explore a work's cultural context, though, papers must still address the more formal aspects of the work itself. A good interpretative essay that evaluates Charles Dickens's use of the philosophy of utilitarianism in his novel *Hard Times*, for example, cannot adequately address the author's treatment of the philosophy without firmly grounding this discussion in the book itself. In other words, any analytical paper about a text, even one that seeks to evaluate the work's cultural context, must also have a firm handle on the work's themes, characters, and language. You must look for and evaluate these aspects of a work, then, as you read a text and as you prepare to write about it.

WRITING ABOUT THEMES

Literary themes are more than just topics or subjects treated in a work; they are attitudes or points about these topics that often structure other elements in a work. Writing about theme therefore requires that you not just identify a topic that a literary work addresses but also discuss what that work says about that topic. For example, if you were writing about the culture of the American South in William Faulkner's famous story "A Rose for Emily," you would need to discuss what Faulkner says, argues, or implies about that culture and its passing.

When you prepare to write about thematic concerns in a work of literature, you will probably discover that, like most works of literature, your text touches on other themes in addition to its central theme. These secondary themes also provide rich ground for paper topics. A thematic paper on "A Rose for Emily" might consider gender or race in the story. While neither of these could be said to be the central theme of the story, they are clearly related to the passing of the "old South" and could provide plenty of good material for papers.

As you prepare to write about themes in literature, you might find a number of strategies helpful. After you identify a theme or themes in the story, you should begin by evaluating how other elements of the story—such as character, point of view, imagery, and symbolism—help develop the theme. You might ask yourself what your own responses are to the author's treatment of the subject matter. Do not neglect the obvious, either: What expectations does the title set up? How does the title help develop thematic concerns? Clearly, the title "A Rose for Emily" says something about the narrator's attitude toward the title character, Emily Grierson, and all she represents.

WRITING ABOUT CHARACTER

Generally, characters are essential components of fiction and drama. (This is not always the case, though; Ray Bradbury's "August 2026: There

Will Come Soft Rains" is technically a story without characters, at least any human characters.) Often, you can discuss character in poetry, as in T. S. Eliot's "The Love Song of J. Alfred Prufrock" or Robert Browning's "My Last Duchess." Many writers find that analyzing character is one of the most interesting and engaging ways to work with a piece of literature and to shape a paper. After all, characters generally are human, and we all know something about being human and living in the world. While it is always important to remember that these figures are not real people but creations of the writer's imagination, it can be fruitful to begin evaluating them as you might evaluate a real person. Often you can start with your own response to a character. Did you like or dislike the character? Did you sympathize with the character? Why or why not?

Keep in mind, though, that emotional responses like these are just starting places. To truly explore and evaluate literary characters, you need to return to the formal aspects of the text and evaluate how the author has drawn these characters. The 20th-century writer E. M. Forster coined the terms *flat* characters and *round* characters. Flat characters are static, one-dimensional characters who frequently represent a particular concept or idea. In contrast, round characters are fully drawn and much more realistic characters who frequently change and develop over the course of a work. Are the characters you are studying flat or round? What elements of the characters lead you to this conclusion? Why might the author have drawn characters like this? How does their development affect the meaning of the work? Similarly, you should explore the techniques the author uses to develop characters. Do we hear a character's own words, or do we hear only other characters' assessments of him or her? Or, does the author use an omniscient or limited omniscient narrator to allow us access to the workings of the characters' minds? If so, how does that help develop the characterization? Often you can even evaluate the narrator as a character. How trustworthy are the opinions and assessments of the narrator? You should also think about characters' names. Do they mean anything? If you encounter a hero named Sophia or Sophie, you should probably think about her wisdom (or lack thereof), since *Sophia* means "wisdom" in Greek. Similarly, since the name *Sylvia* is derived from the word *sylvan,* meaning "of the wood," you might want to evaluate that character's relationship with nature. Once again, you might look to the title of the work. Does Herman Melville's "Bartleby, the Scrivener" signal anything about Bartleby himself? Is Bartleby adequately defined by his job as scrivener? Is this part of Melville's point? Pursuing questions like these can help you develop thorough papers about characters from psychological, sociological, or more formalistic perspectives.

WRITING ABOUT FORM AND GENRE

Genre, a word derived from French, means "type" or "class." Literary genres are distinctive classes or categories of literary composition. On the most general level, literary works can be divided into the genres of drama, poetry, fiction, and essays, yet within those genres there are classifications that are also referred to as genres. Tragedy and comedy, for example, are genres of drama. Epic, lyric, and pastoral are genres of poetry. *Form*, on the other hand, generally refers to the shape or structure of a work. There are many clearly defined forms of poetry that follow specific patterns of meter, rhyme, and stanza. Sonnets, for example, are poems that follow a fixed form of 14 lines. Sonnets generally follow one of two basic sonnet forms, each with its own distinct rhyme scheme. Haiku is another example of poetic form, traditionally consisting of three unrhymed lines of five, seven, and five syllables.

While you might think that writing about form or genre might leave little room for argument, many of these forms and genres are very fluid. Remember that literature is evolving and ever changing, and so are its forms. As you study poetry, you may find that poets, especially more modern poets, play with traditional poetic forms, bringing about new effects. Similarly, dramatic tragedy was once quite narrowly defined, but over the centuries playwrights have broadened and challenged traditional definitions, changing the shape of tragedy. When Arthur Miller wrote *Death of a Salesman,* many critics challenged the idea that tragic drama could encompass a common man like Willy Loman.

Evaluating how a work of literature fits into or challenges the boundaries of its form or genre can provide you with fruitful avenues of investigation. You might find it helpful to ask why the work does or does not fit into traditional categories. Why might Miller have thought it fitting to write a tragedy of the common man? Similarly, you might compare the content or theme of a work with its form. How well do they work together? Many of Emily Dickinson's poems, for instance, follow the meter of traditional hymns. While some of her poems seem to express traditional religious doctrines, many seem to challenge or strain against traditional conceptions of God and theology. What is the effect, then, of her use of traditional hymn meter?

WRITING ABOUT LANGUAGE, SYMBOLS, AND IMAGERY

No matter what the genre, writers use words as their most basic tool. Language is the most fundamental building block of literature. It is essential that you pay careful attention to the author's language and word choice as you read, reread, and analyze a text. Imagery is language that appeals to the senses. Most commonly, imagery appeals to our sense of vision, creating a mental picture, but authors also use language that appeals to our other senses. Images can be literal or figurative. Literal images use sensory language to describe an actual thing. In the broadest terms, figurative language uses one thing to speak about something else. For example, if I call my boss a snake, I am not saying that he is literally a reptile. Instead, I am using figurative language to communicate my opinions about him. Since we think of snakes as sneaky, slimy, and sinister, I am using the concrete image of a snake to communicate these abstract opinions and impressions.

The two most common figures of speech are similes and metaphors. Both are comparisons between two apparently dissimilar things. Similes are explicit comparisons using the words *like* or *as;* metaphors are implicit comparisons. To return to the previous example, if I say, "My boss, Bob, was waiting for me when I showed up to work five minutes late today—the snake!" I have constructed a metaphor. Writing about his experiences fighting in World War I, Wilfred Owen begins his poem "Dulce et decorum est" with a string of similes: "Bent double, like old beggars under sacks, / Knock-kneed, coughing like hags, we cursed through sludge." Owen's goal was to undercut clichéd notions that war and dying in battle were glorious. Certainly, comparing soldiers to coughing hags and to beggars underscores his point.

"Fog," a short poem by Carl Sandburg provides a clear example of a metaphor. Sandburg's poem reads:

The fog comes
on little cat feet.

It sits looking
over harbor and city
on silent haunches
and then moves on.

Notice how effectively Sandburg conveys surprising impressions of the fog by comparing two seemingly disparate things—the fog and a cat.

Symbols, by contrast, are things that stand for, or represent, other things. Often they represent something intangible, such as concepts or ideas. In everyday life we use and understand symbols easily. Babies at christenings and brides at weddings wear white to represent purity. Think, too, of a dollar bill. The paper itself has no value in and of itself. Instead, that paper bill is a symbol of something else, the precious metal in a nation's coffers. Symbols in literature work similarly. Authors use symbols to evoke more than a simple, straightforward, literal meaning. Characters, objects, and places can all function as symbols. Famous literary examples of symbols include Moby Dick, the white whale of Herman Melville's novel, and the scarlet *A* of Nathaniel Hawthorne's *The Scarlet Letter.* As both of these symbols suggest, a literary symbol cannot be adequately defined or explained by any one meaning. Hester Prynne's Puritan community clearly intends her scarlet *A* as a symbol of her adultery, but as the novel progresses, even her own community reads the letter as representing not just *adultery*, but *able, angel,* and a host of other meanings.

Writing about imagery and symbols requires close attention to the author's language. To prepare a paper on symbolism or imagery in a work, identify and trace the images and symbols and then try to draw some conclusions about how they function. Ask yourself how any symbols or images help contribute to the themes or meanings of the work. What connotations do they carry? How do they affect your reception of the work? Do they shed light on characters or settings? A strong paper on imagery or symbolism will thoroughly consider the use of figures in the text and will try to reach some conclusions about how or why the author uses them.

WRITING ABOUT HISTORY AND CONTEXT

As noted above, it is possible to write an analytical paper that also considers the work's context. After all, the text was not created in a vacuum. The author lived and wrote in a specific time period and in a specific cultural context and, like all of us, was shaped by that environment. Learning more about the historical and cultural circumstances that surround the author and the work can help illuminate a text and provide you with productive material for a paper. Remember, though, that when you write analytical papers, you should use the context to illuminate the text. Do not lose sight of your goal—to interpret the meaning of the literary work. Use historical or philosophical research as a tool to develop your textual evaluation.

Thoughtful readers often consider how history and culture affected the author's choice and treatment of his or her subject matter. Investigations into the history and context of a work could examine the work's relation to specific historical events, such as the Salem witch trials in 17th-century Malden, Massachusetts, or the restoration of Charles to the British throne in 1660. Bear in mind that historical context is not limited to politics and world events. While knowing about the Vietnam War is certainly helpful in interpreting much of Tim O'Brien's fiction, and some knowledge of the French Revolution clearly illuminates the dynamics of Charles Dickens's *A Tale of Two Cities,* historical context also entails the fabric of daily life. Examining a text in light of gender roles, race relations, class boundaries, or working conditions can give rise to thoughtful and compelling papers. Exploring the conditions of the working class in 19th-century England, for example, can provide a particularly effective avenue for writing about Dickens's *Hard Times.*

You can begin thinking about these issues by asking broad questions at first. What do you know about the time period and about the author? What does the editorial apparatus in your text tell you? These might be starting places. Similarly, when specific historical events or dynamics are particularly important to understanding a work but might be somewhat obscure to modern readers, textbooks usually provide notes to explain historical background. These are a good place to start. With this information, ask yourself how these historical facts and circumstances might have affected the author, the presentation of theme, and the presentation of character. How does knowing more about the work's specific historical context illuminate the work? To take a well-known example, understanding the complex attitudes toward slavery during the time Mark Twain wrote *Adventures of Huckleberry Finn* should help you begin to examine issues of race in the text. Additionally, you might compare these attitudes to those of the time in which the novel was set. How might this comparison affect your interpretation of a work written after the abolition of slavery but set before the Civil War?

WRITING ABOUT PHILOSOPHY AND IDEAS

Philosophical concerns are closely related to both historical context and thematic issues. Like historical investigation, philosophical research can provide a useful tool as you analyze a text. For example, an investigation into the working class in Dickens's England might lead you to a topic on the philosophical doctrine of utilitarianism in *Hard Times.* Many other works explore philosophies and ideas quite explicitly. Mary Shelley's famous novel *Frankenstein,* for example, explores John Locke's tabula rasa theory of human knowledge as she portrays the intellectual and emotional development of Victor Frankenstein's creature. As this example indicates, philosophical issues are somewhat more abstract than investigations of theme or historical context. Some other examples of philosophical issues include human free will, the formation of human identity, the nature of sin, or questions of ethics.

Writing about philosophy and ideas might require some outside research, but usually the notes or other material in your text will provide you with basic information and often footnotes and bibliographies suggest places you can go to read further about the subject. If you have identified a philosophical theme that runs through a text, you might ask yourself how the author develops this theme. Look at character development and the interactions of characters, for example. Similarly, you might examine whether the narrative voice in a work of fiction addresses the philosophical concerns of the text.

WRITING COMPARISON AND CONTRAST ESSAYS

Finally, you might find that comparing and contrasting the works or techniques of an author provides a useful tool for literary analysis. A comparison and contrast essay might compare two characters or themes in a single work, or it might compare the author's treatment of a theme in two works. It might also contrast methods of character development or analyze an author's differing treatment of a philosophical concern in two works. Writing comparison and contrast essays, though, requires some special consideration. While they generally provide you with plenty of material to use, they also come with a built-in trap: the laundry list. These papers often become mere lists of connections between the works. As this chapter will discuss, a strong thesis must make an assertion that you want to prove or validate. A strong comparison/contrast thesis, then, needs to comment on the significance of the similarities and differences you observe. It is not enough merely to assert that the works contain similarities and differences. You might, for example, assert why the similarities and differences are important and explain how they illuminate the works' treatment of theme. Remember, too, that a thesis should not be a statement of the obvious. A comparison/contrast paper that focuses only on very obvious similarities or differences does little to illuminate the connections between the works. Often, an effective method of shaping a strong thesis and argument is to begin your paper by noting the similarities between the works but then to develop a thesis that asserts how these apparently similar elements are different. If, for example, you observe that Emily Dickinson wrote a number of poems about spiders, you might analyze how she uses spider imagery differently in two poems. Similarly, many scholars have noted that Hawthorne created many "mad scientist" characters, men who are so devoted to their science or their art that they lose perspective on all else. A good thesis comparing two of these characters—Aylmer of "The Birth-mark" and Dr. Rappaccini of "Rappaccini's Daughter," for example—might initially identify both characters as examples of Hawthorne's mad scientist type but then argue that their motivations for scientific experimentation differ. If you strive to analyze the similarities or differences, discuss significances, and move beyond the obvious, your paper should move beyond the laundry list trap.

PREPARING TO WRITE

Armed with a clear sense of your task—illuminating the text—and with an understanding of theme, character, language, history, and philosophy, you are ready to approach the writing process. Remember that good writing is grounded in good reading and that close reading takes time, attention, and more than one reading of your text. Read for comprehension first. As you go back and review the work, mark the text to chart the details of the work as well as your reactions. Highlight important passages, repeated words, and image patterns. "Converse" with the text through marginal notes. Mark turns in the plot, ask questions, and make observations about characters, themes, and language. If you are reading from a book that does not belong to you, keep a record of your reactions in a journal or notebook. If you have read a work of literature carefully, paying attention to both the text and the context of the work, you have a leg up on the writing process. Admittedly, at this point, your ideas are probably very broad and undefined, but you have taken an important first step toward writing a strong paper.

Your next step is to focus, to take a broad, perhaps fuzzy, topic and define it more clearly. Even a topic provided by your instructor will need to be focused appropriately. Remember that good writers make the topic their own. There are a number of strategies—often called "invention"—that you can use to develop your own focus. In one such strategy, called *freewriting*, you spend 10 minutes or so just writing about your topic without referring back to the text or your notes. Write whatever comes to mind; the important thing is that you just keep writing. Often this process allows you to develop fresh ideas or approaches to your subject matter. You could also try *brainstorming*: Write down your topic and then list all the related points or ideas you can think of. Include questions, comments, words, important passages or events, and anything else that comes to mind. Let one idea lead to another. In the related technique of *clustering*, or *mapping*, write your topic on a sheet of paper and write related ideas around it. Then list related subpoints under each of these main ideas. Many people then draw arrows to show connections between points. This technique helps you narrow your topic and can also help you organize your ideas. Similarly, asking journalistic questions—Who? What? Where? When? Why? and How?—can develop ideas for topic development.

Thesis Statements

Once you have developed a focused topic, you can begin to think about your thesis statement, the main point or purpose of your paper. It is imperative that you craft a strong thesis, otherwise, your paper will likely be little more than random, disorganized observations about the text. Think of your thesis statement as a kind of road map for your paper. It tells your reader where you are going and how you are going to get there.

To craft a good thesis, you must keep a number of things in mind. First, as the title of this subsection indicates, your paper's thesis should be a statement, an assertion about the text that you want to prove or validate. Beginning writers often formulate a question that they attempt to use as a thesis. For example, a writer exploring the theme of paralysis in Joyce's *Dubliners* might ask, Why are so many characters in *Dubliners* trapped or paralyzed in their particular situations? While a question like this is a good strategy to use in the invention process to help narrow your topic and find your thesis, it cannot serve as the thesis statement because it does not tell your reader what you want to assert about paralysis. You might shape this question into a thesis by instead proposing an answer to that question: In *Dubliners*, all the main characters are paralyzed, rooted in their unfortunate situations. At the core of this paralysis, Joyce insinuates, is the institution of the Roman Catholic Church and the traditions of Irish society and culture. Notice that this thesis provides an initial plan or structure for the rest of the paper, and notice, too, that the thesis statement does not necessarily have to fit into one sentence. After discussing paralysis in general, and then paralysis specific to a few of the characters, you will examine the ways in which the Roman Catholic Church and the traditions and expectations in Irish culture at the turn of the century cause this paralysis. You would use the particular examples of several characters who are unable to move, both physically (Eveline, frozen on the dock as she watches Frank leave for Buenos Aires without her) and figuratively (the young narrator in "Araby," immobilized by his "vanity" and "anguish").

Second, remember that a good thesis makes an assertion that you need to support. In other words, a good thesis does not state the obvious. If you tried to formulate a thesis about paralysis by simply saying, Paralysis is important in *Dubliners*, you have done nothing but rephrase the obvious. Since several of Joyce's short stories in the collection are centered on the theme of paralysis, there would be no point in spending three to five pages supporting that assertion. You might try to develop a thesis from that point by asking yourself some further questions: What does it mean to be paralyzed in the Joycean context? Why does the young narrator in "The Sisters" fixate on the word *paralysis*? Are there any characters in *Dubliners* who embody momentum and movement as opposed to paralysis? Does Joyce seem to indicate that paralysis is a natural or unnatural phenomenon in this society? Does he present paralysis as the byproduct of the oppression of Catholicism and an overly traditional, conservative Irish society and culture? Such a line of questioning might lead you to a more viable thesis, such as the one in the preceding paragraph.

As the comparison with the road map also suggests, your thesis should appear near the beginning of the paper. In relatively short papers (three to six pages) the thesis almost always appears in the first paragraph. Some writers fall into the trap of saving their thesis for the end, trying to provide a surprise or a big moment of revelation, as if to say, "TA-DA! I've just proved that in *A Portrait of the Artist as a Young Man*, Joyce uses birds to symbolize the protagonist's desires to escape or fly away from what he perceives to be his entrapment in the prison of Ireland." Placing a thesis at the end of an essay can seriously mar the essay's effectiveness. If you fail to define your essay's point and purpose clearly at the beginning, your reader will find it difficult to assess the clarity of your argument and understand the points you are making. When your argument comes as a surprise at the end, you force your reader to reread your essay in order to assess its logic and effectiveness.

Finally, you should avoid using the first person ("I") as you present your thesis. Though it is not strictly wrong to write in the first person, it is difficult to do so gracefully. While writing in the first person, beginning writers often fall into the trap of writing self-reflexive prose (writing *about* their paper *in* their paper). Often this leads to the most dreaded of opening lines: "In this paper I am going to discuss [fill in the blank]." Not only does this self-reflexive voice make for very awkward prose, it frequently allows writers to boldly announce a topic while completely avoiding a thesis statement. An example might be a paper that begins as follows: "The Dead," Joyce's most famous story, takes place at a holiday dinner dance during which Gabriel Conroy, the story's protagonist, has an epiphany about his marriage to his wife, Gretta. In this paper, I am going to discuss the importance of his epiphany. The author of this paper has done little more than announce a general topic for the paper, namely, the epiphany of Gabriel Conroy. While the last sentence might be the starting point for a thesis, the writer fails to present an opinion about the significance of the epiphany. To improve this "thesis," the writer would need to back up a couple of steps. First, the announced topic of the paper is too broad; it largely summarizes the events in the story, without saying anything about the ideas in the story. The writer should highlight what she considers the meaning of the story: What is the story about? The writer might conclude that Gabriel's epiphany serves to reveal his feelings of isolation and frustration in his life, thinking he knows his wife, but all these years she has had a secret in the depths of her heart. From here, the author could select the means by which Joyce explores the emotions of Gabriel as he experiences his epiphany and the significance of the event for the story as a whole. Once the writer has investigated these questions, having returned to the text for a close reading, he or she can then begin to craft a specific thesis. A writer who chooses to explore the moments of mild frustration during the dinner/ dance that lead up to Gabriel's epiphany later that evening when alone with his wife might, for example, craft a thesis that reads, "The Dead" is a story that explores the cumulative effects of isolation and frustration on one man, Gabriel Conroy, whose whole world changes in an evening when his wife, Gretta, tells him about a former love who died for her. The interactions between Gabriel and the dinner guests prior to his epiphany hint at the protagonist's feelings of isolation and frustration, but the confession made by Gretta at the end of the story causes his ultimate disappointment.

Outlines

While developing a strong, thoughtful thesis early in your writing process should help focus your paper, outlining provides an essential tool for logically shaping that paper. A good outline helps you see—and develop—the relationships among the points in your argument and assures you that your paper flows logically and coherently. Outlining not only helps place your points in a logical order but also helps you subordinate supporting points, weed out any irrelevant points, and decide if there are any necessary points that are missing from your argument. Most of us are familiar with formal outlines that use numerical and letter designations for each point. However, there are different types of outlines; you may find that an informal outline is a more useful tool for you. What is important, though, is that you spend the time to develop some sort of outline—formal or informal.

Remember that an outline is a tool to help you shape and write a strong paper. If you do not spend sufficient time planning your supporting points and shaping the arrangement of those points, you will most likely construct a vague, unfocused outline that provides little, if any, help with the writing of the paper. Consider the following example.

Thesis: "The Dead" is a story that explores the cumulative effects of isolation and frustration on one man, Gabriel Conroy, whose whole world changes in an evening when his wife, Gretta, tells him about a former love who died for her. The interactions between Gabriel and the dinner guests prior to his epiphany hint at the protagonist's feelings of isolation and frustration, but the confession made by Gretta at the end of the story causes his ultimate disappointment.

   I. Introduction and thesis

  II. Gabriel
       A. Conversation with Lily
       B. Conversation with his aunts

 III. Conversation with Miss Ivors
       A. Dinner speech

  IV. Sexual frustration

   V. Gretta
       A. Gabriel's epiphany is foreshadowed by the events earlier in the evening.

This outline has a number of flaws. First, the major topics labeled with the roman numerals are not arranged in a logical order. If the paper's aim is to show how Gabriel is frustrated in his personal life, the writer should establish the particulars of that attitude before showing how frustration is evident in individual interactions or conversations. Similarly, the thesis makes no specific reference to the conversation with Miss Ivors, but the writer includes this as a major section of this outline. The dinner speech, which is placed as a point under the major section featuring Miss Ivors, should either be a point on its own or categorized with the Miss Ivors conversation under the Gabriel roman numeral. Certainly both of these scenes contribute to establishing the overall feeling of frustration and isolation that Gabriel experiences, and they certainly have an important place in this paper, but the writer fails to organize these appropriately. Sexual frustration, though it might be relevant to his overall frustration, does not logically merit a major section. The writer could, however, discuss this in another section of the essay. Third, the writer includes a section A in sections III and V. An outline should not include an A without a B, a 1 without a 2, and so on. The fourth problem with this outline is Section V, which is presumably the conclusion, but the writer devotes this section to a discussion of Gabriel's wife, Gretta. Although the writer will certainly use Gretta's confiding her secret to Gabriel as an example of the proverbial last straw in terms of his frustration and isolation, this should not come in the conclusion. A separate section should be devoted to the conclusion. The final problem with this outline is the overall lack of detail. None of the sections provide much information about the content of the argument, and it seems likely that the writer has not given sufficient thought to the support for the paper.

A better start to this outline might be the following:

Thesis: "The Dead" is a story that explores the cumulative effects of isolation and frustration on one man, Gabriel Conroy, whose whole world changes in an evening when his wife, Gretta, tells him about a former love who died for her. The interactions between Gabriel and the dinner guests prior to his epiphany hint at the protagonist's feelings of isolation and frustration, but the confession made by Gretta at the end of the story causes his ultimate disappointment.

    I. Introduction and thesis

   II. Gabriel's feelings of frustration and isolation
       A. In his work
       B. In his relationship with his wife

C. As demonstrated by his thoughts over the course of the evening

  III. Gabriel's interactions with dinner guests
      A. Conversation with Lily
      B. Conversation with his aunts
      C. Conversation with Miss Ivors
      D. Dinner speech

  IV. Gretta's confession
      A. Gabriel does not anticipate what is about to happen
      B. Gretta's secret from her past causes epiphany

  V. Conclusion

This new outline would prove much more helpful when it came time to write the paper.

An outline like this could be shaped into an even more useful tool if the writer fleshed out the argument by providing specific examples from the text to support each point. Once you have listed your main point and your supporting ideas, develop this raw material by listing related supporting ideas and material under each of those main headings. From there, arrange the material in subsections and order the material logically.

For example, you might begin with one of the theses cited above: In *Dubliners,* all the main characters are paralyzed, rooted in their unfortunate situations. At the core of this paralysis, Joyce insinuates, is the institution of the Roman Catholic Church and the traditions of Irish society and culture. As previously noted, this thesis already gives you the beginning of an organization: Start by supporting the notion that all the characters are paralyzed in some way (either physically, spiritually, or emotionally) and then explain how Joyce presents this condition as created by the institutions of Roman Catholicism and Irish society. You might begin your outline, then, with four topic headings: (1) defining Joycean paralysis, (2) examples of paralysis in characters in *Dubliners,* (3) roots of paralysis in Catholicism, and (4) roots of paralysis in Irish culture. Under each of those headings, you could list ideas that support the particular point. Be sure to include references to parts of the text that help build your case.

An informal outline might look like this:

Thesis: In *Dubliners,* all the main characters are paralyzed, rooted in their unfortunate situations. At the core of this paralysis, Joyce insinuates, is the institution of the Roman Catholic Church and the traditions of Irish society and culture.

1. Defining Joycean paralysis
   - Emotional paralysis
   - Physical paralysis
   - Spiritual paralysis

2. Examples of paralysis in *Dubliners*
   - First note that nearly all the characters in the stories suffer some form of Joycean paralysis
     - Focus on example of Eveline for emotional paralysis
     - Focus on example of Father Flynn for physical paralysis
     - Focus on example of Mr. Kernan for spiritual paralysis
   - Eveline wants safety, security, peace of mind that comes with relationship with Frank
     - Plans her escape from Dublin monotony and misery with Frank
     - Gets to docks to board ship for Buenos Aires but is paralyzed with fear and cannot go
   - Father Flynn was physically paralyzed but also suffered emotional paralysis
     - "There was no hope for him this time: it was the third stroke"
     - "there was something queer coming over him lately"

- Mr. Kernan suffers from spiritual paralysis, exacerbated by the insistence on his attending a retreat
    - "Mr Kernan came of Protestant stock and, though he had been converted to the Catholic faith at the time of his marriage, he had not been in the pale of the Church for twenty years."

3. Roots of paralysis in Roman Catholicism
    - Example of Mr. Kernan
        - "Well, Mrs Kernan, we're going to make your man here a good holy pious and God-fearing Roman Catholic"
        - Kernan does not want to go to the retreat but is pressured into it by his wife and "friends"
    - Example of Father Flynn and how the church can be a negative force

4. Roots of paralysis in Irish society and culture
    - Individuals wield virtually no power in this world; life is dictated by cultural norms and expectations
        - Eveline is unable to escape because of the expectation that she must care for her widowed father
        - Kernan must convert to Catholicism in order to marry his wife
    - In order to survive, most of the characters in *Dubliners* sacrifice their lives to Church and culture

Conclusion:
- Flynn's paralysis ends with his death, but other characters in the story remain paralyzed

- Kernan remains spiritually paralyzed due to lack of connection with institutionalized religion
- Eveline will remain a prisoner and will likely become like Maria in "Clay"

You would set about writing a formal outline with a similar process, though in the final stages you would label the headings differently. A formal outline for a paper that argues the thesis about "The Dead" previously cited—that the protagonist's frustration and isolation is revealed not only at the moment of his epiphany, but in moments throughout the entire evening—might look like this:

Thesis: "The Dead" is a story that explores the cumulative effects of isolation and frustration on one man, Gabriel Conroy, whose whole world changes in an evening when his wife, Gretta, tells him about a former love who died for her. The interactions between Gabriel and the dinner guests prior to his epiphany hint at the protagonist's feelings of isolation and frustration, but the confession made by Gretta at the end of the story causes his ultimate disappointment.

I. Introduction and thesis

II. Gabriel's feelings of frustration and isolation
    A. In his work
        1. Teaches at the college
        2. Writes book reviews for the books, not the money
        3. "murmured lamely that he saw nothing political in writing reviews of books"
    B. In his relationship with his wife
        1. Mildly embarrassed when Gretta teases him in front of his aunts

        2. Longs to be intimate with Gretta at the end of the evening

   C. As demonstrated by his thoughts over the course of the evening

        1. Sees himself as different from dinner guests

        2. Questions the tone and level of his speech

III. Gabriel's interactions with dinner guests

   A. Conversation with Lily

        1. "The men that is now is only palaver and what they can get out of you"

        2. Gabriel's awkwardness in giving Lily a Christmas tip

   B. Conversation with his aunts

        1. "Gabriel's solicitude was a standing joke with them"

        2. Joke about galoshes and gentle teasing from his aunts and wife

   C. Conversation with Miss Ivors

        1. Discussion of writing for *The Daily Express*, accusation of being a "West Briton"

        2. Questioning about Gabriel's sense of patriotism, ends in "I'm sick of my own country, sick of it!"

   D. Dinner speech

        1. Questions the contents of the speech intermittently through the evening

           a. Wonders whether references will resonate with listeners

           b. Shifts focus as a means of chastising Miss Ivors

        2. "I am afraid my poor powers as a speaker are all too inadequate"—self-deprecation

3. Reference to Three Graces goes over Aunt Julia's head

IV. Gretta's confession
   A. Gabriel does not anticipate what is about to happen
      1. He cannot read his wife's emotions; is only aware of his own desire for her
         a. Gretta's faraway look as she listens to the music
         b. Gretta is a symbol of something
         c. "Gabriel saw that there was colour on her cheeks and that her eyes were shining. A sudden tide of joy went leaping out of his heart"
      2. Gabriel filled with desire for Gretta on cab ride home, on arrival at hotel
         a. Fond memories of their past together
         b. "But now after the kindling again of so many memories, the first touch of her body, musical and strange and perfumed, sent through him a keen pang of lust"
         c. Gretta kisses Gabriel because of his generosity with Freddy Malins, but he imagines it is a sign of her desire for intimacy
   B. Gretta's secret from her past causes Gabriel's epiphany
      1. "Gabriel stood stock-still for a moment in astonishment"

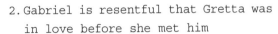

      2. Gabriel is resentful that Gretta was
        in love before she met him
          a. Michael Furey was a "very
            delicate" boy who used to sing
            to Gretta
          b. Furey was in the gasworks
      3. Resentment turns to shame and
        self-loathing for his thoughts and
        actions over the evening

V. Conclusion
    A. How this story comments on the basic
      human need for connection, understanding
    B. Connections to other Joyce characters
      1. The young narrator from "Araby"
      2. Little Chandler from "A Little
        Cloud"

As in the previous example outline, the thesis provided the seeds of a structure, and the writer was careful to arrange the supporting points in a logical manner, showing the relationships among the ideas in the paper.

Body Paragraphs

Once your outline is complete, you can begin drafting your paper. Paragraphs, units of related sentences, are the building blocks of a good paper, and as you draft you should keep in mind both the function and the qualities of good paragraphs. Paragraphs help you chart and control the shape and content of your essay, and they help the reader see your organization and your logic. You should begin a new paragraph whenever you move from one major point to another. In longer, more complex essays you might use a group of related paragraphs to support major points. Remember that in addition to being adequately developed, a good paragraph is both unified and coherent.

Unified Paragraphs

Each paragraph must be centered around one idea or point, and a unified paragraph carefully focuses on and develops this central idea without including extraneous ideas or tangents. For beginning writers, the best way to ensure that you are constructing unified paragraphs is to include a topic sentence in each paragraph. This topic sentence should convey the main point of the paragraph, and every sentence in the paragraph should relate to that topic sentence. Any sentence that strays from the central topic does not belong in the paragraph and needs to be revised or deleted. Consider the following paragraph about how the individual's choices in the turn-of-the-century Dublin of *A Portrait of the Artist as a Young Man* are limited by the Roman Catholic Church and Irish tradition. Notice how the paragraph veers away from the main point that the Church's influence is an impediment to creativity:

In turn-of-the-century Ireland, the setting for *A Portrait of the Artist as a Young Man*, the choices that the characters have available to them are limited by Catholicism and the traditions of Irish society. Stephen Dedalus in particular, as a budding artist, finds it difficult to negotiate the expectations placed on him in his Dublin world. The intellectual side of him finds the ways of Irish society backward and overly immersed in the past. He is not interested in Irish politics or learning to speak the Irish language. He expresses a brief interest in the priesthood but only in response to a fire and brimstone sermon he heard at a retreat. The level of his fervor for the vocation is equal to the fervor with which he frequented prostitutes prior to returning to the church, but it is forced and unnatural for Stephen; he is stifling his true self. The conversation Stephen has with the dean of studies about the tundish/funnel reveals a great deal about Stephen's views of Catholicism and also tells us much about the political dynamics of this relationship, as the priest is British. Thus, the priest highlights and represents both the social and political constraints of the British government as well as the demands and expectations of the Catholic Church.

Although the paragraph begins solidly and the second sentence provides the central idea of the paragraph, the author soon goes on a tangent. If the purpose of the paragraph is to demonstrate that the church and Irish society stifle the artist's individuality, the sentences about Irish politics and language are tangential here. They may find a place later in the paper, but they should be deleted from this paragraph.

Coherent Paragraphs

In addition to shaping unified paragraphs, you must also craft coherent paragraphs, ones that develop their points logically with sentences that flow smoothly into one another. Coherence depends on the order of your sentences, but it is not strictly the order of the sentences that is important to paragraph coherence. You also need to craft your prose to help the reader see the relationship among the sentences.

Consider the following paragraph about the influence of church and society in *Portrait*. Notice how the writer uses the same ideas as the paragraph above yet fails to help the reader see the relationships among the points.

> The choices that the characters in *A Portrait of the Artist as a Young Man* have available to them are very limited by Catholicism and the traditions of Irish society. Stephen Dedalus in particular, as a budding artist, finds it difficult to negotiate the expectations placed on him in his Dublin world. He considers becoming a priest but then sees a girl on the beach and changes his mind. The intellectual side of him finds the ways of Irish society backward and overly immersed in the past. He is not interested in Irish politics or learning to speak the Irish language. He expresses a brief interest in the priesthood but only in response to a fire and brimstone sermon he heard at a retreat. The level of his fervor for the vocation is equal to the fervor with which he frequented prostitutes prior to returning to the church, but it is forced and unnatural for Stephen; he is stifling his true self. He leaves the Catholic Church permanently. The conversation Stephen has with the dean of studies about the tundish/funnel reveals a great deal about Stephen's views of Catholicism, and also tells us much about the political dynamics of this

relationship. The priest highlights and represents both the social and political constraints of the British government as well as the demands and expectations of the Catholic Church.

This paragraph demonstrates that unity alone does not guarantee a paragraph's effectiveness. The argument is hard to follow because the author fails both to show connections between the sentences and to indicate how they work to support the overall point.

A number of techniques are available to aid paragraph coherence. Careful use of transitional words and phrases is essential. You can use transitional flags to introduce an example or an illustration *(for example, for instance)*, to amplify a point or add another phase of the same idea *(additionally, furthermore, next, similarly, finally, then)*, to indicate a conclusion or result *(therefore, as a result, thus, in other words)*, to signal a contrast or a qualification *(on the other hand, nevertheless, despite this, on the contrary, still, however, conversely)*, to signal a comparison *(likewise, in comparison, similarly)*, and to indicate a movement in time *(afterward, earlier, eventually, finally, later, subsequently, until)*.

In addition to transitional flags, careful use of pronouns aids coherence and flow. If you were writing about *The Wizard of Oz*, you would not want to keep repeating the phrase *the witch* or the name *Dorothy*. Careful substitution of the pronoun *she* in these instances can aid coherence. A word of warning, though: When you substitute pronouns for proper names, always be sure that your pronoun reference is clear. In a paragraph that discusses both Dorothy and the witch, substituting *she* could lead to confusion. Make sure that it is clear to whom the pronoun refers. Generally, the pronoun refers to the last proper noun you have used.

While repeating the same name over and over again can lead to awkward, boring prose, it is possible to use repetition to help your paragraph's coherence. Careful repetition of important words or phrases can lend coherence to your paragraph by reminding readers of your key points. Admittedly, it takes some practice to use this technique effectively. You may find that reading your prose aloud can help you develop an ear for effective use of repetition.

To see how helpful transitional aids are, compare the paragraph below to the preceding paragraph about the impact of society and church in *Portrait*. Notice how the author works with the same ideas but shapes them into a much more coherent paragraph whose point is clearer and easier to follow.

> The choices that the characters in *A Portrait of the Artist as a Young Man* have available to them are very limited by Catholicism and the traditions of Irish society. Stephen Dedalus in particular, as a budding artist, finds it difficult to negotiate the expectations placed on him in his Dublin world. Church and society play important roles in the shaping of the young man's life, and although he ultimately decides to turn his back on both, they have a tremendous impact on him, if only because they strictly limit the choices he is able to make. The intellectual side of Stephen Dedalus finds the ways of Irish society backward and overly immersed in the past. He grew up listening to debates (the most striking being one over Christmas dinner) about politics but has no interest in them, seeing no positive outcome of it, sharing with Cranly that "honorable and sincere men" have been "sold to the enemy or failed . . . in need or reviled . . . and left . . . for another." He sees Irish culture as only a restraining force in his life. He also expresses a brief interest in the priesthood but only in response to a fire and brimstone sermon he heard at a retreat. His notions about a vocation, however, change when he sees a beautiful girl on the beach. The level of his temporary fervor for religion is equal to the fervor with which he frequented prostitutes prior to returning to the church, but it is forced and unnatural for Stephen; he is stifling his true self. With the recognition of the "heavenly" beauty of the girl on the beach, Stephen leaves the Catholic Church permanently. Perhaps the best representation of the constraints of church and state combine in the character of the dean of studies with whom Stephen has a conversation about aesthetics, which leads to the discussion of terminology surrounding the words *tundish* and *funnel*.

This exchange reveals a great deal about Stephen's views of Catholicism and also tells us much about the political dynamics of this relationship. The priest highlights and represents both the social and political constraints of the British government as well as the demands and expectations of the Catholic Church.

Similarly, the following paragraph from a paper on Gabriel's feelings of frustration and isolation in "The Dead" demonstrates both unity and coherence. In it, the author argues that Joyce foreshadows Gabriel's epiphany and ultimate disappointment at the end of the story with several failed conversations throughout the evening prior to Gretta's confession.

Gabriel's interactions with the dinner guests throughout the evening work to foreshadow his epiphany at the end of the evening, creating a culminating effect when Gretta confesses her past love. When he first enters his aunts' home, he is greeted by Lily, the caretaker's daughter with whom he has the first conversation of the evening. He asks her about her schooling, and when she tells him that she is done, he happily suggests to her that they should soon be attending her wedding. She "glanced back at him over her shoulder and said with great bitterness: —The men that is now is only all palaver and what they can get out of you." Gabriel is embarrassed by his lack of delicacy and tries to make up for his mistake with a gesture of holiday goodwill: He offers Lily a coin as a Christmas tip. She accepts but only after heartily trying to refuse. Gabriel's next frustration comes in his conversation with his Aunts Julia and Kate. He greets them as Gretta playfully teases him about his insistence on her wearing galoshes, which they all find hysterically funny. Gabriel "laughed nervously and patted his tie reassuringly" as they laugh. Although this is an instance of gently joking at Gabriel's expense, it serves to show him in a particular light. The most obvious scene in which Gabriel is shown as frustrated and isolated is the one in which he goes head to head with Miss Ivors during their dance. She begins by telling him she has a "crow to pluck" with him and then coyly asks him about "G.C." Gabriel considers playing dumb but realizes she will see through the act and defends himself, asking why he should be ashamed of a literary column. She accuses him of being a "West Briton" because the paper for which he writes is *The Daily Express*, a newspaper with British sympathies. She then interrogates him about his summer vacation, urging him to visit the west of Ireland to reconnect with his country and his language. He wants nothing to do with it, retorting, "I'm sick of my own country, sick of it!" She finishes the discussion with one final jab of "West Briton!" The final evidence of Gabriel's isolation and frustration is at the dinner when he gives his speech. He questions and doubts what he has prepared for the speech all evening, wondering whether the references he will make will resonate with his listeners. He also decides, thanks to the conversation with Miss Ivors, to change his speech a bit as a means of passively chastising her. He begins his speech self-deprecatingly but then fills it with erudite references, including the one to the Three Graces in mythology, which goes right over his Aunt Julia's head. Though not entirely a failure, his speech does not have the impact he would have liked because he wrote it more for himself than for the guests. All of these events have a cumulative effect on Gabriel, though perhaps he doesn't recognize it fully until the weight of Gretta's confession falls on him and he understands the extent of his isolation.

Introductions

Introductions present particular challenges for writers. Generally, your introduction should do two things: capture your reader's attention and explain the main point of your essay. In other words, while your introduction should contain your thesis, it needs to do a bit more work than that. You are likely to find that starting that first paragraph is one of the most difficult parts of the paper. It is hard to face that blank page or screen, and as a result, many beginning writers, in desperation to start somewhere, launch into a paper with overly broad, general statements. While it is often a good strategy to start with more general subject matter and narrow your focus, do not begin with broad sweeping statements such as Everyone likes to be creative and feel understood. Such sentences are nothing but empty filler. They begin to fill the blank page, but they do nothing to advance your argument. Instead, you should try to gain your readers' interest. Some writers like to open with a pertinent quotation or with a relevant question. Or, you might begin with an introduction of the topic you will discuss. If you are writing about Joyce's presentation of the effects of frustration in "The Dead," for instance, you might start by talking about how frustration is understood to affect people psychologically. Another common trap to avoid is depending on your title to introduce the author and the text you are writing about. Always include the work's author and title in your opening paragraph.

Compare the effectiveness of the following introductions.

1) Throughout history, people have hated being frustrated. Think how you feel when you are frustrated: It makes you kind of crazy, doesn't it? In this story, Joyce shows Gabriel Conroy's sense of frustration and alienation by focusing on his thoughts and actions over the course of an evening, culminating in an epiphany.

2) Psychologists are well aware that the human psyche, or internal self, is a powerful entity: In some ways, it is more powerful than the individual of which it is a part. The psyche is also a bit of a tyrant; it does not like to be ignored or disregarded. The power of the psyche is such that an individual who tries to circumvent his true nature will, eventually, have to face up to who he is and what he needs. For good mental health, Sigmund Freud advised being true to your psyche, even if your psyche's impulses contradict social niceties. In "The Dead," James Joyce explores the depths of the human psyche and the degrees to

> which we feel alienation and frustration through
> his protagonist Gabriel Conroy, whose whole world
> changes in an evening when his wife, Gretta, tells
> him about a former love who died for her. The
> interactions between Gabriel and the dinner guests
> prior to his epiphany hint at the protagonist's
> feelings of isolation and frustration, but the
> confession made by Gretta at the end of the story
> causes his ultimate disappointment.

The first introduction begins with a vague, overly broad sentence; cites unclear, undeveloped examples; and then moves abruptly to the thesis. Notice, too, how a reader deprived of the paper's title does not know the title of the story that the paper will analyze. The second introduction works with the same material and thesis but provides more detail and is consequently much more interesting. It begins by discussing psychological understandings of the psyche, gives specific examples, and then speaks briefly about one psychologist's philosophy of the individual psyche. The paragraph ends with the thesis, which includes both the author and the title of the work to be discussed.

The paragraph below provides another example of an opening strategy. It begins by introducing the author and the text it will analyze, and then it moves on by briefly introducing relevant details of the story in order to set up its thesis.

> James Joyce's novel *A Portrait of the Artist as a Young
> Man* examines the roles of the Roman Catholic Church and
> Irish society in the lives of the citizens of Dublin at
> the turn of the century. The novel's protagonist, Stephen
> Dedalus, sees these forces as "nets flung at it [a man's
> soul] to hold it back from flight." He aims to "fly by
> those nets." We see Stephen's frustration over the forces
> of church and state at several points in the novel, in
> scenes from his youth and in conversations in his early
> adulthood. At the beginning of the story, religion and
> politics trap Stephen at the Christmas dinner as a young
> boy; he grows confused about why his loved ones are
> arguing so vehemently. The net of religion is thrown

at him again in the sermon at the retreat, forcing him to repent and take on religion with the zeal he had previously devoted to visiting brothels. He frequently finds himself caught up in politics, thanks in part to his name, which is not Irish, and is chastised by his peers for not caring about his country. In each instance of the young artist getting entangled in the snares of religion, politics, and culture, we find the increasing frustration he experiences as a result. His only choice is to escape Ireland entirely and seek out a place where his creativity and intellect can develop unfettered.

Conclusions

Conclusions present another series of challenges for writers. No doubt you have heard the old adage about writing papers: "Tell us what you are going to say, say it, and then tell us what you've said." While this formula does not necessarily result in bad papers, it does not often result in good ones, either. It will almost certainly result in boring papers (especially boring conclusions). If you have done a good job establishing your points in the body of the paper, the reader already knows and understands your argument. There is no need to merely reiterate. Do not just summarize your main points in your conclusion. Such a boring and mechanical conclusion does nothing to advance your argument or interest your reader. Consider the following conclusion to the paper about frustration and alienation in "The Dead."

In conclusion, Joyce presents frustration and isolation as destructive to characters. Gabriel is disappointed that his life, particularly his marriage to Gretta, is not what he had imagined it to be. His sadness at the end of the story indicates that, even when we try hard, we cannot always change our lives. I guess that is true for all of us.

Besides starting with a mechanical transitional device ("In conclusion . . ."), this conclusion does little more than summarize the main points of the outline (and it does not even touch on all of them). It is incomplete and uninteresting (and a little too depressing).

Instead, your conclusion should add something to your paper. A good tactic is to build on the points you have been arguing. Asking "why?" often helps you draw further conclusions. For example, in the paper on "The Dead," you might speculate or explain how Gabriel's frustrations speak to what Joyce is presenting as a human desire for true connections with other people. Another method for successfully concluding a paper is to speculate on other directions in which to take your topic by tying it into larger issues. You might do this by envisioning your paper as just one section of a larger paper. Having established your points in this paper, how would you build on this argument? Where would you go next? In the following conclusion to the paper on "The Dead," the author reiterates some of the main points of the paper but does so in order to amplify the discussion of the story's central message and to connect it to other texts by James Joyce:

> In the end, Gabriel Conroy's growing sense of hope, vitality, and connection on the cab ride to the hotel is thwarted when his wife, Gretta, confesses the love she had for another man when she was young. Gabriel's epiphany after an evening of successive frustrations reinforces the utter isolation of his life. That the story ends with Gabriel crying "generous tears" demonstrates not only his sense of having lost what he believed to be a strong and loving marriage but also emphasizes his isolation from his wife, as he waits for her to fall asleep before allowing his emotions to overcome him. Joyce seems to have acute insight into the psyches of Irish men whose hopes and aspirations are perhaps too lofty for their mundane world. He revisits these frustrated male characters in other stories in *Dubliners*, as well as in the novels *A Portrait of the Artist as a Young Man* and *Ulysses*. Though Joyce's fiction does not offer a solution for the frustration that these men feel in a society stagnating under the social constructs of religion and culture, his deft portraits lend the situation and the experience understanding and dignity.

Similarly, in the following conclusion to a paper on societal influences in *A Portrait of the Artist as a Young Man*, the author draws a conclusion about what the novel is saying about culture and religion.

Ultimately, *A Portrait of the Artist as a Young Man* is a bildungsroman or coming-of-age story in which the protagonist, Stephen Dedalus, develops from a curious and thoughtful young boy into a philosophical and artistic young man. But the reader understands that this process takes place in spite of rather than due to the societal forces that shaped him, namely the Roman Catholic Church and Irish culture. The extent to which Stephen Dedalus manages to "fly by those nets" determines how well he will be able to achieve his full artistic potential. Remaining in Ireland is not an option in Stephen's mind; he feels he will never "encounter . . . the reality of experience" in his native land and must go away in order to "forge in the smithy of my soul the uncreated conscience of my race." The forces that, broadly speaking, shape all humans—culture and religion—are depicted in a negative light in *Portrait*, at least in the case of Stephen. Though the novel is set in a specific locale, Dublin at the beginning of the 20th century, the conflicts faced by the artist with regard to religion and society are universal ones. By showing the extreme decision of exile Stephen makes to become an artist in the world, the reader is led to think about the sacrifices we all make to achieve our goals. Ultimately, Joyce's novel encourages us to "fly by those nets" that work to hold us all back, whatever they may be.

Citations and Formatting

Using Primary Sources:

As the examples included in this chapter indicate, strong papers on literary texts incorporate quotations from the text in order to support their points. It is not enough for you to assert your interpretation without providing support or evidence from the text. Without well-chosen quotations to support your argument you are, in effect, saying to the reader, "Take my word for it." It is important to use quotations thoughtfully and selectively. Remember that the paper presents *your* argument, so choose quotations that support *your* assertions. Do not let the author's voice overwhelm your own. With that caution in mind, there are some guidelines you should follow to ensure that you use quotations clearly and effectively.

Integrate Quotations:

Quotations should always be integrated into your own prose. Do not just drop them into your paper without introduction or comment. Otherwise, it is unlikely that your reader will see their function. You can integrate textual support easily and clearly with identifying tags, short phrases that identify the speaker. For example:

> The narrator describes Eveline's home as one of a series of "little brown houses."

While this tag appears before the quotation, you can also use tags after or in the middle of the quoted text, as the following examples demonstrate:

> "Tell me what it is, Gretta," Gabriel says to his wife as they return to their hotel room after the dinner party, "I think I know what is the matter? Do I know?"

> "When the soul of a man is born in this country there are nets flung at it to hold it from flight," Stephen tells Davin, explaining his views of Ireland. "You talk to me of nationality, language, religion. I shall try to fly by those nets."

You can also use a colon to formally introduce a quotation:

> Cranly offers Stephen his opinion why he should grant his mother's request to fulfill his Easter duty: "Whatever else is unsure in this stinking dunghill of a world a

mother's love is not. Your mother brings you into the
world, carries you first in her body. What do we know
about what she feels? But whatever she feels, it, at
least must be real. It must be. What are our ideas or
ambitions? Play!"

When you quote brief sections of poems (three lines or fewer), use
slash marks to indicate the line breaks in the poem:

In the poem "A Flower Given to My Daughter," Joyce
evokes images of delicacy, purity, and frailty: "Frail
the white rose and frail are / Her hands."

Longer quotations (more than four lines of prose or three lines of
poetry) should be set off from the rest of your paper in a block quotation. Double-space before you begin the passage, indent it 10 spaces from
your left-hand margin, and double-space the passage itself. Because the
indentation signals the inclusion of a quotation, do not use quotation
marks around the cited passage. Use a colon to introduce the passage:

The narrator in the story "Eveline" emphasizes the
dinginess of the protagonist's surroundings, while also
foreshadowing her paralysis:

Home! She looked around the room, reviewing all
its familiar objects which she had dusted once a
week for so many years, wondering where on earth
all the dust came from. Perhaps she would never
see again those familiar objects from which she
had never dreamed of being divided. And yet during
all those years she had never found out the name
of the priest whose yellowing photograph hung on
the wall beside the colored print of the promises
made to Blessed Margaret Mary Alacoque.

By now, the reader should not have any doubts about
Eveline's grim environment, with all the dust and

yellowing photographs. It is old and worn, yet the young woman cannot imagine herself separated from it.

Here is how a writer would do the same for a long passage of poetry:

In his poem "Ecce Puer," Joyce describes the conflicting emotions he experiences on the death of his father, which was closely followed by the birth of his grandson:

> Of the dark past
> A child is born;
> With joy and grief
> My heart is torn.
>
> Calm in his cradle
> The living lies.
> May love and mercy
> Unclose his eyes!
>
> Young life is breathed
> On the glass,
> The world that was not
> Comes to pass.
>
> A child is sleeping:
> An old man gone.
> O, father forsaken,
> Forgive your son!

Written a month and a half after his father's death and on the day his grandson, Stephen James Joyce, was born, the emotions of the poet are real and raw. "Ecce Puer" is perhaps Joyce's most heartrending poem.

It is also important to interpret quotations after you introduce them and explain how they help advance your point. You cannot assume that your reader will interpret the quotations the same way that you do.

Quote Accurately:

Always quote accurately. Anything within quotations marks must be the author's exact words. There are, however, some rules to follow if you need to modify the quotation to fit into your prose.

1. Use brackets to indicate any material that might have been added to the author's exact wording. For example, if you need to add any words to the quotation for clarification or alter it grammatically to allow it to fit into your prose, indicate your changes in brackets:

   > Gabriel's epiphany is like an attack on his psyche and he realizes that "[w]hile he had been full of memories of their secret life together, full of tenderness and joy and desire, she [Gretta] had been comparing him in her mind with another."

2. Conversely, if you choose to omit any words from the quotation, use ellipses (three spaced periods) to indicate missing words or phrases:

   > Gabriel reflects back on the night's events, seeing "himself a ludicrous figure . . . a pennyboy for his aunts, a nervous well-meaning sentimentalist . . . the pitiable fatuous fellow he had caught a glimpse of in the mirror."

3. If you delete a sentence or more, use the ellipses after a period:

   > Gabriel does not want his wife to witness his epiphany, as seen in the following passage: "A shameful consciousness of his own person assailed him. . . . Instinctively he turned his back more to the light lest she might see the shame that burned on his forehead."

4. If you omit a line or more of poetry, or more than one paragraph of prose, use a single line of spaced periods to indicate the omission:

```
Of the dark past
A child is born;
With joy and grief
My heart is torn.

.  .  .  .  .  .  .  .  .  .  .  .  .  .  .  .
A child is sleeping:
An old man gone.
O, father forsaken,
Forgive your son!
```

Punctuate Properly:

Punctuation of quotations often causes more trouble than it should. Once again, you just need to keep these simple rules in mind.

1. Periods and commas should be placed inside quotation marks, even if they are not part of the original quotation:

```
Miss Ivors's baiting of Gabriel is clear: "I
have a crow to pluck with you."
```

The only exception to this rule is when the quotation is followed by a parenthetical reference. In this case, the period or comma goes after the citation (more on these later in this chapter):

```
Miss Ivors's baiting of Gabriel is clear: "I
have a crow to pluck with you" (203).
```

2. Other marks of punctuation—colons, semicolons, question marks, and exclamation points—go outside the quotation marks unless they are part of the original quotation:

> Why does the narrator close the first paragraph
> of "Eveline" with the sentence: "She was
> tired"?

> Before heading to the docks to leave Ireland
> with her lover, Frank, Eveline's thoughts are
> frenzied:"Escape! She must escape! Frank would
> save her. He would give her life, perhaps love,
> too. But she wanted to live. Why should she be
> unhappy?"

Documenting Primary Sources:

Unless you are instructed otherwise, you should provide sufficient information for your reader to locate material you quote. Generally, literature papers follow the rules set forth by the Modern Language Association (MLA). These can be found in the *MLA Handbook for Writers of Research Papers* (seventh edition). You should be able to find this book in the reference section of your library. Additionally, its rules for citing both primary and secondary sources are widely available from reputable online sources. One of these is the Online Writing Lab (OWL) at Purdue University. OWL's guide to MLA style is available at http://owl.english. purdue.edu/owl/resource/557/01/. The Modern Language Association also offers answers to frequently asked questions about MLA style on this helpful Web page: http://www.mla.org/style_faq. Generally, when you are citing from literary works in papers, you should keep a few guidelines in mind.

Parenthetical Citations:

MLA asks for parenthetical references in your text after quotations. When you are working with prose (short stories, novels, or essays) include page numbers in the parentheses:

> Miss Ivors's baiting of Gabriel is clear: "I have a crow
> to pluck with you" (203).

When you are quoting poetry, include line numbers:

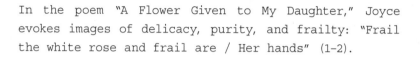

```
In the poem "A Flower Given to My Daughter," Joyce
evokes images of delicacy, purity, and frailty: "Frail
the white rose and frail are / Her hands" (1-2).
```

Works Cited Page:

These parenthetical citations are linked to a separate works cited page at the end of the paper. The works cited page lists works alphabetically by the authors' last names. An entry for the above reference to Joyce's "The Dead" would read:

```
Joyce, James. "The Dead." The Portable James Joyce. Ed.
    Harry Levin. New York: Penguin, 1976. 190-242. Print.
```

The *MLA Handbook* includes a full listing of sample entries, as do many of the online explanations of MLA style.

Documenting Secondary Sources:

To ensure that your paper is built entirely on your own ideas and analysis, instructors often ask that you write interpretative papers without any outside research. If, on the other hand, your paper requires research, you must document any secondary sources you use. You need to document direct quotations, summaries or paraphrases of others' ideas, and factual information that is not common knowledge. Follow the guidelines above for quoting primary sources when you use direct quotations from secondary sources. Keep in mind that MLA style also includes specific guidelines for citing electronic sources. OWL's Web site provides a good summary: http://owl.english.purdue.edu/owl/resource/557/09/.

Parenthetical Citations:

As with the documentation of primary sources, described above, MLA guidelines require in-text parenthetical references to your secondary sources. Unlike the research papers you might write for a history class, literary research papers following MLA style do not use footnotes as a means of documenting sources. Instead, after a quotation, you should cite the author's last name and the page number:

> "The story begins with Eveline framed at her window. She may never escape that frame, immobilized and paralyzed at beginning and at end" (Seidel 53).

If you include the name of the author in your prose, then you would include only the page number in your citation. For example:

> According to Michael Seidel, "The story begins with Eveline framed at her window. She may never escape that frame, immobilized and paralyzed at beginning and at end" (53).

If you are including more than one work by the same author, the parenthetical citation should include a shortened yet identifiable version of the title in order to indicate which of the author's works you cite. For example:

> According to Michael Seidel, "The story begins with Eveline framed at her window. She may never escape that frame, immobilized and paralyzed at beginning and at end" (James 53).

Similarly, and just as important, if you summarize or paraphrase the particular ideas of your source, you must provide documentation:

> At the beginning of the story "Eveline," the protagonist's window frame is symbolic of a prison from which she will never escape. She is clearly just as paralyzed at the beginning of the story as she is at the end (Seidel, Joyce 53).

Works Cited Page:

Like the primary sources discussed above, the parenthetical references to secondary sources are keyed to a separate works cited page at the end of your paper. Here is an example of a works cited page that uses the examples cited above. Note that when two or more works by the same author are listed, you should use three hyphens followed by a period in the subsequent entries. You can find a complete list of sample entries in the *MLA Handbook* or from a reputable online summary of MLA style.

WORKS CITED

Joyce, James. "Eveline." *The Portable James Joyce*. Ed. Harry Levin. New York: Penguin, 1976. 46–51. Print.

Seidel, Michael. *Exile and the Narrative Imagination*. New Haven: Yale University Press, 1986. Print.

———. *James Joyce: A Short Introduction*. Malden, Mass.: Blackwell Publishers, Inc., 2002. Print.

Plagiarism

Failure to document carefully and thoroughly can leave you open to charges of stealing the ideas of others, which is known as plagiarism, and this is a very serious matter. Remember that it is important to include quotation marks when you use language from your source, even if you use just one or two words. For example, if you wrote, Eveline is imprisoned at the beginning of her story, evidenced in her being framed by her window, you would be guilty of plagiarism, since you used Seidel's distinct language without acknowledging him as the source. Instead, you should write: Eveline, "framed at her window," is imprisoned from the very beginning of the story (Seidel 53). In this case, you have properly credited Seidel.

Similarly, neither summarizing the ideas of an author nor changing or omitting just a few words means that you can omit a citation. Richard Ellmann's biography of James Joyce contains the following passage about the poem "Ecce Puer" written not long after his father's death, for which he was still in deep mourning:

> His melancholy was, however, suddenly relieved on February 15, 1932. Helen Joyce, after a difficult pregnancy, gave birth to a son, who was named in his grandfather's honor Stephen James Joyce. In some sense the birth seemed to countervail John Joyce's death, and James wrote the same day his most moving poem.

Below are two examples of plagiarized passages:

> "Ecce Puer" is an example of Joyce working through the melancholy he felt due to his father's death and the joy he experienced with the birth of his grandson, Stephen James Joyce, who was named in Joyce's honor. The grief Joyce felt for his father's loss is offset by the new life.

> James Joyce's grandson was born on February 15, 1932, and his birth seemed to countervail John Joyce's death. Joyce wrote his most moving poem, "Ecce Puer," that same day (Ellmann 646).

While the first passage does not use Ellmann's exact language, it does list the same ideas he proposes as the critical underpinning of the poem without citing his work. Since this interpretation is Ellmann's distinct idea, this constitutes plagiarism. The second passage has shortened his passage, changed some wording, and included a citation, but some of the phrasing is Ellmann's. The first passage could be fixed with a parenthetical citation. Because some of the wording in the second remains the same, though, it would require the use of quotation marks, in addition to a parenthetical citation. The passage below represents an honestly and adequately documented use of the original passage:

> According to Richard Ellmann, "Ecce Puer" is an example of Joyce working through the melancholy he felt due to his father's death and the joy he experienced with the birth of his grandson, Stephen James Joyce, who was named in the author's honor (646). Stephen James Joyce was born on February 15, 1932, nearly a month and a half after the death of Joyce's father, and, as Ellmann notes, "the birth seemed to countervail John Joyce's death" (646). Joyce wrote his most moving poem that same day (646).

This passage acknowledges that the interpretation is derived from Ellmann while appropriately using quotations to indicate his precise language.

While it is not necessary to document well-known facts, often referred to as "common knowledge," any ideas or language that you take from someone else must be properly documented. Common knowledge generally includes the birth and death dates of authors or other well-documented facts of their lives. An often-cited guideline is that if you can find the information in three sources, it is common knowledge. Despite this guideline, it is, admittedly, often difficult to know if the facts you uncover are common knowledge or not. When in doubt, document your source.

Sample Essay

John Smith
Professor Gleed
ENG 101: Introduction to Irish Literature
March 15, 2011

"LITTLE BROWN HOUSES":
PLACE AND COLOR IN JAMES JOYCE'S "EVELINE"

Throughout "Eveline," James Joyce uses color as an important part of his imagery of stagnation and paralysis. These colors are always dark or dull and are contrasted with the kind of light or bright colors that represent the opportunities Eveline will never be able to enjoy or take advantage of and places she will apparently never visit. However, by the end of the story, this pattern is interrupted and undercut by Joyce's use of the traditionally light and bright color white to symbolize the terrifyingly deep stagnation that undoes Eveline at the conclusion.

The story begins with Eveline "[w]atching the evening invade," the darkness of night penetrating the story like a marauding force. She sits at the window, and as Michael Seidel asserts, Eveline "may never escape that frame, immobilized and paralyzed at beginning and at end" (53). This darkness is the hue of a complex pattern of symbols, "dusty" and wistful, that reinforces the stagnant nature of Joyce's Dublin and Eveline's existence. As a man passes beneath Eveline's window and heads toward a group of "new red houses," Eveline recalls that before these houses were built "there used to be a field there in which [Eveline and her brothers] used to play every evening with other people's children" (46). These new red houses are made of "bright brick" with "shining roofs," contrasting sharply to the group of "little brown houses" that includes Eveline's home. The dull brown of the past and Eveline's continued present is at odds with the vibrant red of other people's good fortune and a future that Eveline cannot bring herself to embrace.

Similarly, the next color to find prominence in the story is yellow. Surprisingly, however, this yellow is not related to the bright red of the new homes. As Eveline looks around her room, she contemplates the prospect of leaving her little brown house:

> She looked round the room, reviewing all its familiar objects which she had dusted once a week for so many years, wondering where on earth all the dust came from. Perhaps she would never see again those familiar objects from which she had never dreamed of being divided. And yet during all those years she had never found out the name of the priest whose yellowing photograph hung on the wall above the broken harmonium beside the coloured print of the promises made to Blessed Margaret Mary Alacoque. He had been a school friend of her father. (47)

This yellow, then, is dull and worn, rooted in the past. The face in the photograph is familiar, and yet she does not know the person's name. The yellowing photograph is anonymous, a face lacking a name characterized by its faded hue and its appropriate setting "above the broken harmonium." Moreover, just as the little brown houses were outshone by their more modern, red equivalents, so is the dull yellow photograph contrasted with the bright sunshine of the nameless priest's current home in Australia: "Whenever [Eveline's father] showed the photograph to a visitor her father used to pass it with a casual word: 'He is in Melbourne now.'" (47) The priest has escaped the dull browns and faded yellows of Dublin and made it to the bright world evoked by the "casual word" of Melbourne. Equally, we are told that Eveline's lover, Frank, a man who represents the exotic and the hopeful, the possibility of Eveline's own escape, has a "face of bronze," another shining hue that summons the bright sunshine of a distant land (49).

However, Eveline's inability to escape Dublin is foreshadowed by the return to darker shades in the narrative. After having contemplated the adventures of Frank and the increasing frailty of Eveline's father, the narrator reminds us that Eveline "continued to sit by the window" overlooking the night that began the story. More troublingly, though, Eveline's mind is pulled back to the memory of her mother's death "in the close dark room at the other side of the hall" (50). Ominously, now, the presence of the exotic and the foreign—the possibility of escape—represented by the Italian street musician calls to mind the dark interior of Eveline's little brown house. From this point on, we have no more talk of light, no bright colors (with the exception of the "portholes" of the following passage, though this can be dismissed as something of a dream). Just as the music of the Italian carries her only deeper into her own memory and location, the boat that Eveline hopes will take her to the freedom of lighter skies is forbiddingly imagined as follows:

The station was full of soldiers with brown baggages. Through the wide doors of the sheds she caught a glimpse of the black mass of the boat, lying in beside the quay wall, with illumined

portholes. She answered nothing. She felt her cheek
pale and cold and, out of a maze of distress, she
prayed to God to direct her, to show her what was
her duty. The boat blew a long mournful whistle
into the mist. (51)

The brown baggage of the soldiers harkens back to the
brown houses of Eveline's street, but it is the "black
mass" of the boat that confirms the irresistible hold
of Dublin and the past on Eveline. The "black mass"
of the hull represents not only the darkness of the
unknown and despair but also plays on the religious
cage around Eveline and the Roman Catholic Mass that
is one of the many reasons why she is so paralyzed.
Seeing it, her lips moved "in silent fervent prayer"
(51). As Lee Spinks suggests, "The repressive mechanism
of religious morality and paternal prohibition roots
her to the spot," and "Eveline has internalised the
repressive codes of her culture to the degree that
life is unthinkable without them" (59). The promise of
the "illuminated portholes," never to be fulfilled, is
eclipsed by the dark hulk of the boat itself and the
"long mournful whistle" sounding "into the mist" (51).

This eclipse of the boat's portholes through which,
symbolically, Eveline's untaken future could have been
seen, leads to the most significant shift in the story's
use of light and dark colors. The movement of the
story takes us to the point where white, the lightest
and brightest of all the colors Joyce could have found
in his pallet, is finally associated paradoxically
with the darker, duller shades at the beginning of
"Eveline." Stripped of its bright potential, white
becomes tragically neutral, a cipher symbolizing
not only Eveline's rootedness but also her disabling
passivity. We first see white prominently in the "white
of two letters," intended as farewells to Harry and her
father. The white of the paper here contains the hope

of optimism symbolized by a lighter color, revealing the potential of Eveline's life to improve and grow out of its Dublin confinement. However, this potential is shattered by the transformation of the color white taking place in the story's final image: "He rushed beyond the barrier and called to her to follow. He was shouted at to go on but he still called to her. She set her white face to him, passive, like a helpless animal. Her eyes gave him no sign of love or farewell or recognition" (51). Just as yellow had been drained earlier in the story into a faded, dull color, here the brightness of white is diminished to the quality of paleness, the ghostly color of Eveline's symbolic death at the close of the story.

We see, then, that Joyce's use of color and light in "Eveline" is complex and incorporates some unexpected transformations of bright colors into pale and dull shadows of themselves. They are washed out as if by the seas that tumble around Eveline's heart as she stands frozen by the passenger ship. The dust and darkness of Eveline's street, the dinginess of her little brown house, it seems, pervade Eveline's horizons and blanket out the bright hopes that Joyce briefly flickered in front of her.

WORKS CITED

Joyce, James. "Eveline." *The Portable James Joyce*. New York: Penguin, 1976. 46–51. Print.

Seidel, Michael. *James Joyce: A Short Introduction*. Malden, Mass.: Blackwell Publishers, Inc. 2002. Print.

Spinks, Lee. *James Joyce: A Critical Guide*. Edinburgh: Edinburgh University Press, 2009. Print.

HOW TO WRITE ABOUT
JAMES JOYCE

JAMES AUGUSTINE Aloysius Joyce was born February 2, 1882, in Rathgar, a suburb of Dublin, Ireland. He was the oldest child of John Stanislaus Joyce (from Cork) and Mary Jane (May) Murray, who bore her husband 12 children, 10 of whom survived. When Joyce was young, his father was successful, and for several years the family lived in Bray, a fashionable suburb of Dublin, and James was able to attend the prestigious Clongowes Wood College (just as his future protagonist Stephen Dedalus did). However, John Joyce's poor financial planning and decision making began to take a toll on the family, necessitating their move from Bray to a smaller home in a less expensive neighborhood and their son's move to a Christian Brothers school (considered second rate to the Jesuits at the time). Joyce eventually returned to the Jesuits when he began attending Belvedere College. As John Joyce's fortunes dwindled (he had to sell properties and possessions in Cork and move his family to decidedly less hospitable dwellings in Dublin), his family size continued to increase, and he grew more and more violent and abusive, both verbally and physically. But it seems that he never hurt his son James, who, Richard Ellmann, Joyce's biographer, tells us, "got along easily" with his father, as opposed to his siblings who hated John (40).

Joyce's boyhood surroundings, acquaintances, and experiences frequently worked their way into his writing, blurring the lines between fact and fiction. He lived on North Richmond Street, the setting for his short story "Araby" in *Dubliners,* and many of the characters in that collection as well as in *Ulysses* are derived from this time in his life. A day of skipping school with his brother Stanislaus morphed into "An Encoun-

49

ter," and the Boardman family who lived down the street gave him Edy Boardman from the "Nausicaa" episode of *Ulysses*. Joyce began his sexual life very young, meeting with a prostitute at age 14, and similar to Stephen Dedalus, he was concurrently involved in the religious aspects of his education, holding the position of prefect of the sodality of the Virgin Mary. Also like Stephen, Joyce experienced a brief period of religious devotion (Ellmann 43–47).

Joyce graduated from Belvedere College, where he performed well, especially his first years there, studying English and foreign languages—French, Latin, and Italian. In 1898, Joyce continued his education at University College, Dublin, keenly aware of this institution's second-place standing at the time when compared with Trinity College. He fancied himself the "cleverest man at University College," and many of the friends he made there appear under different names in *A Portrait of the Artist as a Young Man* (Ellmann 61). At this point in his life, Joyce had all but split with the Catholic Church and was also beginning to despise the sort of Irish nationalism that caused his companions to protest W. B. Yeats's play *The Countess Cathleen*. In his second year at University College, Dublin, Joyce officially began his career as a writer with his first essay, "Ibsen's New Drama," published in the *Fortnightly Review*. Ibsen, one of Joyce's literary idols, wrote to Joyce to thank him for his positive review of the play *When We Dead Awaken*, and Joyce was exultant. He set himself to studying languages and literature even more seriously as a result, seeing this letter as a "benison at the beginning of his career" (Ellmann 74).

In 1902, Joyce met George Russell (the theosophist writer who used the pseudonym Æ or AE), as well as W. B. Yeats and Lady Gregory, three of the main players in the Irish literary renaissance. They saw a rising star in Joyce and did what they could to help the young writer, who was about to begin his medical studies. When Joyce decided that medical school in Dublin was not for him, he investigated his options in Paris. Lady Gregory provided assistance in this regard, and he left Dublin in December 1902 (Ellmann 98–110). His time in Paris was wasted in regard to the progression of his medical studies (he gave up the idea of becoming a doctor relatively soon after arriving in France) but allowed him to more fully explore his ideas as an artist, immersed in a more free-thinking, tolerant society. It was the telegram from his father—"MOTHER DYING COME HOME FATHER"—that forced his premature departure from Paris and prompted his return to Dublin. It was during this year and a half that Joyce would meet the love of his life, Nora Barnacle, and formally begin their life together on June 16, 1904, the date he would memorialize in his masterpiece, *Ulysses* (Ellmann 111–28).

Joyce persuaded Nora to leave with him, unmarried, for mainland Europe in October 1904, where, with the exception of a few short trips back to Ireland, they remained for the rest of their lives. They began in Pola, the Austrian port city that is now Pula, Croatia. They then moved to Trieste, which was then part of Austria but today is under Italian rule, where they spent the next 10 years, with the exception of the one year they lived in Rome. Their two children, Giorgio and Lucia, were both born in Trieste, and so were Joyce's first two literary children, *Dubliners* and *A Portrait of the Artist as a Young Man.* During his Triestine period, Joyce met Harriet Shaw Weaver, the editor of the literary magazine *Egoist,* which serialized *Portrait.* She would later become Joyce's benefactor. It was also in Trieste that Joyce began writing *Ulysses,* in 1914, though he had been planning the novel in his head for many years prior. It was also in 1914 that Joyce wrote his play, *Exiles.*

When World War I broke out in 1914 and when Italy entered the war in 1915, Joyce decided it would be in his best interest to move his family to neutral Zurich, Switzerland. The Joyces remained there for five years before moving on to Paris, and it was in Zurich that he wrote much of *Ulysses,* seeing Switzerland not only as a refuge but, as Ellmann points out, as "a symbol of artistic detachment, *au-dessus de la mêlée,*" or above the battle (386). The next 19 years of Joyce's life were spent in Paris, where he completed *Ulysses* and *Finnegans Wake.* It was also in Paris that he added many individuals to his list of benefactors and allies, including Valery Larbaud, Adrienne Monnier, Sylvia Beach, Stuart Gilbert, and Eugene and Maria Jolas. When the German occupation of France began during World War II, Joyce and his family again returned, in December 1940, to Zurich. He lived there for the final 13 months of his life, dying of a perforated ulcer on January 13, 1941. He is buried in Fluntern Cemetery in Zurich.

James Joyce was a complicated and complex man. He left Ireland at age 22 for his self-imposed exile on the European continent, returning for only brief visits, but in a way, he never really left. He also left the Roman Catholic Church but was so indoctrinated into its theology and rites that we see Catholicism seeping through in his work, both intentionally and unconsciously. He spent his entire life at the mercy of the charity of others, from his youth, when his father's fortunes dwindled, to his adulthood when he and his family were supported mainly by patrons of the arts. He was a generous man who was devoted to his wife and children, refusing social invitations if they were not included. His health plagued him though his adulthood, particularly problems with his eyes, and the many surgeries on his eyes did not do enough to help improve his sight. Much of his life experiences made their way into his fiction, some more thinly veiled than others, which tempts the reader to make a parallel between Joyce and his protagonists and wonder about which real-life people his characters represent. He was an arrogant, egotistical man who was fully aware of the artistic power of his mind yet was painfully sensitive about the fact that his wife, Nora, never bothered to read a word he wrote. Joyce was a man whose own personal complexities are mirrored in the complexity of his literary work.

Included in this chapter, in addition to many general, overarching questions in regard to Joyce's work, are a few questions pertaining to Joyce's final novel, *Finnegans Wake*; his only play, *Exiles*; and his poetry. The novel has not been accorded a chapter of its own in this volume since it is rarely studied except at the graduate level. The questions included in this section should offer writers a range of starting points from which to begin an essay on that novel.

TOPICS AND STRATEGIES

Writing about James Joyce in broad terms will certainly require incorporating an understanding of one or more of his works. While the following chapters focus primarily on an individual text in order to develop specific essays, the topics and suggestions in this chapter ask the reader to look at several texts for commonalities within the Joycean canon. If you plan to write your essay on *Portrait* or *Ulysses* and cannot find a topic here that you would like to explore, read the chapters discussing those individual works as well to get some ideas. You may even find that you can combine an idea from this section with another from a different chapter to construct your ideal essay topic. Remember, the suggestions presented in this volume are merely prompts, meant to serve as springboards or points of departure, and are certainly not the only essay topics at your disposal. Your essay on Joyce should be limited only by your own creativity and imagination.

Themes

Religion and Ireland are undeniably important themes in Joyce. Despite having left the Catholic Church and his native land, they really never left Joyce and weave their way through every text he produced. A dedicated family man, Joyce also presented some intriguing portraits of family life in his work, meriting further study.

Sample Topics:

1. **Religion:** What overall impression do we have of religion based on reading Joyce? What place does religion have in Joyce's society? What power does it yield?

Because he grew up in predominantly Roman Catholic Dublin, Ireland, and was educated by priests (mainly Jesuits), Joyce was fully indoctrinated into the Catholic Church, and the marks that this Catholic upbringing left on his character were indelible. As Richard Ellmann chronicles, Joyce left the Catholic Church sometime between 1897 and 1901, probably having taken his last communion in 1897 but still participating in some Catholic organizations through 1901. When Joyce was asked late in life when he left the Catholic Church, he responded "That's for the Church to say" (65). Ellmann suggests that, for Joyce, "of the two ways of leaving the Church that were open to him, denial and transmutation, he would choose the second. He would retain the faith, but with different objects. He would still reprove others for pretending to be Christian and not being so" (65).

What role does religion, specifically, Irish Roman Catholicism, play in Joyce's works? Look at the first portrayals of religion in the stories in *Dubliners*. What do we make of Father Flynn in "The Sisters"? Why does Mrs. Mooney know that the threat of exposing Bob Doran to his "great Catholic wine-merchant" employer will force him to marry her daughter? What roles does religion play in Eveline's decision to remain in Ireland? Then, look at *Portrait*, and the portrayal of the priests who teach Stephen and his classmates at Clongowes and Belvedere. What assessment of the priesthood can we make based on these men, many of whom have parallels in Joyce's own life?

Think, too, about the retreat in the novel which drives Stephen to confess his sins and repent, as well as consider a vocation, albeit briefly. Finally, look at the role of the church in *Ulysses*, focusing on the "Telemachus" and "Hades" episodes to round out your impression of Catholicism in Joyce. What does Joyce tell us about Catholicism and religion in general? What power does it have over society and the individuals in it? Does Joyce present any characters who have a positive relationship with organized religion? If so, what does he want us to think about those individuals?

2. **Ireland:** What overall impression do we have of Ireland based on reading Joyce? What do we make of Joyce's portrayal of his native land, its inhabitants, and its politics?

When we think about Irish literature, James Joyce is frequently the first writer to come to mind. This is, of course, ironic since his relationship with his native land was a very complicated one. While he lived there, he disparaged it, disappointed in its reliance on the church and state to determine and shape social norms. In *Portrait*, Joyce's protagonist (and parallel) Stephen Dedalus recognizes that he must leave Ireland, the "old sow that eats her farrow," to fly by the nets of "nationality, language, religion." Yet, once away from Ireland in his self-imposed exile on the continent, Joyce often waxed nostalgic for his birthplace, and even considered returning later in life. When asked by an acquaintance why he did not return to Ireland, he replied: "Have I ever left it?" (Ellmann 704). His geographical description of Dublin was so accurate, he felt, that historians would be able to rebuild the city based on his work if it were ever to be destroyed. He was inextricably tied to his native land and culture, but needed to keep it at arm's length in order to fulfill his artistic potential.

When we look at the depiction of Ireland in Joyce's works, we necessarily begin with *Dubliners*, searching for clues in the text that help to create an overall impression. *Dubliners* is filled with images of decay, decrepitude, and disenchantment. The Emerald Isle of popular imagination is now brown, yellow, and dusty. The characters in these stories are paralyzed with fear, overcome with anger and resentment, and forced to repress natural human feelings and desires. The impact of politics is also portrayed negatively, with forces on both sides of the Home Rule debate. These themes follow through in *Portrait* and *Ulysses* to create an overall image of Ireland that is not very flattering. What do we make of Joyce's portrayal of his homeland? Why would he present such a negative image of Ireland? Was he alone in doing so at the turn of the century? Use specific examples from the texts that help to support your argument.

3. **Family:** How would we classify a "typical" Irish family as presented by Joyce? What are some of the common characteristics? Does Joyce present mainly stereotypes?

Although the term *dysfunctional* had not come into the vernacular during Joyce's lifetime to describe the family unit, it can certainly be applied to the families he presents in his works. He came from what might be considered a typical, or at least a stereotypical, family for Ireland at the time: His father was an alcoholic who drove the family into poverty, his mother was a martyr for her husband and children, and he had eleven siblings, nine of whom survived. It goes without saying that his upbringing was dysfunctional, and his adult life was not what most would consider "typical," either. Certainly the circumstances of his own family life influenced the characters he created in his fiction.

How does Joyce present the concept of family in his work? How is family a theme for Joyce? What kind of family does Joyce generally present? Many of the families in *Dubliners* are not traditional family units. In "Araby," it seems as though the protagonist is being raised by his aunt and uncle; in "Eveline," the mother is dead and the young title character must look after the family; Mrs. Mooney in "The Boarding House" has separated from (but not divorced) her alcoholic husband. Even the family units that are intact and appear "typical," the Conroys in "The Dead," the Sinicos in "A Painful Case," and the

Chandlers in "A Little Cloud," betray those appearances to the reader who learns the true story. In *Portrait* and *Ulysses,* the Dedalus family, which corresponds greatly to Joyce's own, is in dire straits, and the Blooms' marriage is in jeopardy. The family presented in *Exiles,* which mirrors Joyce's own as an adult, with Richard Rowan and his partner, Bertha, whom he has not married but with whom he has a son, is again not typical for the time period. Finally, the family Joyce creates in *Finnegans Wake,* with HCE, ALP, Shem, Shaun, and Issy defies the norm as well. Why does Joyce give us these models for family life? Does he play into Irish stereotypes (many children, alcoholism), or does he merely present life as he knows it? How do we define a "typical" Joycean family? What are some of their common characteristics?

Character

Joyce's characters—Stephen Dedalus, Molly and Leopold Bloom, Gabriel Conroy—are famous. He develops character personalities so acutely that we come to know them quite intimately by the end of their story. Joyce presents much of the human condition in his protagonists, creating unlikely modern heroes for his readers.

Sample Topics:

1. **Joyce's women:** Are Gretta Conroy, Eveline, Molly Bloom, and Bertha typical examples of women of Joyce's time? Based on the women characters Joyce creates, what conclusion might we make of his understanding of women?

   Gretta Conroy seems haunted by the memory of a man who died for her when she was a teenager but is simultaneously dedicated to her husband and children. Eveline yearns for a new life outside the confines of Ireland but is paralyzed when faced with the opportunity to leave. Molly Bloom is an earth goddess who is fully in touch with her sexuality, but longs for a loving connection that she lacks both in her marriage to Bloom and in her newly begun affair with Boylan. Bertha in *Exiles* is also nontraditional, possibly ahead of her time, and similar to Molly with the exception that her partner Richard openly encourages her to pursue her interest in another man, while Bloom only passively allows Molly's affair with Boylan.

What is Joyce trying to communicate about women in the characters he creates? Are these characters stereotypes? Are they realistic? Do they elicit the reader's sympathy? Can the female reader identify with any of these women? How do they compliment the male characters in the texts? What do they reveal to the reader about Joyce? Did he understand women? Did he capture what it meant to be a woman in turn-of-the-century Dublin? Why or why not? Give specific examples from the texts to support your thesis.

2. **Joyce's men:** How would we characterize the men in Joyce? Are Simon and Stephen Dedalus, Gabriel Conroy and his fellow *Dubliners,* Leopold Bloom and Richard Rowan typical men? What does Joyce teach us about men?

This question is very similar to the one on Joyce's female characters, above, except you will be looking at the male protagonists he has created. Gabriel Conroy, by the end of "The Dead," has become a symbol of the isolation of the modern man. Stephen Dedalus, the burgeoning artist, is also isolated. His father Simon, though not isolated, suffers the stereotypical fate of the Irishman: alcoholism, poverty, and a too-large family. Leopold Bloom is an outsider in his own country, and is cuckolded by his wife. Richard Rowan is a non-conformist writer whose freethinking causes him the pain of jealousy and doubt.

When much of Joyce's own personality is built into the character of his protagonists, it is difficult to separate the writer from his creation. Stephen, Rowan, and even Bloom all have some characteristics of Joyce. Many of Joyce's other male characters were based on people he knew; for example, his father was the model for Simon Dedalus. What does Joyce teach us about men through his characters? What do we learn about the writer? Are the female characters as multidimensional as the male ones? How would we characterize these men? Would we consider them typical for their time? How do they complement the female characters in the texts?

3. **Joyce's priests:** What is the reader's assessment of the priesthood as a result of reading Joyce? Are Joyce's priests any different from his other male characters?

This question would necessarily incorporate some aspects of the question about religion in general found above, but the focus would be more specific, looking closely at Joyce's characterization of the priesthood. Priests appear as characters in the stories in *Dubliners,* in *Portrait,* and in *Ulysses* as well. This should not strike the reader as excessive, as they played a very important role in Irish society at the time. There was no shortage of priests, and they held positions of power not only in the church and education, but they also, as we learn during the Christmas dinner scene in *Portrait,* had tremendous influence over the political environment of the time. Joyce presents us with several characterizations of the priesthood, which seem as varied as the individuals who took up the vocation.

The first priest we meet, working through Joyce's texts chronologically, is Father Flynn, the paralytic simoniac who has died, leaving the narrator (and, in turn, the reader) with many questions about the priest's true character. The priest who inhabited the home on North Richmond Street into which the young narrator in "Araby" has moved left behind some articles that the reader should recognize as a bit odd for a priest, including a novel by Walter Scott, a crime novel, and a phallic bicycle pump. We learn that he left "all his money" to charity, but Roman Catholic priests frequently take a vow of poverty, so he really should not have had money to donate, let alone a substantial sum as indicated by the narrator's "all." *Portrait* is filled with priests, from the stern Father Arnall, to the violent Father Dolan, to the seemingly benevolent Father Conmee, who jokes with Stephen's father about Stephen's incident with Father Dolan and betrays the boy's confidence. The dean of studies at University College, Dublin, with whom Stephen has a philosophical conversation, is no match for his student's intellect. In *Ulysses,* Father Francis Coffey, the priest who buries Dignam in the "Hades" episode, is described by Bloom as a "Muscular christian [sic]" who is "Bully about the muzzle" and "Bosses the show." Father John Conmee, from *Portrait,* also reappears in *Ulysses,* in the "Wandering Rocks" episode, musing about his days at Clongowes.

What does Joyce communicate about the priesthood through these characters? Are they any different from the other men in Joyce's works? How does the reader react to these priests? Is Joyce's depiction realistic and honest? Is there a bias in his presentation?

History and Context

When we study Joyce we cannot ignore three important and influential relationships he had: with his wife, Nora, his brother Stanislaus, and his sometime protégé, Samuel Beckett. Other important people not presented below but whose impact on Joyce would warrant further study are his father, John Joyce, his benefactress Harriet Shaw Weaver, and his daughter Lucia Joyce.

Sample Topics:

1. **Nora Barnacle Joyce:** Who was Nora Barnacle Joyce? How would we describe the Joyces' marriage? How did Nora impact Joyce's writing?

   Nora Barnacle Joyce was born in Galway, in western Ireland, in March 1884 to a middle-class Roman Catholic family. As the family grew, they moved to smaller homes in less desirable areas of Galway. According to her biographer Brenda Maddox, Nora was spared most of the financial problems faced by her parents, however, since she was sent to live with her maternal grandmother, Catherine Mortimer Healy, when she was very young (12). She was educated in convent schools until she was 12, which was typical for the time for both boys and girls, and on finishing, went to work as a portress at the Presentation Convent on Galway (13). Maddox suggests that it "is a solid testimony to Nora's appearance and affability that the Mercy Sisters put her forward to open the Presentation's door. To act as a go-between between the silent world of the cloister and the rough world outside was not inappropriate training for what Nora's future held in store" (13). Similar to Gretta Conroy, whose girlhood love died for her, Nora had two teenage loves who died. She left Galway in 1904 for Dublin, where she found a position at Finn's Hotel near Trinity College, working as a chambermaid and waiting tables (Maddox 26). She met James Joyce on June 10, 1904, and the two arranged to meet for a walk on June 15, but Nora did not appear. They met the next day for their first "date," one that Joyce memorialized in *Ulysses*. She left Ireland with Joyce in October 1904 and became pregnant that same month with their first child, Giorgio, who was born in July 1905. Their second child, Lucia, was born in July 1907. Nora married James Joyce in London on July 4, 1931, after 27 years together (268). She supported her husband's career, despite never having read his work. She moved with him from apartment to apartment, country to country, and she respected James's wishes up to the end, refusing a Mass of Christian burial for him when he died.

What was Nora's influence on her husband? What assumptions do we have about Nora? Are these assumptions correct? Is Molly really Nora? Was Nora also a model for Bertha in *Exiles*? For Anna Livia Plurabelle? Based on Joyce's biography by Ellmann and Nora's biography by Maddox, what might we deduce about their life together? How was Nora her husband's muse?

2. **Stanislaus Joyce:** What role did Stanislaus Joyce play in his brother's life? How did Joyce treat Stanislaus? How did Stanislaus view his older brother?

Stanislaus Joyce, James's younger brother, was born December 17, 1884. Stanislaus, whose nickname was Stannie, was close with his brother growing up, but once they entered the university and Joyce began to meet more people, he started to leave his brother behind. Stanislaus resented being overshadowed by James, and Ellmann shares the following passage from Stanislaus's diary in Joyce's biography: "But it is terrible to have a cleverer older brother. I get small credit for originality"

(134). Despite his frustrations with Joyce, however, Stanislaus praised his brother's early writing, offered him feedback, and eventually followed him and Nora to Trieste where he worked to sort out the many domestic squabbles between the couple. His relationship with James was complicated and had periods where the two would not speak, and then reconcile, and then not speak again. Stanislaus chronicles this relationship in his memoir, *My Brother's Keeper: James Joyce's Early Years,* which will be required reading for the writer of this essay, along with Ellmann's biography of Joyce.

As you plan your essay, consider the importance of Stanislaus in Joyce's life. Unlike many of the people who surrounded the author, Stanislaus seems not to have been immortalized as a character in one of Joyce's works. Why is that? Is this simply a case of sibling rivalry, or is there more to their problematic relationship? How did Joyce treat Stanislaus? How did Stanislaus view his older brother (the title of his memoir may give us a not so subtle hint)?

3. **Samuel Beckett:** What was the relationship between Joyce and Beckett? Was there a meeting of the minds between these two great Irish expatriates?

Samuel Beckett was born on April 13, 1906, in the outskirts of Dublin, Ireland, nearly two years after Joyce had left the country. In academic interests, Beckett and Joyce shared a great deal—both men studied French, Italian, and English at the university level, but Joyce did his studies at University College, Dublin, the Roman Catholic, less prestigious, and less expensive school, while Beckett attended Trinity College, which was Protestant affiliated, had an excellent reputation, and was very expensive. He moved to Paris and took a position as lecturer in English at the École Normale Supérieure, and it was during this time that he was introduced to James Joyce. From 1928 through to 1931, Beckett worked closely with Joyce and the two became close friends. Some critics saw the relationship as one of a mentor and protégé, but it seems from further investigation that it was mutually beneficial. Joyce, whose eyesight was growing increasingly worse despite surgeries, benefitted greatly from Beckett's help with the transcription of *Finnegans Wake,* which was then known as *Work in Progress* (Ellmann 649). Beckett, in the company of Joyce, learned more about the art of fiction, and he seems to have inherited some of Joyce's sense of irreverent humor and modernist style. Joyce enlisted Beckett's assistance for the translation into French of the "Anna Livia Plurabelle" section of *Finnegans Wake,* but as Lucia Joyce expressed an interest in the young writer that he did not return (indeed, some critics say that he trifled with Lucia's emotions in order to be around her father), Nora and James Joyce broke with Beckett. They eventually reconciled and were in contact with each other through to the end of Joyce's life.

This essay would require not only research into the Joyce-Beckett relationship but also a familiarity with Beckett's works, especially those associated with Joyce. Beckett is sometimes considered the last of the modernist writers, sometimes the first of the postmodernists, but no matter how he is classified, his writing reveals echoes of Joyce. Joyce's writing, specifically *Finnegans Wake,* reveals some influence by Beckett as well. How did these two Irish expatriates impact each other? How would we describe their friendship? How important was this relationship?

Philosophy and Ideas

The reading and study of Joyce's texts invariably leads the reader to consider key recurring philosophical ideas or approaches: modernism, exile, and the difference between readerly text and a writerly one. Any of these would provide an excellent topic for an essay on Joyce.

Sample Topics:

1. **Exile:** What does Joyce tell us about exile? Why did he choose exile for himself and for his protagonist Stephen Dedalus? Was exile necessary to achieve his artistic goals?

Stephen Dedalus, toward the end of *Portrait,* comes to the understanding that for him to become an artist, he must leave Ireland and "fly by" the nets of "nationality, language, religion." He follows through on this, and in the final pages of the novel, we find him leaving for Paris. When we meet him again in *Ulysses,* approximately two years have elapsed, and he was called home to be with his dying mother. She has passed away, and Stephen still remains in Ireland, working temporarily as a schoolteacher, but by the end of that novel, the reader understands he does not intend to stay much longer. In both novels, Stephen spends a great deal of time disparaging Ireland, asserting that is it a not a country where an artist can thrive. Too many forces hold him back.

Recognizing that *Portrait* is semiautobiographical, and considering the fact that Joyce, too, left Ireland for Paris, returned when his mother was dying, and then left permanently (with the exception of a few short visits), what conclusion might we draw about Joyce's decision to exile himself? Richard Ellmann suggests that "Joyce needed exile as a reproach to others and a justification of himself. . . . That Joyce could not have written his books in Ireland is likely enough, but he felt the need for maintaining his intimacy with his country by continually renewing the quarrel with her which was now prompting him to leave for the first time" (109). Ellmann goes on to explain that Joyce did not want to create an exile for his characters that would cause readers to interpret them as helpless victims but, rather, as individuals who "seek freedom, which is also exile, by will and by compulsion" (109). How do we define Joycean exile? How does Joyce take this concept and adapt it, both for his own personal definition as well as in his writing? Is exile for Joyce only the physical distancing from a native land, as he and his protagonist experience? Is Joycean exile more than physical? Can it be spiritual? Think of Richard Rowan in *Exiles* and Leopold Bloom in *Ulysses*—are these men in exile? What does Joyce tell us about exile? Does the Joycean hero require it?

2. **Readerly versus writerly:** Are Joyce's texts "readerly" or "writerly"? How would you support your assessment?

The terms *readerly* and *writerly* were coined by French philosopher and literary critic Roland Barthes in the 1970s as a way to describe the style of a literary text and the way a reader approaches or interacts with it. Barthes describes these concepts in full in *S/Z,* but for our purposes, all we need to know is that when Barthes uses the word *readerly,* he refers to a work of literature that expects little interaction and requires no special effort on the part of the reader. In a readerly text, the meaning is there for the reader, neatly laid out. The writerly text is the opposite of the readerly one: it requires the reader to make meaning from what is on the page. Not everything (and indeed, sometimes very little) is handed to the readers of a writerly text, and they must do their share of the creative work. A writerly text is open to interpretation, and language is frequently used in an unexpected, unconventional way.

With this summary definition of Barthes differentiation between readerly and writerly, where would you say Joyce's writing falls? Is there a difference between his early works, for example, the short stories in *Dubliners,* and his final novel *Finnegans Wake* with regard to these terms? Does Joyce move from readerly to writerly over the course of his career? To write this essay, it would be best to look at the progression of literary style in the Joycean canon, giving examples of where his writing is readerly and/or writerly to support your assessment.

3. **Modernism:** What is modernism, and how do Joyce's works fit into that definition? What were the modernists trying to do? How do we define the movement?

Broadly defined, modernism was the cultural movement that began in the late 19th century and lasted into the first half of the 20th century. It is characterized by the expression of discontent with what was perceived as outdated modes of interacting with the world, specifically critiquing organized religion, traditional social structures, and classical art forms. Modernist artists and thinkers defied the traditions in place in society and worked to create a new understanding of being in the world. Some early modernists include Charles Darwin, whose theory of evolution turned the world of science (and religion) upside down, and Karl Marx, who criticized the capitalist system for imprisoning the individual. Sigmund Freud and Carl Jung's work in psychoanalysis were also important milestones in modernism, as was the philosophy of Friedrich Nietzsche, which spoke about the power of the individual. Modernist painters include Wassily Kandinsky, Pablo Picasso, and Henri Matisse, whose canvasses reflected much of the thought and philosophy of the time period. Finally, modernism in literature features writers such as T. S. Eliot, Marcel Proust, Ezra Pound, William Faulkner, Virginia Woolf, Gertrude Stein, W. B. Yeats, and, quite obviously, James Joyce.

What makes Joyce a modernist? How does Joyce fit into this movement? How do his works match the definition of modernism? What outdated modes did Joyce critique in his writing? What mark did Joyce make on this movement? How was Joyce influenced by the early modernists and his peers within the movement? What was his influence on later modernists and even postmodernists? Do we see a progression in his texts over the course of Joyce's lifetime, becoming gradually more modernist? Give examples from his works to support your assessment.

Form and Genre

When we think of Joyce, most people usually think of his three most widely read texts: *Dubliners, A Portrait of the Artist as a Young Man,* and *Ulysses.* Less widely studied are his most experimental novel, *Finnegans Wake*; his play, *Exiles*; and his poetry. We will look at ways to write about these here.

Sample Topics:

1. ***Finnegans Wake:*** How do we read *Finnegans Wake?* What is a reader to make of this text? How do we approach it?

   Finnegans Wake, which Joyce began writing in 1922 while living in Paris, is his novel of the night, a counterpart to *Ulysses,* his novel of the day. Called *Work in Progress* up until the end of its composition, Joyce wanted to keep the title a secret, including from his publisher. The only person who knew it until 1938 was his wife, Nora, who was sworn to secrecy (Ellmann 543). *Finnegans Wake* began appearing in installments in literary magazines in 1928, and the first copy was in Joyce's hands on his birthday, February 2, 1939. (Being quite superstitious, Joyce placed a great deal of significance on dates, and his birthday was important to him.) As he was writing it, some of his usual supporters, including Harriet Shaw Weaver, Ezra Pound, and his brother Stanislaus, were unenthusiastic about his new endeavor, but others rallied around Joyce and his novel, composing essays to be collected in a volume hailing *Finnegans Wake*. The collection, titled *Our Exagmination Round His Factification for Incamination of Work in Progress*, brought together Samuel Beckett, Frank Budgen, Stuart Gilbert, Thomas MacGreevy, and William Carlos Williams, to name a few. Beckett's essay, "Dante . . . Bruno. Vico . . . Joyce," is perhaps the best known, and in it, the young Beckett offers his famous advice about the *Wake* to the reader: "Here form *is* content, content *is* form. You complain that this stuff is not written in English. It is not written at all. It is not to be read— or rather it is not only to be read, it is to be looked at and listened to. His writing is not *about* something; *it is that something itself*" (14). This is perhaps the best guidance available to the reader as he or she is tackling this novel, which Joyce himself referred to several times as "the monster" (Ellmann 716).

The novel gets its name from the Irish ballad of the same name in which Tim Finnegan appears to have died. He is taken home to be laid out, and the famous Irish wake, with food, drink, and celebration of the life of the deceased, begins. In the course of the evening, a fight breaks out, and whiskey splashes on Tim and he wakes up, never having been dead in the first place. Joyce uses this story to open his novel, with his Finnegan (a parallel for the Irish legend Fionn mac Cuhmaill/Finn MacCumhal/MacCool) laid out for his wake, and the mourners prepared to eat him, emphasizing what Joyce felt was the psychologically cannibalistic nature of his fellow countrymen. He, like Tim in the song, awakens but is told he is better off dead. In regard to its central plot, *Finnegans Wake* tells the story of a family whose father/husband, Humphrey Chimpden Earwicker or HCE, is Scandinavian by birth but who has settled in Dublin, becoming the new Fionn perhaps. He has gotten himself in some trouble in Phoenix Park (we never get the true story but several versions of it). His wife, Anna Livia Plurabelle or ALP, writes a letter to try to clear his name. We learn of ALP mostly through what others say about her, similar to Molly Bloom in *Ulysses.* They have three children, twin boys Shem and Shaun, who are near opposites and seem to be in constant competition. Shem the Penman is an unconventional artist, and Shaun the Post is a more traditional postman. Their daughter, Issy, who seems to suffer from a split personality, is the object of desire for the men in the novel, including her father and brothers. The novel begins *in medias res,* and the end of the novel cycles back to the beginning, reinforcing the cycles of life and nature, especially rivers.

If, as Beckett suggests, the *Wake* is not meant to be read or only read, how do we approach the novel? What do we "do" with *Finnegans Wake?* If you plan to write an essay on this topic, you might want to choose one of the more accessible passages, for example, the "Anna Livia Plurabelle" section, and look at what Joyce is doing there. How does he tell his story? What techniques does he use? How would we describe his language? What do we do with all the puns and wordplay? How about the river imagery? Because the plot of the novel is relatively loose and open to much interpretation, due to the fact that it is being told in the night when it is dark and things are not what they seem, it is more fruitful to look at the poetry of the language and allow the words to wash over you. What is the essence of *Finnegans Wake?*

2. *Exiles:* What do we make of Joyce's only dramatic work? How does *Exiles* fit into the Joycean canon? Is it identifiably Joycean?

Written during Joyce's most productive period, 1914, between finishing *Portrait* and beginning *Ulysses,* and published in 1918, the play *Exiles* reveals a debt to the Norwegian playwright Henrik Ibsen, one of Joyce's favorite writers. It is one of the least studied works by Joyce, and many critics consider it somewhat mechanical. The plot is fairly simple: A writer, Richard Rowan and his common-law wife Bertha (they are not married), live in Dublin with their son Archie who is eight years old. Archie takes piano lessons from Beatrice Justice, an old friend of Richard's. Richard and Beatrice have another friend in common, Robert Hand, a journalist. The play features two love triangles: Richard-Bertha-Robert and Richard-Beatrice-Robert. Jealousy and doubt are the overarching emotions in this drama, which features the freethinking Rowan encouraging Bertha to yield to the advances of Hand if she so desires. She somewhat reluctantly takes him up on the offer, and spends the night with Hand, though the event is not dramatized and the reader does not know precisely what happened overnight. Rowan, who believed himself to be above jealousy, is distraught. Hand, who is leaving for England, stops in to say goodbye and he and Bertha share a moment recalling their evening together and agree that it was "a dream." Hand then tells Rowan what happened (though it is not clear which version of the story is true), revealing that he failed in his pursuit of Bertha, and that she "went away." Bertha and Rowan are reconciled at the end of the play, and she wishes to be with her "strange wild lover," meaning Rowan.

This play picks up one of the themes of "The Dead" and foreshadows some of the thoughts on Bloom's mind as he makes his way through the day in *Ulysses:* marital jealousy and doubt. Joyce's own doubts and insecurities about Nora's past are brought out here, and he projects some of his characteristics onto his protagonist Richard Rowan. Robert Hand is modeled on Vincent Cosgrave, a friend of Joyce's who tried to convince Nora that Joyce did not love her and that "in any case the man was mad" (Ellmann 160). It is certainly no coincidence that Rowan and Bertha are not married and that they have a child out of wedlock.

What do we make of Joyce's one and only drama? How does it fit into the Joycean canon? Why is it seldom studied? Is there more to *Exiles* than meets the eye? What was Joyce's purpose in writing this play? Is it identifiably Joycean? Why or why not? Use specific passages in the play to support your thesis.

3. **Joyce's poetry:** How do we approach *Chamber Music* and *Pomes Penyeach?* How does Joyce's poetry fit into his oeuvre? How might the reader classify it?

Along with his drama *Exiles,* Joyce's poetry is not frequently studied. His first volume, *Chamber Music,* is a collection of 36 love poems written when Joyce still lived in Dublin, before he met Nora and before they left for continental Europe together. By the time Joyce had found a publisher for his collection, he was having second thoughts about publishing them at all. He saw them as "poems for lovers, and he was no lover" (Ellmann 260). His brother Stanislaus, who liked the book, persuaded him to go through with the publication, arguing that he should "publish *Chamber Music* with all its dishonesty so that he may publish his other books with all their honesty. As so often, Stanislaus was sensible and practical, but James had cause to feel that *Chamber Music* was pale beside his other work" (260). *Pomes Penyeach* is a collection of 13 poems published in 1927, written over the 20 years since *Chamber Music.* The poem "Ecce Puer," written on the death of his father and birth of his grandson, was published in 1936 in Joyce's *Collected Poems* (which consisted of his two volumes and the one new addition). Other poems by Joyce include "The Holy Office" (1904) and "Gas from a Burner" (1912), which were circulated within the Joycean circle but not formally published until after his death, and the posthumous "Giacomo Joyce," a love poem written in 1907 and published in 1968.

What does Joyce's poetry reveal about the author? Do we see a different side of Joyce through his poetry? If so, what side do we see? How would we describe the poet Joyce as opposed to the novelist Joyce? Are their voices different? How would we characterize Joyce's poetry? Why is it so infrequently studied?

Language, Symbols, and Imagery

Joyce, with his classical educational background and training, borrows a great deal from mythology and the symbols contained within myth for his texts, especially *Ulysses* and *Finnegans Wake.* He also uses geography, specifically rivers and the cities through which they run, as a recurrent image in the *Wake.* Finally, it would be appropriate here to consider how Joyce, himself a talented linguist, has been translated into other languages, both during his lifetime and after his death.

Sample Topics:

1. **Rivers in *Finnegans Wake:*** What is the importance of river imagery in this novel? What role do rivers play in the text? How are rivers symbolic? How does the water imagery work within the text?

   Anna Livia Plurabelle, the female protagonist in *Finnegans Wake,* is Anna Liffey, the colloquial name for the Liffey River that runs through Dublin. The Irish for Liffey is *An Life* or *Abhainn na Life,* and although the Irish word *life* is not pronounced the same as the English word "life," certainly Joyce would have appreciated the wordplay. He uses Anna Livia Plurabelle, or ALP, to symbolize life, and the life-giving properties of water are emphasized throughout the text. In the "Anna Livia Plurabelle" section of the *Wake,* the washerwomen are working at opposite sides of the river, holding a conversation while they do the laundry. As night falls and the tide comes in, they grow more distant and more indecipherable. The water separates them, and they can no longer hear or understand each other. At the end of the novel, Anna Livia Plurabelle flows out to the sea, saying "I'll slip away before they're up. They'll never see. Nor know. Nor miss me." Her final words connect to the opening words of the novel, emphasizing the cyclical, interconnected nature of water and rivers.

   What role do rivers play in *Finnegans Wake?* What is the importance of river imagery in this novel? Joyce has woven hundreds of river names into the text, particularly in the "Anna Livia Plurabelle" section, and he uses his neologism "riverrun" to begin the novel. How does the water imagery and sound make its way into the *Wake?* What impact does it have on the reading? Does the flow of water mimic the flow of language (or vice versa)? Why did Joyce choose rivers? What is their significance in the progress of human history? Can we make a parallel to the progress of literary history? What is Joyce trying to tell us here?

2. **Mythology in Joyce:** How does Joyce use myth in his fiction? How does he adapt Greek myth in *Ulysses* and Irish myth in *Finnegans Wake?* Does the reader need to know the mythology that Joyce adapts to fully appreciate these texts?

Joyce's educational background and avid reading habits gave him a solid understanding of mythology, both classical Greek and Roman as well as native Irish. It is from these myths that he draws storylines for his novels *Ulysses* and *Finnegans Wake.* Obviously *Ulysses* parallels the Greek epic tale that features Odysseus's famous journey home and all the obstacles he faced along the way. (For more background on the *Odyssey/Ulysses* correspondences, see the first chapter on *Ulysses:* "The Telemachiad.") *Finnegans Wake* takes its inspiration from both the Irish street song of the same name and the legend of Fionn mac Cumhaill (Finn Mac-Cumhal or Finn Mac Cool), who was a hunter-warrior in Irish legend and whose stories formed what is called the Fenian Cycle. As a boy, Fionn was a protégé to a druid whose life's work consisted of trying to catch the salmon of knowledge. He finally accomplished his task and asked Fionn to cook it for him. As the story goes, Fionn burned his thumb while cooking the fish and instinctively put his thumb in his mouth. There was some salmon skin on his thumb, and as a result Fionn received the salmon's knowledge. Fionn mac Cumhaill's followers were called the Fianna, and his son was Oisín the poet. As legend has it, Fionn never died but sleeps somewhere under the city of Dublin with his Fianna warriors, waiting for the moment when Ireland needs him most. Several accounts tell us that Fionn was a giant, and some of Ireland's geography is attributed to him, including the Giant's Causeway in Northern Ireland, which legend says Fionn created so that he could hop across to Scotland without getting his feet wet. The myth of Fionn figures heavily especially at the beginning of *Finnegans Wake*, and Joyce shared that "he conceived his book as the dream of old Finn, lying in death beside the Liffey and watching the history of Ireland and the world—past and future—flow through his mind like flotsam on the river of life" (Ellmann 544).

How does Joyce adapt the *Odyssey* and the legend of Fionn mac Cumhaill for his purposes? Can a reader make his or her way through *Ulysses* without knowing the correspondences? Can we say the same for *Finnegans Wake?* Look for ways the source and adaptation are similar and different. Does knowing the source text enhance our understanding of Joyce's novel? If so, how? If not, why?

3. **Joyce in translation:** How does the very act of translating the seemingly untranslatable *Ulysses* and *Finnegans Wake* reinforce the infinite possibility of language?

In 1924, while Joyce was living in Paris, Ludmila Savitsky's French translation of *A Portrait of the Artist as a Young Man*, which she titled *Dedalus*, was published. As a result, Joyce became insistent on *Ulysses*, which he had previously deemed untranslatable, being translated into French. Some sections of it had already been completed for the lecture Valery Larbaud gave on Joyce's work in December 1922, but now Joyce hoped to have the entire novel completed. The translation was a monumental task that required the work of a team of four men: Auguste Morel, who was the main translator, and Larbaud, Stuart Gilbert, and Joyce himself who reviewed and edited Morel's work. There were heated discussions about word choice and by the end the men were not speaking to one another. The same types of problems surrounded the translation of the "Anna Livia Plurabelle" section of *Finnegans Wake* into French. The work was begun by Samuel Beckett and his friend Alfred Péron, but when Beckett broke with the family due to what the Joyces felt was his trifling with Lucia Joyce's feelings, the work was taken up by Paul Léon, Eugene Jolas, Ivan Goll, Philippe Soupault, and the author. The five men met once a week to collaborate on the translation, and when it was complete, Joyce proclaimed: "There is nothing that cannot be translated" (Ellmann 632). The complete French translation of the *Wake* was not published until 1982.

The statement Joyce made when the "Anna Livia Plurabelle" translation was complete certainly rings true: If this section of the *Wake* could be translated, anything could. To write this essay, and to do it well, the author should be fluent in another language in order to be able to make a comparative analysis of the source (original text) and target (translation) side by side. *Ulysses* has been translated into nearly every modern language but *Finnegans Wake* only into a handful, so your choice of text and language may be dependent on what is available. Once the preliminaries are done, choose a passage in the text and do a close reading of the English and foreign language texts. Look for places where the translator had to make a difficult decision, perhaps where a word or phrasing in Joyce had several layers of meaning, contained a double entendre, pun, or wordplay that could not easily translate into the target language. What is the task of the translator in undertaking the works of Joyce? How does translating Joyce reinforce the infinite possibility of language?

Compare and Contrast Essays

Possibilities abound here—a writer might compare two works or two characters within the Joycean canon, or compare a work or character in Joyce with another author's. The suggestions offered below are just a few of the many options in this category, and since *Finnegans Wake* does not have its own chapter, all three questions revolve around that novel.

Sample Topics:

1. ***Ulysses* and *Finnegans Wake*:** How do these two novels compare? In what ways are they similar? In what ways are they different? Does *Ulysses* provide a natural progression into *Finnegans Wake?*

   Joyce called *Ulysses* his novel of the day and *Finnegans Wake* his novel of the night. Unlike *Portrait* and *Ulysses*, *Ulysses* and the *Wake* share no common characters, and one does not pick the story up where the other left off. Nonetheless, there are similarities and the reader is able to see a stylistic progression from one to the next. In *Ulysses,* Joyce takes on the themes of familial relationships, an individual's struggle with identity, the power of gossip and rumor, the human need for connection, and navigating the problems of everyday life, including death, isolation, and despair. *Finnegans Wake* addresses those issues as well, though in a much more convoluted and complicated way. HCE is an outsider, an immigrant to Dublin, who has been charged with a crime he may or may not have committed. Much of what we learn about these characters, especially ALP, is filtered through others, much as we learn about Molly through gossip and innuendo until her monologue. Issy, like Milly Bloom, is coming into womanhood and men are beginning to view her as a sexual partner. Stephen is similar to Shem the Penman, as both are aspiring artists, and, critics suggest, both are parallels for Joyce.

How are *Ulysses* and *Finnegans Wake* similar? In what ways are they different? If a reader makes his or her way through the Joycean canon chronologically, do the final episodes of *Ulysses* prepare him or her for what is to come in *Finnegans Wake?* What overall comparison can we make between these two works?

2. **Anna Livia Plurabelle and Molly Bloom:** What commonalities do Joyce's female protagonists share? How do they contrast? How does Joyce portray these women?

Molly Bloom is the earth goddess in *Ulysses,* and Anna Livia Plurabelle is the river goddess in *Finnegans Wake.* They both stand as symbols in Joyce's works of what he imagines woman to be. Both of them are mothers to young women, Milly and Issy, who are about to replace them as sexual objects of desire. Both have husbands who are outsiders and about whom other characters speculate. We learn about Molly and ALP through the opinions of others who gossip about them, and it is left to the reader to wonder what is the truth. Both characters are given the final words in their novels, presenting stream-of-consciousness monologues as Molly drifts off to sleep and ALP drifts into the sea.

What do Molly and ALP have in common? How are they different? To write this essay, look closely not only at the monologues these two characters deliver but also at how the other characters in the books perceive them. For ALP, look at the washerwomen's conversation about her and what assumptions they make. For Molly, consider the way in which the men with whom Bloom interacts throughout the day make allusions to her character and personality, both to his face and behind his back. How does Joyce portray these two women? Does he want them to stand as universal symbols of womanhood? If so, what does that tell the reader about Joyce's opinion or understanding of women? Has he created sympathetic, realistic characters? Who are Anna Livia Plurabelle and Molly Bloom?

3. **Humphrey Chimpden Earwicker and Leopold Bloom:** How do Bloom and HCE compare? What does Joyce tell us about husbands and fathers through these characters?

Leopold Bloom and Humphrey Chimpden Earwicker, the unlikely heroes of Joyce's final two novels, *Ulysses* and *Finnegans Wake*, are both outsiders. Bloom, though born in Ireland and baptized Catholic, is seen as a Hungarian Jew, and the fact of his wife's adultery with Blazes Boylan ostracizes him further. Humphrey Chimpden Earwicker is Scandinavian, making him an immigrant to Dublin, where he marries Anna Livia Plurabelle, the life source of the city. His alleged crime in Phoenix Park involving two young girls results in his being snubbed and mistrusted, the subject of much gossip and curiosity. Both men have daughters whose budding sexuality is a cause for concern and, perhaps more unconsciously for Bloom than for HCE, desire. Unlike HCE, Bloom has no sons with whom he must compete for power, but he makes up for that with the character of Boylan.

How do Bloom and HCE compare? What traits do they have in common? What makes them different? Does Joyce expect the reader's sympathy for both? Is one more likeable than the other? What does Joyce tell us about husbands and marriage through these characters? What does he tell us about fathers? How would we describe these two men?

Bibliography and Online Resources

Attridge, Derek, ed. *The Cambridge Companion to James Joyce.* Cambridge: Cambridge University Press, 1990. Print.

Beckett, Samuel, et. al. *Our Exagmination Round His Factification For Incamination Of Work In Progress.* London: Faber and Faber, 1929. Print.

Campbell, Joseph and Henry Morton Robinson. *A Skeleton Key to Finnegans Wake.* New York: Buccaneer Books, 1976. Print.

Carey, Phyllis and Ed Jewinski, eds. *Re: Joyce 'n Beckett.* New York: Fordham University Press, 1992. Print.

An Chomhairle Leabharlanna. [The Library Council.] "Ask about Ireland." Web. <http://askaboutireland.ie/>

Ellmann, Richard. *James Joyce.* New York: Oxford University Press, 1982. Print.

———, ed. *Letters of James Joyce: Volume II.* New York: Viking, 1966. Print.

———, ed. *Letters of James Joyce: Volume III.* New York: Viking, 1966. Print.

Fargnoli, A. Nicholas. *Critical Companion to James Joyce: A Literary Companion to His Life and Works.* New York: Facts on File, 2006. Print.

Gilbert, Stuart, ed. *Letters of James Joyce: Volume I.* New York: Viking, 1966. Print.

Gluck, Barbara Reich. *Beckett and Joyce: Friendship and Fiction.* Pennsylvania: Bucknell University Press, 1979. Print.

Gordon, John. *Finnegans Wake: A Plot Summary.* Syracuse, N.Y.: Syracuse University Press, 1986. Print.

Gorman, Herbert. *James Joyce.* New York: Farrar and Rinehart, 1939. Print.

Joyce, James. *Collected Poems. The Portable James Joyce.* New York: Penguin Books, 1967. Print.

———. *Dubliners. The Portable James Joyce.* New York: Penguin Books, 1967. Print.

———. *Exiles. The Portable James Joyce.* New York: Penguin Books, 1967. Print.

———. *Finnegans Wake.* New York: Penguin Books, 1976. Print.

———. *A Portrait of the Artist as a Young Man. The Portable James Joyce.* New York: Penguin Books, 1967. Print.

———. *Ulysses*. New York: Vintage Books, 1990. Print.

Joyce, Stanislaus. *My Brother's Keeper: James Joyce's Early Years.* New York: Viking, 1958. Print.

Maddox, Brenda. *Nora: The Real Life of Molly Bloom.* Boston: Houghton Mifflin, 1988. Print.

McHugh, Roland. *Annotations to Finnegans Wake.* Baltimore: Johns Hopkins University Press, 1991. Print.

Nash, John. *James Joyce and the Act of Reception: Reading, Ireland, Modernism.* Cambridge: Cambridge University Press, 2006. Print.

O'Brien, Edna. *James Joyce.* New York: Viking Penguin, 1999. Print.

Schloss, Carol Loeb. *Lucia Joyce: To Dance in the Wake.* New York: Farrar, Straus and Giroux, 2003. Print.

Seidel, Michael. *James Joyce: A Short Introduction.* Malden, Mass.: Blackwell Publishers, 2002. Print.

Senn, Fritz. *Joyce's Dislocutions: Essays on Reading as Translation.* Baltimore: Johns Hopkins University Press, 1984. Print.

Spinks, Lee. *James Joyce: A Critical Guide.* Edinburgh: Edinburgh University Press, 2009. Print.

Vichnar, David, ed. "Hypermedia Joyce Studies: An Electronic Journal of James Joyce Scholarship." Web. <http://hjs.ff.cuni.cz/main/hjs.php?page=index_page>

DUBLINERS

READING TO WRITE

JAMES JOYCE's *Dubliners,* a collection of 15 short stories, was first published in London in 1914 after a nine-year struggle that included three publishing houses, several lawyers, and quite a bit of the author's personal savings. The stories, most of which seem quite tame by today's standards, shocked early readers, and publishers feared audience reception of them, as well as possible lawsuits for libel and obscenity. Each of these stories presents an episode in the life of a resident of Ireland's capital city, and each of these episodes ends with the main character having an epiphany, a moment of sudden realization and understanding. The bleakness of Irish life at the turn of the century as portrayed by Joyce cannot go unnoticed. As we read *Dubliners,* we would find it difficult to miss the symbolism and imagery calling to mind decay, stagnation, and hopelessness. Joyce is also sharply critiquing the Catholic Church in Ireland, certainly another reason why publishers were reluctant to print his work.

As we read *Dubliners,* we should allow ourselves to be guided by the young narrator in "The Sisters" and his fixation on three critical words that can shape how we write about these stories. He muses: "Every night as I gazed up at the window I said softly to myself the word *paralysis.* It had always sounded strangely in my ears, like the word *gnomon* in the Euclid and the word *simony* in the Catechism." These three words, *paralysis, gnomon,* and *simony,* are elements that weave through the entire tapestry of *Dubliners.* Paralysis is evident in nearly every story, with the protagonists frozen in their bleak situations. The meaning of the word *gnomon,* which in Euclidean geometry is the shape left behind after removing a small parallelogram from a larger one, is expanded by Joyce to encompass whatever is missing or incomplete. As a narrative device, gnomon leaves the reader (and sometimes the narrator) wondering what is really happening and what he or she has missed. Finally the term *simony,* strictly defined, is the act of accepting payment for holy offices or church favors. It is a sin in Roman Catholicism. Joyce also expands this term to include not simply the selling of spiritual favors but the debasement of anything sacred. For Joyce, simony is also closely connected with all forms of secular corruption. In developing an essay topic about *Dubliners,* we must pay close attention to the narrators and their fixations, as they give us the best insights into the stories. Nothing in Joyce is accidental.

One of the most commonly anthologized and read stories from *Dubliners* (with the exception of "The Dead," which will be treated in its own chapter) is "Araby." Though one of the shorter stories in the collection, it contains nearly all of Joyce's main themes. In the following passage, the young narrator describes his feelings when he sees Mangan's sister, on whom he has a boyhood crush:

> Her image accompanied me even in places the most hostile to romance. On Saturday evenings when my aunt went marketing I had to go to carry some of the parcels. We walked through the flaring streets, jostled by drunken men and bargaining women, amid the curses of labourers, the shrill litanies of shop-boys who stood on guard by the barrels of pigs' cheeks, the nasal chanting of street-singers, who sang a come-all-you about O'Donovan Rossa, or a ballad about the troubles in our native land. These noises converged in a single sensation of life for me: I imagined that I bore my chalice safely through a throng of foes. Her name sprang to my lips at moments in strange prayers and praises which I myself did not understand. My eyes were often full of tears (I could not tell why) and at times a flood from my heart seemed to pour itself out into my bosom. I thought little of the future. I did not know whether I would ever speak to her or not or, if I spoke to her, how I could tell her of my confused adoration. But my body was like a harp and her words and gestures were like fingers running on the wires.

This passage is rich in symbolism and the themes that run through all of the short stories in *Dubliners.* The young narrator begins the paragraph by providing the reader with a clear sense of setting, showing an unpleasant side to Ireland's marketplace, which he tell us is "hostile to romance." The streets are filled with drunken men, cursing laborers, (injecting an immediate class distinction into the scene), and the singers and their traditional Irish tunes, come-all-ye's or ballads about Irish politics. The narrator envisions himself as a knight carrying the Holy Grail to safety. Mangan's sister has become his grail, his prize. He admits that he does not quite understand his emotions for the girl and the physical manifestations of those feelings—"Her name sprang to my lips at moments in strange prayers and praises," and "my eyes were often full of tears." His ecstasies over Mangan's sister mimic the religious ecstasies he certainly would have read about in Catholic Lives of the Saints books. Indeed, in this passage and in others, the religious overtones reveal to the reader exactly how entrenched and intertwined Irish life is in its dominant religion (at least at the time), Roman Catholicism. The final image in this passage is unequivocally Irish. The narrator shares that his "body was like a harp and her words and gestures were like fingers running on the wires." One of the symbols of Ireland is the harp, and here the young boy offers himself up as this symbol, allowing himself to be played by Mangan's sister. Certainly there is a sexual connotation to the image of the girl's fingers running along the harp wires since the boy is standing in for the instrument, but we can also read more into this sentence. Mangan's sister, throughout the story, recognizes the power she has over the boy. She is coy with him, takes advantage of him, and he seems to recognize this in the passage, but does not seem to mind. The narrator's shame and anger at the end of the story might allow the reader to interpret this symbolism further. If the young boy is a harp being played by the young girl, we may understand that the boy is Ireland and the girl symbolizes one of the institutions controlling that country, the Roman Catholic Church. "Araby" is filled with church imagery, not only in this passage but throughout the story. The family lives in a home that used to be inhabited by a priest (who left behind some of his belongings), and Mangan's sister cannot go to the Araby bazaar because of a convent retreat. The rich array of symbols Joyce presents would certainly be a promising avenue to pursue in writing about this story.

TOPICS AND STRATEGIES

Dubliners presents and suggests any number of viable directions to pursue when developing a topic and essay. The following prompts and sug-

gestions should give you a good starting point from which you can begin to flesh out your paper.

Themes

Joyce plays with several overarching themes throughout *Dubliners,* working them through his short stories in such a way that we, as readers, quickly begin to see the commonalities among the tales and characters. In almost every story, the main character or characters have an epiphany, but each of their moments of understanding comes in a different way and with very different consequences.

Sample Topics:

1. **Gnomon, paralysis, simony:** How do these three words collectively suggest a theme in the stories of *Dubliners?* Certainly they work to frame "The Sisters," but in what other tales do we find evidence of this three-part theme?

   The narrator in "The Sisters" provides us with these three themes in the first paragraph of the story. He obsesses over the words, and it is certainly no coincidence that they provide a thematic foundation for this story as well as others in the collection. A paper that addresses this question would begin by clearly defining for the reader what Joyce meant in using these words and how our young narrator understands them. How are the definitions of these words expanded in the Joycean text? The essay would then move to provide examples of these three themes in "The Sisters" through what is explicitly seen and stated in the text as well as what is missing (nicely providing evidence of the theme of gnomon). In what other stories in *Dubliners* do we find these themes? When considering the concept of gnomon, think about what stories leave the reader feeling a bit in the dark and uncertain about what is truly happening. Ellipses in dialogue or narration are certainly a hint for the reader of the presence of a Joycean gnomon, but also consider other signs of absence as well, such as places in the stories where the narrator witnesses an event "offstage" and we as readers do not have the benefit of seeing it ourselves. For example, what does the "queer old josser" do in the field in the story "An Encounter"? What were the objects Maria handled on the saucers in "Clay"? For paralysis, a writer should certainly consider physical ailments (the priest in "The Sisters" and Mr. Kernan in "Grace"), but more importantly, look for the multitude of characters who experience a mental or emotional paralysis, which is how Joyce wants us to understand this state. Joycean paralysis is one of the spirit or mind, a sense of being caught in a truly unfortunate position with no way out. The most obvious example of paralysis in the Joycean sense is seen in "Eveline," with the tragic heroine paralyzed with fear at the end of the story, unable to move forward and make a life for herself. What other characters seem spiritually or emotionally paralyzed? Finally, in discussing simony, certainly the characters with religious connections in these stories will need to be mentioned, including the priests in "The Sisters," "Araby," and "Grace," but when writing on this theme, you must expand your definition to include the degradation of anything sacred. Consider the institution of marriage in "The Boarding House" and how Mrs. Mooney reduces it to a business deal. What does Joyce do to the sacredness of family in "Counterparts" and "A Little Cloud"?

2. **Decay and desperation:** Where do we see the themes of decay and desperation in *Dubliners?* How would you provide evidence of these themes? What stories in particular reinforce them?

Evidence of decay and desperation can be found in every story in *Dubliners*. Joyce evokes this theme in the physical descriptions of the city of Dublin, its homes and its outdoor spaces. We see material decay everywhere, but we also observe decay of the spirit in nearly all of Joyce's characters. This spiritual decay frequently leads to acts of desperation. When writing this essay, a reader should probably focus on a few stories rather than the entire text and then re-read those stories very closely for signs of decay and darkness. For example, in "A Painful Case," the reader quickly forms an idea about the sad state of affairs in the life of James Duffy after reading only the first full paragraph. Joyce chooses his words with extreme care, and knows the impact of language on the reader. Duffy's home is "sombre" and is situated next to a "disused distillery" on the banks of a "shallow river." His furnishings are sparse and austere, and the description of his dwelling does not evoke the comforts of home. How do his surroundings foreshadow or predict the desperation and unhappiness that inform this story? Similarly, signs of decay are prevalent in "Two Gallants," and the characters in this tale are among the most desperate and despicable in *Dubliners*. What signs in the story does Joyce provide to indicate decay? Think about how language and word use suggest the moral and spiritual decay of the characters. In what other stories do we find decay and desperation?

3. **Epiphany:** How would you classify a Joycean epiphany? How is it different from what a reader might traditionally expect? Which characters experience the most profound epiphanies?

All of the main characters in *Dubliners* experience epiphanies, or moments of revelation or understanding, but contrary to what we might expect, these flashes do not function to bring them contentment but rather further fuel their frustration and anxiety. Their epiphanies do not serve as solutions to their problems but instead add to their existential crises, causing them to question everything. The epiphany at the end of "Araby" is certainly one worth discussing in an essay, as it is obvious and dramatic, but look for and discuss the somewhat more subtle moments of revelation experienced by the characters in "The Boarding House" and "A Painful Case." What can we understand about Little Chandler's character from his epiphany at the end of "A Little Cloud"? What impact do the epiphanies have on the characters in the stories? How do they impact the reader? Do the epiphanies provide the protagonist and the reader with a satisfying dénouement or conclusion to the story? How does Joyce adapt epiphany, and what purpose does it serve in his writing?

4. **Homecoming:** Where in *Dubliners* do you see the theme of homecoming? How have the characters changed over the course

of their travels, and how do they approach their original setting as a result?

Certainly the theme of homecoming is an obvious one in Joyce's *Ulysses,* but we find it playing out in some of the stories in *Dubliners* as well. Joyce began experimenting with the circular story in which the protagonist starts and ends his or her day in essentially the same physical location. A great place to begin when writing this essay would be to look for the stories in *Dubliners* that begin and end at home. Certainly "An Encounter" would provide an excellent example of the theme of homecoming, especially since the young protagonist set out on his quest with very high expectations for his day of adventure and returns home with more than he bargained for. Consider how the boy's travels in the course of his day changed him, perhaps moving him from innocence to experience. Similarly, the young narrator of "Araby" follows a circular route from his home to the bazaar and back again, but returns a different person. And the reader knows that Eveline, in the story of the same name, will return to her dusty little brown house a changed woman as well. Finally, the homecomings in "Counterparts" and "A Little Cloud" are scenes of utter desperation and despair. Reflect on how Joyce plays with our perception of homecoming, which we generally assume to be a joyous event, and turns it into something unsettling at best and shocking at worst. Can the protagonists in *Dubliners* ever go home again after their experiences? Why is Joycean homecoming so disappointing?

Character

Joyce's characters in *Dubliners* provide the writer with a multitude of paper topics. In even the shortest of these stories, Joyce develops elaborate character sketches, allowing the reader to form an understanding about that individual. Indeed, even Joyce's supporting characters have personalities that are distinct enough that the writer might successfully build an essay around one of them.

Sample Topics:

1. **Polly Mooney:** How would we characterize Polly Mooney? Is she in control, or is she being controlled? What can we say about Polly Mooney from what is revealed through the text?

Although the reader is provided a fuller portrait of Mrs. Mooney in "The Boarding House," Joyce also gives quite a bit of insight into her daughter Polly's character. The first thing we learn about her is that she is fond of singing and chooses appropriately titled contemporary songs—"I'm a Naughty Girl" from the musical comedy *A Greek Slave.* Joyce, fond as he was of the stage, would have known this and so would the readers of the time, but it still resonates with us today. Polly is clearly a flirt. We are told she is "a slim girl of nineteen" with "light soft hair and a small full mouth." Joyce refers to her as a "little perverse Madonna." An essay on Polly Mooney would benefit from a character analysis of not just the young woman but also who she is in relation to her mother and in the eyes of her future husband, Mr. Doran. Joyce tells us a great deal about Mrs. Mooney and Mr. Doran, but much of what we know about Polly is inferred, hinted at, or learned secondhand. We have a physical description of her, and find out that she had been training to be a typist when she caught the unwanted attention of a "disreputable sheriff's man." What can we surmise from this? Polly knows she is being watched by her mother as her relationship with Mr. Doran develops but does nothing to hide her secret. It is only once Mrs. Mooney decides to address the problem that Polly becomes concerned, breaking down as she tells Doran of her mother's intentions. What do we make of Polly's tears and threat to "put an end to herself"? How do Mr. Doran's impressions and memories of Polly impact our opinion of the young woman? Joyce ends his story with the omniscient narrator writing from Polly's point of view. What do we learn about her in these final paragraphs? Does it reinforce what we have already concluded? Discuss how Joyce builds the character of Polly in a piecemeal fashion and the effect this has on the reader.

2. **Eveline:** How does the story represent Eveline? What causes her paralysis? Is Eveline a victim? If so, of what?

The title character in Joyce's "Eveline" is perhaps one of the most paralyzed individuals in *Dubliners* and, as a result, one of the most tragic. Her life is miserable, and she is charged with taking on the role of woman of the house after the death of her mother. She cares for her abusive father and her siblings, as well as provides for the family financially by working as a shop attendant. While much of her situation is brought on by outside circumstances, consider the ways in which Eveline's unhappiness and paralysis is the result of her self-destructive behavior and mindset.

The writer of this essay would certainly begin with a close analysis of what Joyce tells us about Eveline, including the information we can take at face value: her job, her dusty home, her exhaustion. But of course Joyce wants us to move from these surface details into a more critical, deeper understanding of Eveline's character. What are the roots and underlying causes of her paralysis? Does the reader anticipate her inability to leave with Frank at the end of the story? Are we surprised that she cannot board the ship? Look for instances in the text where Eveline is passive, acted on rather than acting. How do the supporting characters in the story, specifically Frank and Eveline's father, but also Miss Gavan in the Stores, reinforce for the reader Eveline's submissive nature? Would you characterize Eveline as the embodiment of feminine passivity? If so, what passages specifically support this? What are your impressions of her relationship with Frank? Look at the paragraphs detailing their courtship. Does she love Frank or the "idea" of Frank? Before the section break at the end of the story, we learn that Eveline expects Frank to save her, and then after the section break, as she approaches the boat, she prays that God will direct her, "show her what was her duty." How do Eveline's expectations of Frank and God further point to her passive nature? The final paragraphs of the story provide excellent evidence for the theme of self-destructive obedience and paralysis.

3. **Mrs. Kearney:** How does Joyce present Mrs. Kearney as an example or type of mother? How would you describe her, based both on her words and actions as well as the unspoken elements in the text, namely the reactions of the supporting characters in the story?

The meddlesome mother in Joyce's "A Mother" provides an excellent case for character study. Indeed, Joyce's choice of a title for this story tells the reader that Mrs. Kearney is a distinct type (or stereotype) of a mother. As you begin to develop your essay, think first about what we know of Mrs. Kearney's personal history. The first paragraph of the story presents us with the fact that Mrs. Kearney "arranged everything," setting the tone for what is to come. Then, Joyce flashes back to the past, giving us a glimpse into how she became the "nice lady" we are left with at the end of the story. Was Mrs. Kearney (even as Miss Devlin) ever a genuinely nice lady? What impression does the reader have of her as a young woman? How does Joyce's characterization of her in her youth predict the events later in the story? What can we say about her in relation to her daughter? What do we think about her determination "to take advantage of her daughter's name" during the Irish Revival? How would we describe Mrs. Kearney's relationship with her husband? We are told early in the story that she married out of spite, but Joyce presents us with a rather sympathetic portrait of Mr. Kearney, who, unlike other fathers in *Dubliners*, is "sober, thrifty and pious," and was a "model father." However, Mrs. Kearney views her husband in the same way she views the General Post Office: something large, secure, and fixed; and though she knew the small number of his talents she appreciated his abstract value as a male." Is this utilitarian attitude about her husband in line with what we know of her personality? Does she have the same utilitarian approach toward her daughter? Study the text and develop an in-depth character assessment of Mrs. Kearney based not only on what Joyce tells us, but moreover on what Joyce shows us through the actions of the other characters.

4. **Father Flynn:** What do we really know about Father Flynn? Can we form a reliable character sketch of him based on the details provided by the narrator? How do the cryptic references to the priest by the adults in the story help to fill in the blanks? Is Flynn a typical or stereotypical priest? If so, what does Joyce communicate about Catholicism?

The priest in "The Sisters," already dead when the story opens, offers the reader an interesting choice for character analysis because we learn about him through a series of narrators whose reliability may be questionable. The young narrator has an innocence that prevents him from fully understanding what is really happening in the story and who Father Flynn really was, and the adults in the story leave ellipses (Joycean gnomons) to confound both the boy and the reader. Nobody gets a full picture of Father Flynn, which makes this essay challenging for the writer, but attention-grabbing for the reader.

As with all character analysis papers, this one should begin with what we are told in the text. What does Joyce reveal to the reader though the young narrator? The boy, after learning of Father Flynn's death, cannot fall asleep: "In the dark of my room I imagined that I saw again the heavy grey face of the paralytic . . . It murmured; and I understood that it desired to confess something." The boy's youth and innocence prevent him from comprehending why he is afraid of the priest, but he is. Then, just a few sentences later, a hint of his adult self filters into the narrative when he recognizes that he smiled "to absolve the simoniac of his sin." What other details about Father Flynn are revealed by the young narrator? How do some of these details hint at something being not quite right with the priest? For example, the boy felt "uneasy" at the man's smile because he "used to uncover his big discolored teeth and let his tongue lie on his lower lip." What other evidence from the narrator do we have to develop a character analysis of Flynn? What input do we get from the supporting characters in the story, including Flynn's sisters, the narrator's aunt and uncle, and Old Cotter? Their conversations are filled with ellipses, but frequently those ellipses tell the reader more than words would. Cotter clearly did not like Father Flynn, saying he would not like his children spending time with a "man like that." Later in the story, when the aunt and the narrator go to the home to pay their respects, we learn more about the priest from his sisters' perspectives. How do their recollections add to the character sketch?

History and Context

Although by the time Joyce was writing *Dubliners* he was no longer living in Ireland, he kept fully up to date on what was happening in his homeland through newspapers and letters from family and friends. His notion that one could reconstruct the city based on his writing is clear in *Dubliners*, as Joyce provides landmarks for the reader as he or she is traveling through the text with the narrator. He also incorporates a great deal of Irish history, which forces readers to brush up on their knowledge to fully appreciate what Joyce is trying to convey.

Sample Topics:

1. **Parnell and turn-of-the-century Irish politics:** What makes "Ivy Day" such an important text within the framework of *Dubliners?* Is it worth the extra effort required to appreciate and understand the story? Can we read "Ivy Day" without knowing the history and still take something away?

   "Ivy Day in the Committee Room" was one of Joyce's favorite tales in *Dubliners,* a fact that alone makes it worthy of close study. However, "Ivy Day" presents many obstacles to modern readers, especially ones who are unfamiliar with Irish politics at the turn of the century as well as Irish slang. A reader who is willing to do his or her research will be able to take great satisfaction in a deeper and clearer understanding of this story.

   Before writing an essay on Irish history and politics as seen through the lens of "Ivy Day," one must first become acquainted with the person of Charles Stewart Parnell, the Irish patriot who fought for Home Rule. Parnell, considered Ireland's uncrowned king, was a powerful politician who garnered many followers. His vision of an Ireland free of British rule won him support from Catholics and Protestants alike.

His political downfall and, some argue, the decline of the Home Rule movement stemmed from a scandal in his personal life: Parnell was in love with a married woman, Katharine (Kitty) O'Shea, the estranged wife of Captain William O'Shea. Captain O'Shea was aware of his wife's affair with Parnell for some years, filing for divorce only after she came into a sizeable inheritance. Captain O'Shea named Parnell as the cause for the divorce, marking him as an adulterer, which for many Irish Catholics was an irreconcilable offense. He married Kitty O'Shea, but the anti-Parnell movement and the attacks he faced because of his personal life took a toll on his health. Parnell died less than two years after the story broke at the age of 45. He is remembered on October 6, the date of his death, by wearing a sprig of ivy.

With this brief background, the reader/writer can then begin an in-depth study of "Ivy Day." Discuss Irish politics as presented in the story. The men are returning from a day of canvassing for a Dublin election and are discussing local politics as well as national issues. They have been paid to campaign for a man named Tierney, and several of the men are lukewarm at best about him as a city councilman. The passion comes into their conversation when talking about a possible visit to Dublin by the current king of Great Britain and Ireland, Edward VII. The men, being nationalist, cannot get excited about this visit, and this leads into their exchange about Parnell. What do we learn about Parnell through their dialogue? What do we learn about the men? In this story, more than any other, Joyce employs dialogue among the men, allowing us to hear their voices. Why did he choose this technique? He also uses gossip as a way of providing insight into these characters. How does gossip fit with the theme of politics? What is Joyce telling us about Irish politics in the late 1800s and early 1900s? Joyce, in "Ivy Day," looks closely at local politics; what can we extrapolate from this to get a sense of his opinion of national politics?

2. **The Irish condition in Dublin:** Based on what Joyce presents in *Dubliners*, how would we characterize the Irish condition in the early 1900s? Was Joyce's assessment accurate, or is he pre-

senting his own gnomon (only giving part of the whole)? How does Joyce portray not only Dublin and its inhabitants, but also the Catholic Church, politics, and economics to create a more complete impression for the reader?

The state of Ireland and, specifically, Dublin at the turn of the century is another subject of Joyce's criticism in *Dubliners.* The themes of paralysis, hopelessness, decrepitude, decay, and stagnation are prevalent throughout the stories and paint a very grim image of the city at the turn of the century. As you prepare to write this essay, you can speak generally about the impressions Joyce creates about his setting and characters, but you will be best served by focusing on several specific passages to support your thesis. "After the Race" would certainly be a good choice because it has several nationalities represented (and stereotyped) by characters who offer their views on Ireland. For example, Jimmy Doyle, the Irishman, has a father who hosts a dinner party for the "continentals," going out of his way to express "a real respect for foreign accomplishments." Despite being considered a "merchant prince" and having made his fortune several times over, Mr. Doyle is still intimidated by the young men whom he imagines are more worldly and more important. After the dinner, Joyce emphasizes Dublin's second-class ranking, writing, "That night the city wore the mask of a capital." Dublin cannot live up to the glamour of continental Europe (or even England) or the gluttonous wealth of the United States, as represented in the overweight Farley. How do these characters uphold Joyce's overall impressions of Dublin? What passages in this text support this? The same impressions of Ireland as second class come through in "A Little Cloud." Little Chandler, who is average sized but gives the "idea of being a little man," has the opportunity to meet up with his friend Gallaher who is returning from London for a visit to his family and friends in Dublin. Chandler, like many other Joycean characters and, indeed, like Joyce himself, believes "if you wanted to succeed you had to go away." Does the character Gallaher reinforce this notion? Chandler, who considers himself a poet, presents a vivid portrait of Dublin in his walk to meet Gallaher, musing: "The glow of a late autumn sunset covered the grass plots and walks. It cast a shower of kindly golden dust on the untidy nurses and decrepit old men who drowsed on the benches; it flickered on all the moving figures—on the children who ran screaming along the gravel paths and on everyone who passed through the gardens." This scene makes him sad, but then he grows annoyed once the sun sets and a "horde of grimy children populated the street. They stood or ran in the roadway or crawled up the steps before gaping doors or squatted like mice on the thresholds." These images of Dublin are bleak and desperate, and his mindset matches the setting. What other passages in *Dubliners* work to create this bleak image of the city? If *Dubliners* is a type of ethnography, what does the reader take away from this? What is the role of the Roman Catholic Church at the time? What role does class play, and where do we see class differences? Is the image Joyce presents fair and balanced? Your analysis will benefit from some research into Irish history to get a sense of the economy and state of affairs in Dublin in the early 1900s.

Philosophy and Ideas

Although *A Portrait of the Artist as a Young Man* and *Ulysses* showcase Joyce's philosophy more obviously and thoroughly than *Dubliners* does, we can still find several interesting essay topics within this category. Joyce begins to question and test what he has learned in all his years of Catholic school in *Dubliners,* and this is clear in the stories focused on religion in Ireland. In other stories, we find evidence of Joyce's modernist and existentialist ideals at their very beginning.

Sample Topics:

1. **Religion:** How is religion inextricably intertwined into Irish daily life? What does Joyce think about that relationship? How are the characters in *Dubliners* impacted by the role religion plays in their lives?

Although Joyce rejected Roman Catholicism in his midteens, the influence of the church on his writing or worldview lasted his entire life. That said, religion, and specifically the Irish brand of Roman Catholicism, makes its way into nearly every story in *Dubliners*. A discussion of the role of the church in Ireland would be a broad topic for an essay, and the writer would necessarily need to narrow his or her focus to either one aspect of Catholicism or religion as portrayed in just one or two stories.

In preparation for this essay, a writer unfamiliar with Roman Catholicism in the early 1900s in Ireland would need to do some research on church practices and dogma. The Irish brand of Roman Catholicism features a special and significant dedication to the Blessed Mother or Virgin Mary, the mother of Jesus. You may also find your research leading you into a comparison of Irish Catholicism with Celtic paganism, and this would also be a strong line of inquiry. The next step would be to decide what stories or what aspects of religion you will spotlight in your essay. If you choose to focus on devotion to the Virgin Mary, you would want to consider using "Araby" for its portrayal of Mangan's sister and the young narrator's idolatry of her. He venerates her, and Joyce's staging of the narrator's encounters with the girl emphasize this, as she is always higher than he, on a symbolic pedestal, and backlit to provide a halo. We also have a version of the Blessed Mother, ironically, in the "slavey" or servant girl-turned-prostitute. The traditional colors of the Virgin Mother are blue and white, and it is not accidental that the housekeeper in this story also wears those colors. Of course, we know the nameless slavey is no virgin. A writer could also focus on corruption in the church as seen in these stories. Certainly "The Sisters" would be included, as well as "Grace." Although we do not get the entire story behind Father Flynn's questionable behavior, it is clear that there was some scandal and cover-up involving the priest. In "Grace," the corruption within the church is seen through its members, Mr. Kernan's friends who convince him to go on a retreat to renew his faith. The men, though perhaps they mean well and hope to help Kernan overcome his alcoholism, are simply perpetuating stereotypes about other religions and getting much incorrect about their own. The priest at the retreat may not be corrupt, but he does not know his Bible, either. He tries to explain a difficult verse and relate it to the lives of the men in attendance, but he gets it wrong. Show the ways Joyce tries to steer the reader to an opinion of the Roman Catholic Church in Ireland. Discuss the ways in which religion (Catholicism as well as Protestantism) guides the decisions made by the characters in these stories.

2. **Modernism in *Dubliners*:** What makes *Dubliners* "modern"? Could a modern hero or heroine achieve fulfillment in Dublin? Is Dublin, seen through Joyce's lens, prepared for the ideas and ideals of the modern world?

Joyce is one of the great, if not the greatest, modernist writer, and we can readily note the themes and preoccupations associated with this movement throughout *Dubliners*. Modernism, broadly defined, is the cultural movement that questioned and frequently rejected "traditional" forms of thought and practice in favor of new, more modern ways of being in the world. Modernist philosophy was socially progressive and forced individuals to rethink the status quo. We see these ideas and ideals come through in *Dubliners,* as Joyce's narrators find themselves in situations in which they are faced with the decision to change and adjust to the modern world or remain prisoner of the past and its outdated methods.

As you begin to consider stories for inclusion in this essay, you might want to decide what aspects of modernism you will address. If you choose to look at religion, and specifically how this outdated institution prevents its participants from moving forward in their lives, stories such as "Grace," "The Boarding House," and "Eveline" would be excellent choices. Would Mr. Doran in "The Boarding House" have agreed to marry Polly, a girl he does not love, if it were not for the influence of the Catholic Church? Does religion prevent Eveline from leaving Ireland for Buenos Aires and a new, free life? Another angle you could pursue is to consider the impact of the modern, industrialized world of capitalism on a society that seems reluctant or unable to keep up. Look for stories in *Dubliners* where outside influences play a role in Dublin, such as in "An

Encounter," as the boys journey though the city and encounter not only industry but also the foreign sailors with exotically colored eyes. "Araby" also provides an example of how the modern, exotic world blends into Dublin society, though only briefly. The young boy is overwhelmed and paralyzed not only by his vanity but also by this entirely new and foreign experience, and he has no reference point for behaving in this environment. How does the insularity and isolation of Dublin society stand as the antithesis to modernist thought and ideals? What other examples from the stories reinforce this notion? Are there any characters in *Dubliners* who might represent a modernist hero or heroine? Could we make the argument that Mrs. Emily Sinico in "A Painful Case" is a modernist heroine destroyed by the social and moral traditions and expectations of turn-of-the-century Ireland? What about Parnell in "Ivy Day in the Committee Room"? Though not a character who is physically present in the story, his presence is keenly felt by the men who lament his downfall and death. Although *Ulysses* and *Finnegans Wake* offer the writer more evidence of modernism, *Dubliners* provides a glimpse into Joyce's early experimentations within the movement.

3. **Existentialism in *Dubliners*:** How would we classify Joyce's existentialism? Where do we see Joyce's version of existentialist thought playing out in *Dubliners*?

It was after Joyce's death that Jean-Paul Sartre penned the popular quote "Hell is other people" ("L'enfer, c'est les autres" in the original French) in his play *No Exit*, but Joyce seems to anticipate this phrase in several stories in *Dubliners*. Sartre's three main characters in the drama, Garcin, Estelle, and Inez, are trapped in a room in hell. They wait there, expecting some form of torture to begin but gradually realize that they are one another's torture. Of course, existentialism as a philosophical movement or branch of thought existed long before Sartre, and certainly Joyce would have been familiar with its tenets. Indeed, existentialism and modernism concern themselves with similar notions in regard to the human being in his or her world. Both focus on the individual and the choices that person makes to improve his or her life. Early existentialist thinkers, Søren Kierkegaard specifically, placed the sole responsibility for individual happiness on the shoulders of the individual, reasoning that we are responsible for creating a meaningful life, even when faced with despair, angst, and crisis. Later philosophers, including Sartre, argued that while we must take action to improve our own situations, outside forces could frequently be blamed for the anguish and suffering in an individual's life.

Existentialist thought plays out obviously in "A Little Cloud" and "Counterparts" but can be noted in other stories as well. Indeed, any of the stories in *Dubliners* in which characters are used and abused by others or cannot seem to escape the lot dealt them by the world would fit an essay with this theme. In "A Little Cloud," Gallaher seems to be idolized and idealized by Chandler but in the end is really Chandler's own personal hell. Gallaher symbolizes everything Chandler wants to be but is not—a successful journalist, cosmopolitan, charming, experienced. Spending time in Gallaher's company only reinforces what Chandler perceives to be shortfalls in his own life. He fancies himself a poet but has been unable to get published. His most recent travels "abroad" were to the Isle of Man, a small island not very far away in the Irish Sea. His married life is not what we would call blissful. At the end of their meeting, Chandler "felt acutely the contrast between his own life and his friend's, and it seemed to him unjust." The final provocation for Chandler is when Gallaher tells him he is not ready to marry, supposing that being with one woman "must get a bit stale," just as Chandler prepares to head home to his family. Of course, the end of the story finds Chandler at home, feeling imprisoned, and taking his frustration out on his child. "Counterparts" provides an excellent foil to "A Little Cloud" because the main characters are essentially interchangeable, though Chandler feels remorse for losing his temper with his son while Farrington does not. Farrington is the victim of the condescending boss, Mr. Alleyne, at his law firm. At the end of a humiliating workday, Farrington pawns his watch to get money for drinks, spends it all, loses in arm wrestling to a "mere boy," and arrives home to an empty kitchen and dark home. He beats his son with a rage directed more at his own circumstances than at the boy himself. Chandler and Farrington would likely agree that hell is other people, but they go on to create a hell for someone else. Can we see an end to this cycle? What is Joyce's vision of human nature as seen in the characters in *Dubliners?* Do we find any of Kierkegaard's existentialist beliefs in any of the stories?

Form and Genre

As Samuel Beckett wrote of *Finnegans Wake* in his article "Dante . . . Bruno. Vico . . . Joyce," "Here, form *is* content, content *is* form" (14). While this certainly applies to the *Wake,* we also see early signs of this melding of form and content in *Dubliners.* And although each of the stories in the collection can stand on its own and be understood and appreciated in itself, *Dubliners* is a rich tapestry in which the life stories of the characters in its pages are woven together to become an inseparable whole.

Sample Topics:

1. **Shifts in narrative style:** Where in *Dubliners* do we encounter shifts in narrative style? What do these shifts or changes do to the reader? Why do you think Joyce used this technique?

   The newspaper insert in "A Painful Case," the poem in "Ivy Day in the Committee Room," and the song in "Clay" all mark shifts in Joyce's narrative style. We move from narrative prose to something else, breaking the text for the reader. But what is the real purpose of this technique? Why, for example, do we learn of Mrs. Sinico's death through a newspaper article? Mr. Duffy reads about Mrs. Sinico's death as he begins to eat his dinner in a pub while looking at the newspaper, but it is only once he arrives home that we as readers get the full story. And when we do find out what happened, it comes to us as a distant, unemotional paragraph in the *Mail.* Why does Joyce present Mrs. Sinico's death in this manner? Do we need the shift in narrative style to fully appreciate Mr. Duffy's reaction to her death? In "Ivy Day," the shift in style comes in the form of a poem recited by Mr. Hynes commemorating the death of Parnell. Indeed, all of "Ivy Day" is a shift from the overall narrative style of *Dubliners*, as much of the story is told in the form of dialogue. What does this poem inserted in dialogue do to the reader? What is its purpose? How does Joyce frame the poem within the text? Finally, look at "Clay" and the song Maria sings in the story, "I Dreamt that I Dwelt" from the opera *The Bohemian Girl* by Michael Balfe (incidentally but certainly not accidentally, this is the same opera Frank takes Eveline to see in "Eveline"). In "Clay," we are told that Maria sings the first verse twice instead of moving to the second verse, which is about suitors and romantic love. Whether Maria's repeating the first verse was a mistake, as suggested by the omniscient narrator, or if she purposely omitted the second verse because it was too painful for her to sing, remains up for question. Certainly, though, the reader during Joyce's time would know the song well and understand what was missing. For the modern-day reader, that might not be the case. How does this song within the narrative shift how the reader understands the text? What does it do to guide our impression of Maria?

2. **Joycean gnomon:** The Joycean gnomon is a theme in *Dubliners*, but it is also a stylistic form that the author uses in several of the stories. How and why does Joyce use this form? What effect does it have on the narrative and on the reader?

Joycean gnomon is first experienced in the opening story "The Sisters" but is found throughout all of the tales in *Dubliners*. The unfinished sentences and ellipses leave the reader in the same uncertain position as the narrator in some instances, while in others, completely in the dark, left to assume what is happening in the narrative. In "The Sisters," the ellipses in the adult's conversations leave the narrator feeling confused while the reader can intuit what is really going on. Old Cotter is especially fond of the Joycean gnomon, "No, I wouldn't say he was exactly . . . but there was something queer . . . there was something uncanny about him. I'll tell you my opinion . . ." We later hear the narrator share: "He [Old Cotter] began to puff again at his pipe without giving us his theory," though we realize that he probably did not share his theory because he was in the presence of a woman and child. All of the ellipses in "The Sisters" occur because the narrator is deemed too young by the adults in the story to hear what would have been said. The adults are able to fill in the blanks and so is the reader to some extent, but the ellipses serve only to frustrate the narrator. Another variation on the Joycean gnomon occurs in "An Encounter" when the "queer old josser" likely masturbates in the field, offstage, so to speak. Although the young narrator does not explicitly say what is happening, we as readers can deduce this from the text. Why does Joyce choose to have this incident happen the way he does? Was it merely the case of turn-of-the-century norms in publishing, or is there something else happening here? In addition to ellipses and intimations of what is happening, there are also textual gnomons in the form of section breaks within the stories. Sometimes these act to show some passage of time, but they can also indicate a change in narrative style or point of view. They can be found in "Eveline," "The Boarding House," "A Little Cloud," "Counterparts," and "Grace." Consider how these section breaks work as gnomons in the stories and what their purposes might be for the narratives.

3. **Parts to a whole:** How can we view the stories in *Dubliners* as both individual texts as well as parts of a larger narrative tapestry? Do we read the stories differently when taken out of the context of the collection? Would we read the collection differently if it were missing some of the stories?

Although *Dubliners* is a collection of short stories that can be read on their own and appreciated as works of art in their own right, Joyce intended for us to read them as a collection, ordering the stories to lead us to an observation or series of insights that build on each other cumulatively. The first stories are about childhood, the next about adolescence, then come the stories about young adulthood and, finally, maturity. The personalities of narrators/protagonists come through clearly in the tales, and some of the adolescent characters, the reader may assert, could easily grow up into versions of the adult ones. For example, if we follow the young narrator in "Araby" through to adulthood, he might grow up to be a Gabriel Conroy from "The Dead." Eveline in her story is a young version of Maria in "Clay." What other characters from the early stories make appearances under different names in the later ones? Is Joyce revealing to us universal character traits or the result of years of oppression under Irish Catholicism and provincialism? What is Joyce trying to convey within the context of the collection? Taken individually, the stories have a certain meaning or give a certain impression. As a whole, however, the cumulative effect has a much stronger impact. Discuss how the themes in the stories are layered and fused to create one overarching theme. Consider how the collection would change if one or more of the stories were omitted.

Language, Symbols, and Imagery

Joyce was a consummate wordsmith, and there are no linguistic coincidences in his work. He used images and symbols in the same way he used words in his texts—carefully and with precision. A word is almost never just a word, and an object is almost never just an object. A close, critical reading of Joyce will help to unlock some of these symbols.

Sample Topics:

1. **Maria and "Clay":** What symbolism do we find in the story "Clay"? How do these symbols work within the text? Is Maria herself a symbol?

   For a reader unfamiliar with Irish Halloween customs, the symbolism in "Clay" would likely not register. However, some research would provide a great deal of insight into what Joyce is really trying to convey to us. The parlor game played at the Donnelly household is a variation on a traditional Irish fortune-telling game played Halloween night. The story tells us that saucers were placed on the table and children were led to them, blindfolded. One of them got a prayer book, three got water, and one got a ring. The prayer book symbolizes entrance into a religious calling, the water indicates a long journey (at the time, it probably suggested emigration) and the ring foretells marriage. Maria's experience with the divination game, however, is not as straightforward. The soft, wet substance she finds on the saucer is the clay from the title of the story, and it represents an early grave. Mrs. Donnelly chastises the girls for allowing Maria to pick the saucer with the clay, and Maria had to have known what was happening. She "understood that it was wrong that time and so she had to do it over again: and this time she got the prayer book." How do the symbols in this game work within the text? Why did the girls not rig the game so the second time Maria would find the ring? Or the water?

Next, you might consider whether Maria herself is a symbol. Look closely at the description Joyce provides for us. Her physical appearance is given to us quite vividly: "Maria was a very, very small person indeed but she had a very long nose and a very long chin." We see later in the story, as she sets out tea for her mistress and then again when the children are blindfolding her, that when Maria laughs, the tip of her nose nearly meets the tip of her chin. The fact that her face is reminiscent of that of a witch or crone is certainly no mistake, and that Maria is unmarried only emphasizes this. However, we have some contrasting descriptions of her as well. When she changes from her work clothes to her outfit for the evening at the Donnelly's, she admires her figure, looking "with quaint affection at the diminutive body which she had so often adorned. In spite of its years she found it a nice tidy little body." She then flirts with the "colonel-looking" gentleman on the tram, reinforcing the notion that although she is likely beyond the marriageable age, she is still excited by the attention of the opposite sex and feels buoyed by this interaction. How does Joyce use Maria as a symbol?

2. **Symbolism in "Araby":** How does Joyce use symbolism in "Araby"? On what symbols does the young narrator fixate? What do the narrator's obsessions reveal about him?

As you prepare to write this essay, keep in mind that Joyce chose the objects, images, and symbols in his stories with extreme care. Nothing is coincidental or extraneous. Reread "Araby" with that in mind, making note of the details in the story. The first several paragraphs alone could provide enough symbolism for an entire essay, so you need to decide how you will approach Joyce's use of symbolism in "Araby." You can take the approach of using religious symbolism and discuss how the objects in the story call to mind the Catholic Church and emphasize the devotion the boy has for Mangan's sister, similar to devotion to the Virgin Mother. To do this, identify those passages in which the boy places the young woman on a proverbial pedestal. Notice how Mangan's sister is always lit from behind, as if to create a halo effect around the girl. She is also always a few steps above the narrator when they interact. Her name springs to the narrator's lips "at moments in strange prayers and praises" that he does not understand. Alternatively, there is the case of the "charitable priest" who occupied the narrator's house before he did—how are the symbolism and imagery connected with the priest used? Is the symbolism lost on the young narrator? You could also look at symbols and images of blindness, darkness, and obstructed vision, beginning with the first words of the story, "North Richmond Street, being blind," and culminating in the final sentence: "Gazing into the darkness I saw myself as a creature driven and derided by vanity; and my eyes burned with anguish and anger." Much of the story takes place after sunset, which emphasizes the symbolic blindness of the narrator. We find cases of obstructed vision in the narrator's peeping Tom antics, peering out the blinds to catch a glimpse of Mangan's sister. The partial darkness of the Araby bazaar tells the boy he is too late to accomplish his goal of bringing back a trinket for his crush. Where else do we find darkness and blindness in this story? What is their overall effect? Another approach you could take would be to identify romantic symbols and images. The narrator certainly has a romantic approach to the world, and we see this in his thoughts, words, and actions. He is preoccupied with grail imagery ("I imagined that I bore my chalice safely through a throng of foes"), as well as Irish revivalism ("But my body was like a harp and her words and gestures were like fingers running along the wires."). The Araby bazaar itself is romantic, calling to mind the idealized representation of the foreign and exotic known as Orientalism. Where else do we see signs of the boy's romantic nature? How does Joyce's use of romantic symbolism guide our opinion of the narrator?

3. **"After the Race" and foreign perceptions:** What does this story tell us about the Irish perception of foreigners? What do the foreigners in "After the Race" tell us about the perception of Ireland internationally at the turn of the century?

In the first paragraph of "After the Race," Joyce writes: "At the crest of the hill at Inchicore sightseers had gathered in clumps to watch the cars careering homeward and through this channel of poverty and inaction the Continent sped its wealth and industry. Now and again the clumps of people raised the cheer of the gratefully oppressed. Their sympathy, however, was for the blue cars—the cars of their friends, the French." These two sentences set the tone for the entire story. As always, Joyce's word choice is precise. "Clumps" is not generally used to describe people, but something unpleasant or dirty such as mud or fur. Joyce tells us the people are "gratefully oppressed." What impression does this give the reader? Why would these people cheer for the French? As we move through the story and meet the characters, what stereotypes does Joyce reinforce? We see the same types of perceptions and assumptions at the dinner party at Doyle's home, with his parents being "unusually friendly" and expressing a "real respect for foreign accomplishments." Why does Jimmy's father, who is a successful Dublin businessman, feel required to show such deference to a bunch of young men? How does Joyce typecast the characters? How would you describe Ségouin, Villona, Rivière, Routh, Farley, and Doyle? How do they represent their respective countries? What is Joyce trying to convey at the end of the story with the result of the card game? Is there a broader meaning here?

Compare and Contrast Essays

Dubliners provides the writer with a multitude of possibilities for compare and contrast essays. The most obvious choice would be to compare characters, but you can also compare themes and symbolism among the stories.

Sample Topics:

1. **Young narrators:** The narrator of a story controls the reader's understanding of the events. How do the young narrators in "The Sisters," "Araby," and "An Encounter" steer the reader through the tale? We often think about the reliability of the narrator, so as you read to write, consider whether the narrator is reliable or if there are errors or omissions that result in misunderstandings. How does Joyce use the narrator to manipulate the reader? How are these three young narrators similar? How are they different?

   To write this essay, you would first need to read closely to determine some basic elements of the narrator's style. Are the narrators writing as young people or retrospectively as adults? Where can you find clues in the stories to support this assessment? How does a retrospective narrative change the reading? How does Joyce use the technique of gnomon (the sense of something being missing) in these three stories, and how do the narrators respond to it? Do the narrators themselves employ this technique? For example, we do not "see" what the old man does in the field in "An Encounter," but certainly the young boy does. On the other hand, the missing pieces in "The Sisters" seem just as confusing to the narrator as they do for us as readers. Compare and contrast the styles of these and the overall tones of their narratives.

2. **Parents:** Joyce paints quite a grim portrait of fathers in *Dubliners*, presenting us with men who are abusive ("Eveline," "A Little Cloud," and "Counterparts"), absent ("The Boarding House"), or essentially useless ("A Mother"). Similarly, mothers in *Dubliners* are not safe from Joyce's criticism either. They range from overtly manipulative (Polly Mooney in "The Boarding House"

and Kathleen Kearney in "A Mother") to nurturing caregivers (Maria and Mrs. Donnelly in "Clay" and Annie in "A Little Cloud") who are dealt miserable situations in life. Compare and contrast Joyce's mothers and fathers in these tales.

This essay would require some preliminary decisions on the part of the writer. First, will you compare and contrast only fathers or mothers, or will you compare and contrast fathers with mothers? What stories provide you with the best examples to support your thesis? If you choose to compare and contrast only fathers, consider what your focus will be: Will you look at abusive fathers compared with "good ones" (Joe in "Clay")? Or will you study the impact of an absent father versus one who is in the picture but essentially a nonpresence? How are the fathers in the tales similar? How are they different? The same can be asked about the mothers or mother figures (aunts often replace mothers in *Dubliners*) in the stories. Certainly Mrs. Mooney and Mrs. Kearney stand out as examples of a type of mother in Joyce's work; how do they compare with other mothers and mother figures? You may also choose to compare the parents in one story with those in another. "Clay," with its relatively positive portrait of home and hearth and parental love (Maria is a stand-in for Joe's biological mother), is a stark contrast to the family life depicted in "Counterparts," with an abusive husband and father and a wife who "bullied her husband when he was sober." What does Joyce, a dedicated family man who refused any invitation that did not include his wife and children, tell us about parenting and family life?

3. **Symbolism:** Joyce's use of symbolism in *Dubliners* guides the reader through the tales. His symbols frequently stand in for a larger concept, such as Ireland, religion, or decay and death. Do the symbols carry the same meaning throughout the stories? How does Joyce direct our interpretation of the stories through his use of symbolism? Compare and contrast Joycean symbolism in *Dubliners*.

A good starting point for this essay would be to reread closely and critically several of the stories in order to decide which ones to use. There is symbolism in every story, and the best approach is to decide what Joyce is symbolizing in the tale. For example, an essay on religious symbolism would certainly use "The Sisters," "Araby," "Two Gallants," and "Grace." How do the symbols present guide the readers in understanding Joyce's point of view? What impact do the symbols in these stories have on our comprehension of religion and, specifically, Roman Catholicism in Ireland at the time? An essay on Irish symbolism would have to include "After the Race," "Clay," and of course "Ivy Day in the Committee Room," though there are symbols of Ireland in nearly all of the stories. How does Joyce use symbols of Ireland, and what do we as readers take from this? What impression does he give us of his native country and, specifically, its capital Dublin? Are the symbols Joyce uses in *Dubliners* positive or negative? Compare and contrast his use of symbolism among the tales.

Bibliography and Online Resources for *"Dubliners"*

Attridge, Derek, ed. *The Cambridge Companion to James Joyce.* Cambridge: Cambridge University Press, 1990. Print.

Benstock, Bernard. *Narrative Con/Texts in Dubliners.* Urbana: University of Illinois Press, 1994. Print.

Bloom, Harold. *James Joyce's Dubliners.* New York: Chelsea House, 1998. Print.

Blumberg, Roger B., and Wallace Gray. "World Wide *Dubliners.*" Web. <http://www.mendele.com/WWD/home.html>

Bosinelli Bollettieri, Rosa Maria, and Harold Frederick Mosher, eds. *ReJoycing: New Readings of Dubliners.* Lexington: University Press of Kentucky, 1998. Print.

An Chomhairle Leabharlanna. [The Library Council.] "Ask about Ireland." Web. <http://askaboutireland.ie/>

Ellmann, Richard. *James Joyce.* New York: Oxford University Press, 1982. Print.

Fargnoli, A. Nicholas. *Critical Companion to James Joyce: A Literary Companion to His Life and Works.* New York: Facts on File, 2006. Print.

Frawley, Oona, ed. *A New and Complex Sensation: Essays on Joyce's Dubliners.* Dublin: Lilliput, 2004. Print.

Hobby, Blake. "Alienation in James Joyce's *Dubliners*." *Alienation*. New York: Bloom's Literary Criticism, 2009. 61–69. Print.

Hong, Dauk-Suhn. "The Narrative Silence of *Dubliners*." *James Joyce Journal*. 10.2 (2004): 191–210. Print.

Joyce, James. *Dubliners*. *The Portable James Joyce*. New York: Penguin Books, 1967. Print.

Mickalites, Carey. "*Dubliners* IOU: The Aesthetics of Exchange in 'After the Race' and 'Two Gallants'." *Journal of Modern Literature*. 30.2 (2007): 121–38. Print.

Nash, John. *James Joyce and the Act of Reception: Reading, Ireland, Modernism*. Cambridge: Cambridge University Press, 2006. Print.

Norris, Margot, ed. *Dubliners: Authoritative Text, Contexts, Criticism*. New York: Norton, 2006. Print.

Osteen, Mark. "'A Regular Swindle': The Failure of Gifts in *Dubliners*." *Twenty-First Joyce*. Florida: University Press of Florida: 2004. 13–35. Print.

Seidel, Michael. *James Joyce: A Short Introduction*. Malden, Mass.: Blackwell Publishers, 2002. Print.

Simmons, Allan H. "Topography and Transformation: A Postcolonial Reading of *Dubliners*." *Joyce, Imperialism, and Postcolonialism*. Syracuse, N.Y.: Syracuse, N.Y. University Press, 2008. 12–40. Print.

Spinks, Lee. *James Joyce: A Critical Guide*. Edinburgh: Edinburgh University Press, 2009. Print.

Thacker, Andrew, ed. *Dubliners: James Joyce*. New York: Palgrave MacMillan, 2006. Print.

"THE DEAD"

READING TO WRITE

"THE DEAD," the last of the 15 stories collected in *Dubliners,* is frequently studied both in the context of the work as a whole as well as a novella separate from the rest. While it clearly provides the finale for the collection and completes the trajectory begun with "The Sisters," it is too grand in scope to be combined with the rest of the stories and is, thus, deserving of additional individual scrutiny.

The themes and ideas found in the other stories in *Dubliners* can also be found in "The Dead," including paralysis, decay, hopelessness, epiphany, and homecoming, but Joyce presents them much more in-depth in his novella. He also develops his characters more fully, giving the reader more vivid descriptions of them, especially the protagonist, Gabriel Conroy. Although religion, music, and politics played roles in the other stories, here they take center stage, acting as catalysts for the action in "The Dead" to unfold.

The climax of the story occurs in Gabriel and Gretta's hotel room after the evening's festivities. He is filled with desire for his wife but does not know her well enough to accurately read her mood. She kisses him for his generosity in lending a friend a pound, but he imagines she is ready to yield to him. When Gretta bursts into tears over the song "The Lass of Aughrim" and then explains why, Gabriel's mood swiftly changes from victory to astonishment to anger and then to humiliation, as we see in the following passage:

> Gabriel felt humiliated by the failure of his irony and by the evocation of this figure from the dead, a boy in the gasworks. While he had been full of memories of their secret life together, full of tenderness and joy

and desire, she had been comparing him in her mind with another. A shameful consciousness of his own person assailed him. He saw himself as a ludicrous figure, acting as a pennyboy for his aunts, a nervous, well-meaning sentimentalist, orating to vulgarians and idealising his own clownish lusts, the pitiable fatuous fellow he had caught a glimpse of in the mirror. Instinctively he turned his back more to the light lest she might see the shame that burned on his forehead.

He tried to keep up his tone of cold interrogation, but his voice when he spoke was humble and indifferent.

"I suppose you were in love with this Michael Furey, Gretta," he said.

"I was great with him at that time," she said.

Her voice was veiled and sad. Gabriel, feeling now how vain it would be to try to lead her whither he had purposed, caressed one of her hands and said, also sadly:

"And what did he die of so young, Gretta? Consumption, was it?"

"I think he died for me," she answered.

A vague terror seized Gabriel at this answer, as if, at that hour when he had hoped to triumph, some impalpable and vindictive being was coming against him, gathering forces against him in its vague world. But he shook himself free of it with an effort of reason and continued to caress her hand. He did not question her again, for he felt that she would tell him of herself. Her hand was warm and moist: it did not respond to his touch, but he continued to caress it just as he had caressed her first letter to him that spring morning.

In this passage, we see three of the main themes in *Dubliners*, hopelessness, epiphany, and decay, coming to a climax. These three work hand in hand, one leading to the next. The hopelessness and decay are symptoms of Gabriel and Gretta's married life. At the beginning of "The Dead," we meet what appears to be a happily married couple, and we are potentially amused at their playful teasing of each other in front of Gabriel's aunts. Later, we see a man admiring his wife's beauty from the bottom of the stairs, imagining she is a symbol of something and anxious to get her alone. It is only once they are alone in their hotel room that the reader is allowed into Gretta's mind; prior to this, we had only Gabriel's point of view. We witness Gretta's despair and hopelessness at the same time as her husband, and simultaneously we see the decay of their marriage. The secret Gretta has kept about Michael Furey humiliates Gabriel, and he realizes that his wife has been comparing him to the boy. More than a mere childhood crush, the existence of which Gabriel (and their marriage) could have withstood, the relationship Gretta had with Michael Furey was tender and significant, terminating in the most romantic of ways when the young boy died for her. Gabriel knows he cannot compete with this, and we witness his epiphany as a result. In the preceding passage, his epiphany begins in humiliation and shame and then progresses to terror, but later in the story, once Gretta has fallen asleep, his realization of "how poor a part he, her husband, had played in her life" hardly pains him. He then recognizes that his feelings for Gretta are not as strong as her young lover's were and weeps at that thought. Gabriel's epiphany has several stages, similar to the stages of the grieving process, which is thoroughly appropriate since he is grieving the loss of his happy marriage. Though we do not anticipate divorce (it would have been more than scandalous in turn-of-the-century Ireland, and Gabriel does not seem the type to make waves), certainly their relationship will never be the same again after Gretta's confession, at least not for Gabriel. There are many areas open for exploration in this short passage, but a close analysis of the progression of Gabriel's epiphany beginning with the preceding text through to the end of the story would make for an excellent essay topic.

TOPICS AND STRATEGIES

"The Dead," with its brooding, elegiac themes and layered narrative, offers numerous avenues for critical exploration. The following prompts and topic suggestions should give you a good starting point from which you can begin to flesh out your paper.

Themes

The themes to explore and write about in "The Dead" are similar to the ones in *Dubliners* overall, but because of the length of the story and the development of the characters in it, the themes are more expansive in scope. You could take a cue for possible themes from the young narrator in "The Sisters" and write about simony, paralysis, and gnomon, all three of which are present in "The Dead," or you could explore one of the suggestions below, which are by no means exhaustive.

Sample Topics:

1. **Life and death:** How does Joyce use life and death as themes in "The Dead"? Which characters exemplify life? Which ones represent death?

This essay on the themes of life and death in "The Dead" would begin with a discussion of the title of the story. Joyce chose "The Dead" for his title, and it is only at the end that we meet the individual who is dead and has been for many years. Although Gabriel's aunts are everyday moving toward death, nobody actually dies in the story. What is Joyce perhaps suggesting with his title? Do the characters in the story live their lives as though they are already dead? Are the characters in "The Dead" shades or ghosts? Gabriel, at the end of the story, muses to himself: "One by one they were all becoming shades. Better pass boldly into that other world, in the full glory of some passion, than fade and wither dismally with age." Does Gabriel have it right?

As you prepare to write, look closely at the main characters and decide whether they live their lives as Gabriel recommends. Does he follow his own advice? Does Gabriel live boldly and with passion? Is Gretta "alive"? Gabriel notices as Gretta sleeps that her face is "no longer the face for which Michael Furey had braved death." Gretta, though Gabriel is hesitant to admit it and really only notices it after she has confessed about the young lover in her past, is withering dismally with age. What can we say about Lily, the caretaker's daughter, one of the youngest characters in the story? We are told that she is pale and "run off her feet," but her exchange with Gabriel in the opening pages provides us even more evidence that this young girl does not really live her life. Indeed, two of only a handful of characters in the story who truly live are Aunt Julia and Aunt Kate, the oldest people in "The Dead." Where in the text can we find evidence for this? Can we make the same case for the drunkard Freddy Malins and the high-spirited Miss Ivors? When you make the differentiation between alive and dead characters, consider whether they live in the past or the present, whether they take advantage of what life has to offer or not.

2. **Love and marriage:** How are love and marriage portrayed in
"The Dead"? Does Joyce present us with a positive picture of
either?

There are few happily married couples in *Dubliners.* The
aunts and uncles who act as guardians for the young narrators in "The Sisters" and "Araby" seem happy enough despite
how they may frustrate the boys. We might consider Joe and
his wife in "Clay" to be happy, but a hint of a problem comes
when Maria hopes that Joe isn't drunk since he was "so different when he took any drink." The rest, including the Kearneys
in "A Mother," the Sinicos in "A Painful Case," the Chandlers
in "A Little Cloud" and the Farringtons in "Counterparts,"
are all rather miserable in their matches. When we arrive at
"The Dead" and see the playful, teasing interactions between
Gabriel and Gretta Conroy, we imagine we have finally found
evidence of marital happiness. When we learn of Gretta's
secret, however, we witness the disintegration of that supposed bliss.

Love seems impossible in "The Dead." Lily is tired of the
men who are "only all palaver and what they can get out of
you," and Gabriel's aunts Julia and Kate and his cousin Mary
Jane are all unmarried. Miss Ivors seems married to her political cause and Freddy Malins to his drink. Certainly Gabriel
loves Gretta, evidenced in his thoughts about her all night
during the party and especially as they are making their way
homeward. He admires her decorously from afar all night, and
his desire for her gradually builds to a climax once they are
alone in their hotel room. But it is Gretta's admission that she
once loved another man that changes everything. Is Gretta's
love for Michael Furey and vice versa the only real romantic
love we have in "The Dead"? Does anything change for Gretta?
Is Gabriel being irrational in his reaction?

3. **Nostalgia:** What is the significance of nostalgia in "The Dead"?
Does it have a positive or negative impact on the characters in
the story?

Nostalgia, a sentimental longing for the past and the people, places, and things long gone, is a major theme in "The Dead." The title itself is nostalgic, and the characters in the story serve to reinforce this idea. Nearly every character, from Gabriel and Gretta to Lily and Miss Ivors, has one foot in the past, idealizing the days gone by as compared with the current environment. Lily disdains "the men that is now," and in her criticism, we understand that she believes men in earlier generations must have been more gentlemanly. Miss Ivors is certainly nostalgic, swept up in the passion of the Irish Revival, working to resurrect the language and culture from the near-dead. The tradition of the annual party at the Misses Morkans is also steeped in nostalgia, as all tradition tends to be. Julia, Kate, and even Mary Jane serve as symbols of times past, in their mannerisms, their decorating style, and their taste in music, and Gabriel highlights this in his speech, equating them with the Three Graces in mythology.

Much of the discussion at the party centers on the old times and how things were better years ago. The music was better, as displayed by the choices of songs played and sung. The singers were better, though not everyone at the dinner table has heard of Parkinson, Aunt Kate's favorite tenor. Gabriel's speech at dinner only further emphasizes and extols the traditions of an Ireland that is changing thanks to a new generation living in a "thought-tormented" age. He says that the days gone by were "spacious" and hopes that at future gatherings "we shall still speak of them with pride and affection, still cherish in our hearts the memory of those dead and gone great ones whose fame the world will not willingly let die." Of course, Gabriel has in mind dead relatives, including his parents, but he is also anticipating that his Aunt Julia will not be at the dinner table at next year's party. However, he certainly does not anticipate that his speech, along with Bartell D'Arcy's song at the end of the night, will cause his wife, Gretta, to recall another "gone great one." Does Gabriel's speech at dinner foreshadow what will come later? Are we as surprised as he is at Gretta's confession? Although Gabriel's speech centers on nostalgia, he seems to at least try to live in the present. Can we say the same for Gretta? Where else in the text do we find nostalgia?

Character

Because "The Dead" is significantly longer than any other story in *Dubliners*, Joyce was able to more fully develop the characters in this piece. They are more complicated and complex and much more nuanced than the characters in the other stories in the collection. As a result, they lend themselves nicely to a character analysis.

Sample Topics:

1. **Gabriel:** Does Joyce want us to identify with Gabriel? Does he present a sympathetic character?

   Although the style of narration in "The Dead" is omniscient, the narrator seems to be closest to Gabriel Conroy, and we hear his thoughts more clearly than we do anyone else's. Indeed, once he arrives at the party, it is only seldom that we learn the thoughts of another character. As such, we get to know Gabriel better than any other individual in the story. What do we think of him? How does Joyce guide our assessment? Can we identify with Gabriel Conroy? Our first encounter with Gabriel comes as he enters the party and makes small talk with Lily, the caretaker's daughter who does housework for the Misses Morkan. Gabriel has known the girl since she was young and speaks with her in a friendly way, inquiring after her schooling and the prospect of her marriage. He unintentionally strikes a nerve with her and is embarrassed. He further annoys her by giving her a Christmas tip, which she does not want to accept. He is then teased by his wife, Gretta, about his insistence that she wear galoshes. He is subsequently humiliated by the outspoken nationalist Miss Ivors for being a "West Briton" and not keeping in touch with his own language and country. He questions himself over his dinner speech, whether to quote Browning or if it will be above everyone's head. Is Gabriel's confidence in his intellect a sign of arrogance? What can we say about his speech? Is he giving the speech for the benefit of his listeners (does he consider his audience?) or is it for his own aggrandizement? What do we think of Gabriel by the end of the story? After his epiphany as the story comes to a close, we encounter a different man from the beginning of the story. How does Gretta's admission of love for another man change Gabriel? Do we, as readers, sympathize with him?

2. **Gretta:** How would we characterize Gretta? What impact does learning so much about her in a short time span have on the reader?

We know surprisingly little about Gretta Conroy until the end of "The Dead" when she makes her confession, and much of what we do learn is filtered through other characters, especially her husband, Gabriel. The first thing he says about Gretta is that she "takes three mortal hours to dress herself." Then we have the teasing conversation about galoshes, in which we learn that Gretta is not afraid to make a joke at her husband's expense. In a moment alone, Gabriel muses about his mother's "sullen opposition" to his marriage to Gretta, whom she considered "country cute" which he felt was not true at all. We learn that Gretta, who must have known of her mother-in-law's feelings, still nursed the woman when she was ill. From this, we can gather that Gretta has a clear sense of moral obligation and duty, and we later wonder if this sense of duty has spilled over into her relationship with her husband as well. We see very little of Gretta through the dinner, and we encounter her again through Gabriel's eyes as she listens, transfixed, to Bartell D'Arcy singing "The Lass of Aughrim." He finds her very beautiful and imagines she is a symbol of something. He is sexually aroused by his wife and is anxious to get her back to their hotel. We know that Gabriel feels "proud and happy," but Gretta is silent and withdrawn, and it is only once Gabriel presses her that she makes her confession about Michael Furey. She clearly does not want to talk about it, seen through her body language and verbal cues, but Gabriel misses these outward signs.

Because we do not know much about Gretta except what we have come to believe through Gabriel, her admission of love for the dead Michael Furey at the end of the story is surprising. We find out about Gretta's past at the same time as her husband, and as readers we feel a sense of shock as her tale unfolds. Has Gretta changed for the reader? If so, how? Do you believe Gretta is haunted by her past and specifically Michael Furey? Gabriel believes Gretta has been comparing him with Michael Furey—do you think he is correct in this assumption? Does Gretta love Gabriel? Will life change for her now that she has told her secret?

3. **Michael Furey:** Is Michael Furey a foil to Gabriel? How would we characterize him? Although he has been dead for years, is he omnipresent in Gretta's life?

Making his grand entrance at the end of the story, Michael Furey, though a ghost, changes the married life of Gabriel and Gretta Conroy, at least in Gabriel's eyes. However, on closer analysis, we might argue that Furey has been in the tale all along. If, as Gabriel imagines, Gretta is in the habit of comparing him with Furey, we can see how this would bring about Gabriel's "shameful consciousness of his own person" as a result. Gabriel is a man ruled by the head—he is thoughtful and planning, aware of his intellect and guided by it. It is only at the end of "The Dead" that we see him directed by his heart and his desires for his wife, but even then he is careful and cautious about following through. Michael Furey, on the other hand, clearly throws caution to the wind, which is obviously part of what contributed to his death. He was ill and supposed to be recovering in bed when he snuck out in the rain to see Gretta one last time before she left for school. We cannot imagine Gabriel doing this. Michael Furey was impulsive and romantic; he was gentle and delicate, Gretta tells us, and had a "very good voice." He is nearly the exact opposite of Gabriel, who is "a stout tallish young man" whose colored cheeks reveal good health. Gabriel's love of literature is academically based, while Furey's musical talents were unstudied. Although we are not in Gretta's head to get the comparisons between the two men from her point of view, as readers we can easily see them ourselves. Is the ghost of Michael Furey a constant presence in Gretta's life? Or does hearing the song "The Lass of Aughrim" bring him back to life? Certainly Gretta's attitude changes on hearing the song, and she is in another world as a result. Who is Michael Furey, really? Consider whether his ghost is a new presence in the life of the Conroys or if he has been there, but completely unnoticed by Gabriel, all along.

Philosophy and Ideas

Religion is always an element in a Joycean work, and "The Dead" is certainly no exception. Joyce also explores class distinctions more fully in this text and gives us another opportunity to have a view into the complicated nature of Irish politics at the turn of the century in the character of Miss Ivors and her exchange with Gabriel.

Sample Topics:

1. **Class distinctions:** What differences in class do we observe in "The Dead"? How do Joyce's characters react to these differences?

Joyce was fully (and painfully) aware of class distinctions, having grown up in a family that had money at the start but progressively lost it through the years. He understands from experience the differences between being comfortable and being destitute, and he is able to convey this difference in his text. In "The Dead," we are told that Julia, Kate, and Mary Jane Morkan lived modestly, but we also know that they spare no expense on their annual party, that they "believed in eating well," and kept Lily has a housemaid. The Conroys also have a housemaid and can afford to spend the night at a hotel in Dublin, and Gabriel speaks of a yearly trip to continental Europe to go cycling with his friends. Gabriel's thoughts through the evening also suggest an upper-class mindset, and we know he attended Royal University and is now a teacher. What other clues do we get about the characters' situations in terms of class?

At the end of the story, when Gretta is telling Gabriel about Michael Furey, it seems as though he is not only upset by the fact that his wife had a lover when she was young, before he had met her, but humiliated by Furey's having been of such little means. He was in the gasworks, a factory job, and could not study music because of his poor health. We may wonder if his poor health was the result of his poverty in rural western Ireland. Although the Great Famine would have been over by the time the two young lovers were courting, that entire area would still have been recovering. Gretta probably did not come from much money, and certainly Michael Furey did not either. What does the fact that Gabriel is especially humiliated by Furey's class standing tell us about him? Does Joyce guide our opinions of these characters based on class?

2. **Religion:** How does Joyce use "The Dead" to critique religion? What are his overt and covert criticisms?

Mr. Browne, the only guest at the party who is "of the other persuasion" (in other words, he is Protestant) is the perfect device for Joyce to reveal his thoughts about the Catholic Church in Ireland. The first criticism of the Church comes immediately following Aunt Julia's performance of "Arrayed for the Bridal," when she is being praised for her voice. Her sister Kate openly disapproves of Julia's having devoted so much time to the church choir only to be replaced by boys, thanks to a directive by Pope Pius X. When Mary Jane reminds her Aunt Kate that Mr. Browne is listening, she backpedals, assuring the audience, "O, I do not question the pope's being right. I'm only a stupid old woman and I wouldn't presume to do such a thing. But there's such a thing as common everyday politeness and gratitude. And if I were in Julia's place I'd tell that Father Healy straight up to his face . . ." She is again silenced by her niece so as not to "give scandal" to Browne. The topic of religion comes up again at dinner when Mrs. Malins, Freddy's mother, mentions that her son soon will be going to Mount Melleray Abbey. For Freddy, an alcoholic who has taken the pledge, a religious oath of abstinence, and has clearly already broken it, this will probably be equivalent to rehab, but the guests at the table speak highly of the monks' hospitality. Mr. Browne is amazed that someone can "put up there as if it were a hotel and live on the fat of the land and then come away without paying a farthing." He wishes his church had an institution like that, not understanding that, as Mary Jane says, most people leave a donation, and indeed that one is expected. He does not understand, either, that in Catholicism, rules are rules, and there is not much room for questioning. Joyce overtly questions the Catholic Church through the character of Browne, but is there a covert questioning present in "The Dead"? He perhaps hints at it with Freddy Malins taking the pledge. What about Miss Ivors who is wrapped up in the Irish Revival? What about the "University question"? Think not only about the obvious references to religion in "The Dead" but also about the ones that are more veiled. How does religion impact these characters?

3. **Irish nationalism:** What impression does the reader get of Irish nationalism as it is depicted in "The Dead" through the character of Miss Ivors? Does Joyce present the movement favorably?

Miss Molly Ivors is thoroughly involved in the Irish Revival and stands as a symbol of Irish nationalism in "The Dead." The movement, which was both cultural and political, sought to diminish and remove the influence that England had over Ireland. They did this through the endorsement of anything traditionally Irish, including music, language, literature, and mythology. Gabriel tells us on first encountering Miss Ivors that she is a "frank-mannered talkative young lady, with a freckled face and prominent brown eyes. She did not wear a low-cut bodice and the large brooch which was fixed in the front of her collar bore on it an Irish device." She immediately confronts Gabriel, albeit playfully, about a column he wrote in *The Daily Express*, a respectable newspaper if not for its pro-English political views. She chides her colleague for being

a "West Briton," an insult which suggests he has more alle-
giance to England than Ireland (so called because Ireland is
west of Britain). Gabriel wants the chance to explain himself
but does not know quite where to begin. He knows that telling her "literature was above politics" would be too "grandi-
ose" a phrase for her, and perhaps he does not even believe
it himself. Instead, he "murmured lamely that he saw nothing political in writing reviews of books." She lets him off the
hook for that but then soon after criticizes him for traveling
abroad rather than keeping in touch with his own language
and culture. When pressed as to why, Gabriel exclaims, "O, to
tell you the truth . . . I'm sick of my own country, sick of it!" Do
we as readers side more with Miss Ivors or with Gabriel in this
exchange? Does she represent the Irish nationalism movement
accurately? What opinion do we form of the movement based
on Miss Ivors? What were Joyce's own political views? Do they
come through in the text?

Form and Genre

"The Dead" provides many opportunities to examine form and genre
in an essay. It's a bit too long for a standard short story, but too short
to be deemed a novel. Additionally, the entire piece is shaped by music,
which weaves its way through the text and underpins and emphasizes
the events occurring. Finally, we see Joyce experimenting with the textual device *roman à clef,* in which characters in the fiction stand in for
people in real life.

Sample Topics:

1. **"The Dead" as novella:** Does "The Dead" match the standard
   definition of a novella? If we view it as such, rather than the final
   short story in a collection, what changes in the reading? How
   does it fit into the Joycean canon?

   A novella, as defined by Merriam-Webster's dictionary, is "a
   work of fiction intermediate in length and complexity between
   a short story and a novel." There are no fixed rules about number of pages or word count, so the designation of "novella"

seems somewhat arbitrary. According to Webster, the word came into use in the English language in 1898, in time for Joyce to be aware of it. Considering how well read he was, it is likely he knew of the genre that was becoming popular at the turn of the century with Joseph Conrad, Henry James, and Thomas Mann. As far as we know, Joyce never called "The Dead" a novella, but in many ways it can fit into that category. What argument can you make for it as a novella? What argument can you make that it is a short story? In writing this essay, consider the ways in which "The Dead" fits the definition of a novella. It is twice as long as the second-longest short story, "Grace," in *Dubliners*, and it is much more complex than any of the others. There are more characters, and each one of them is much more fully developed. The story itself is also much more layered and nuanced. At the same time, however, "The Dead" was published in a collection of short stories and, as the final tale in the collection, ends *Dubliners* with a perfect Joycean dénouement (which in some ways is an anti-dénouement). In Joyce, there never seems to be a happy resolution to a conflict. There is never a complete catharsis for the reader, which would typify a traditional, conventional dénouement. Over the course of *Dubliners* (and in Joyce's other works as well), the reader witnesses many conflicts but only incomplete resolutions, leaving him or her to feel similar to the characters in the stories. At the end of "The Dead," Gretta is asleep, having shared her secret with her husband and painfully reliving the loss of Michael Furey. Perhaps in some ways she experiences catharsis, but certainly Gabriel's entire world has changed and he is still coming to grips with it. Although Gabriel cries "generous tears," which could outwardly indicate a catharsis, there is no real resolution for him. However, the story provides the reader with a sense of closure of all the action in the stories that preceded it, reinforcing the case to be made for "The Dead" being a short story. As you write, keep in mind Joyce's decision to include "The Dead" in a collection of short stories, but at the same time, consider the ways in which this tale is different from the rest in *Dubliners*.

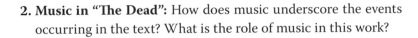

2. Music in "The Dead": How does music underscore the events occurring in the text? What is the role of music in this work?

Music was central to Joyce's own life, and certainly music is very important in "The Dead." Indeed, music is very nearly a character in the story, as its presence is felt and is even a catalyst for action. Julia, Kate, and Mary Jane Morkan are all music teachers, and many of their students are present at the party, ready to perform for the guests' listening and dancing enjoyment. As you begin to brainstorm for this essay, think of the many ways music is featured in this text and how Joyce presents it for his readers.

We first encounter music in "The Dead" as Gabriel walks upstairs after his uncomfortable exchange with Lily. He hears a waltz playing and waits to enter until it finishes, when the "indelicate clacking of the men's heels and the shuffling of their soles reminded him that their grade of culture differed from his." The music over, the men leave the dance floor and provide Gabriel an opportunity to be a bit of a snob. Another waltz ends with a flourish and clapping, underscoring the entrance of Freddy Malins, another person who allows Gabriel to feel superior. Music offers another glimpse into Gabriel's mind as he cannot listen to the "Academy piece" that Mary Jane plays which "had no melody for him." Then, music plays an important role in the following scene in which Gabriel and Miss Ivors dance to a quadrille, a type of square dance. The dancing and the music reinforce what is happening in the conversation. However, the most obvious role of music in "The Dead" is the moment when Gabriel observes his wife Gretta listening to Bartell D'Arcy singing "The Lass of Aughrim." The song provides the catalyst for the rest of the story, and very likely changes the course of the rest of Gabriel's life. Can we make a case for music being a character in this story? What is the significance of the particular songs Joyce used in the text? Finally, as you prepare for this essay, you might consider investigating the Broadway musical adaptation of this story, *James Joyce's "The Dead"* which ran from January–April 2000 and make comparisons with the text.

3. **"The Dead" as *roman à clef:*** How does "The Dead" reflect elements of the *roman à clef*? Is the integration of these elements effective? Does having the "key" provide the reader with deeper understanding of the characters and events?

This essay would require quite a bit of research on the part of the writer, but if you like to put literary puzzles together and enjoy historical criticism, this would be an enjoyable paper for you to write. The *roman à clef,* French for "novel with a key," was a literary technique that came into fashion in France in the 17th century. In a *roman à clef,* the writer describes characters and plotlines that are based on actual people and events but gives the people pseudonyms and sometimes changes the setting. The technique fell out of fashion for quite some time because of the fear of libel, but writers in the 1900s began to popularize it again.

The first step in writing this essay would be to do your research on Joyce and his early years. Richard Ellmann's biography is a great resource for this (indeed, he devotes an entire chapter to "The Backgrounds of 'The Dead'"). Then begin to draw connections between text and real life, making a key for the characters and their counterparts. Is Gabriel a stand-in for Joyce? Gretta for Nora? Several sources tell us that Nora Barnacle had a young love, Michael "Sonny" Bodkin, in Galway before she met Joyce, and the author was jealous about this former love interest. It should come as no surprise that Bodkin had tuberculosis, was bedridden, and snuck out to sing to Nora one rainy night. Bodkin, like Michael Furey, died not long after (Ellmann 243). This story from Joyce's own life provides the focal point of the story, but these three characters are not the only ones with cognates in the real world. Your investigation into "The Dead" will reveal the keys for nearly all the characters in the story, some of whom are amalgams of a few people Joyce knew. Once you have completed the key, discuss whether putting these pieces in place is a worthwhile exercise. Does it enrich our understanding of the story? Of Joyce? Why does Joyce use the *roman à clef* technique?

Language, Symbols, and Imagery

The symbolism in "The Dead" suggests many possible paper topics. As stated earlier, Joyce wrote with great precision, and there are no coincidences in his texts. Language is exact, and Joyce chose his symbols carefully. The following examples are just three of the many possibilities to pursue.

Sample Topics:

1. **Snow:** What is the effect and impact of the snow in "The Dead"? How does Joyce use it as an extended metaphor for what is happening in the text?

Winters in Ireland, Dublin especially, are relatively mild, with temperatures rarely dropping to freezing. Snow, as a result, is also quite rare, and when it does snow, it is usually in the form of flurries, not the type of snowfall Joyce writes about in "The Dead." In addition, snow is not prevalent throughout Ireland. The weather in this story is certainly an anomaly, and clearly Joyce is using the snow as a symbol, but of what?

As you plan this essay, think about snow as a symbol. What does it stand for? How do we view it? Snow is clean, white, and cold, obviously, but it is also fleeting and short lived. It blankets and covers everything, hiding from view what is really there. Finally, it is an element (water, in its frozen state) and is thus symbolic of the natural world. Then, keeping in mind the abnormality of this Dublin snowfall, think about how Joyce might want us to perceive it. How do his characters react to it? Look to the text and read closely for their attitudes toward the weather. Gabriel scrapes the snow from his galoshes, keen to remove traces of it from himself. His aunts imagine that Gretta has "perished alive" because of the weather, perhaps foreshadowing what we will learn later about the weather and the problems it causes. The ailing Michael Furey braved the rain to see Gretta one last time, very different from Gabriel who is quick to be rid of the snow on his overcoat and shoes. He wants to protect himself and his wife from the "dangers" of the weather by wearing galoshes, keeping nature at bay as much as possible. He stands in stark contrast to Furey, a country boy who was comfortable in the elements. What does the snow represent? Why does Joyce set his story during a snowfall, an out-of-the-ordinary weather event in Ireland?

2. **The "Three Graces":** Is Gabriel's comparison of the Misses Morkan with the Three Graces appropriate, given what we know about them? How do the Three Graces in mythology function as a symbol in the text?

To begin this essay, do some research on the Three Graces and what they represent. In Greek mythology, the Three Graces, or Charites, are Aglaea, who represents beauty or splendor, Euphrosyne, who represents mirth, and Thalia, who represents good cheer or comedy. Aglaea is the oldest and Thalia the youngest. They are alternately described as the daughters of the gods Zeus, Dionysus, or Helios and their various mates and are frequently associated with the goddess Aprhodite (who may or may not have been their mother). The Graces frequently crop up in mythology and in art, and Joyce, through Gabriel, brings them into "The Dead" as well. How do the Misses Morkan represent the Three Graces? Is the reference there simply for Gabriel to show off his intelligence?

Look closely at the descriptions of the Morkan women in the text. Gabriel first encounters his aunts as he ascends the stairs to enter the party. His aunts are described based on their physical features, and we get a sense of their characters in the dialogue that follows. But it is in Gabriel's speech, during which he makes the connections to the Three Graces, that the reader is better able to make the connections and parallels. Gabriel says that his Aunt Kate, the chief hostess, has a "too good heart," which "has become a byword with all who know her." Julia Morkan "seems to be gifted with perennial youth," and her "singing must have been a surprise and a revelation" to everyone at the party. Finally, the youngest, Mary Jane, is "talented, cheerful, hard-working and the best of nieces." Based on Gabriel's assertion in his speech and on what you encounter in the text, which woman represents which of the Three Graces? Do they each embody some elements of all three? What is the significance of this reference?

3. **Gretta as a "symbol of something" for Gabriel:** What does Gretta symbolize for Gabriel? What does this tell the reader about their relationship?

Gabriel, watching his wife listening to Bartell D'Arcy sing "The Lass of Aughrim," muses, "There was a grace and mystery in her attitude as if she were a symbol of something." He continues, imagining himself a painter and capturing the moment, calling the finished work *Distant Music.* Gabriel is quick to see symbols in many things, and we have already encountered his equating the Morkan women with the Three Graces, so it should come as no surprise that he does the same with his wife. He admires his wife at the beginning of the story and is proud of her beauty and charm. He resents the fact that his mother called Gretta "country cute," and when Miss Ivors asks him if his wife is from the west of Ireland, Gabriel, who associates the west with a lack of culture and education, says "Her people are." Gretta, for Gabriel, is a refined woman whose past, he imagines, is long behind her. We do not encounter Gretta much again until Gabriel spies her at the top of the stairway in the passage quoted previously in the chapter. From that moment on, he becomes filled with desire for her and is desperate to get her alone. He begins to notice the small details about Gretta, including the "rich bronze of her hair" and the "colour on her cheeks." He sees that her eyes are shining but is not aware enough to understand why. He imagines that her quiet hesitation to his advances is a sign of her modesty. Up until the point where Gretta reveals her secret, she is a symbol for Gabriel, but what does she represent? Is she still a symbol for him after he learns of Michael Furey? How does Gabriel's view of Gretta change at the end of the story? What does the fact that Gabriel sees Gretta as a symbol tell the reader about him? About their marriage?

Compare and Contrast Essays

"The Dead" lends itself to compare and contrast essays, and a reader/ writer has many possibilities to explore here. Because it has been made into a film and into a stage musical, "The Dead" can be discussed in relation to its adaptations. Because it is part of the Joycean canon, and specifically *Dubliners*, the characters in the story can be compared and contrasted with their counterparts in the collection.

Sample Topics:

1. **Adaptation of "The Dead":** How does the movie version of "The Dead" compare to the text? What changes were made, and what is the effect of those changes?

John Huston's 1987 film *John Huston's "The Dead"* was the last movie he directed. It starred his daughter Anjelica Huston in the role of Gretta Conroy and Donal McCann, an Irish stage actor, as Gabriel Conroy. The screenplay was written by Tony Huston, John Huston's son, and his work on the adaptation of Joyce's short story earned him an Academy Award nomination for Best Writing (Screenplay Based on Material from Another Medium). The film was also nominated for an Academy Award for Best Costume Design by Dorothy Jeakins.

As you watch the film, keep an eye out for changes the screenwriter and director made to the original. In adapting "The Dead" for the medium of film, what decisions were they forced to make for the story to "work" on the screen? Many of the discoveries made by the reader in the text happen thanks to the omniscient narration, which allows us to see what is happening in Gabriel's head. The film uses limited voiceover, only at the end, and relies on the actors revealing through their facial expressions and body language what they are feeling and thinking. Does the acting in the film stand up to this demand? Do we have the same sense of isolation, frustration, and longing in Gabriel? In the film, Gretta seems wistful nearly all evening, but Joyce's text does not indicate that. Was the change required in adaptation? Why or why not?

Then, look specifically at the drastic changes made as the story was translated from text to screen. Tony and John Huston add a completely new character, Mr. Grace, to the film. He plays an important role onscreen, reciting a poem he calls "Broken Vows" but which is actually titled "Donal Óg," or "Young Donal," translated by Lady Augusta Gregory from an anonymous Middle Irish lyric. Neither the recitation of this poem nor the character who shares it are present in the original, but the purpose of their inclusion seems clear: It causes Gretta to recall Michael Furey, foreshadows her confession, and causes Gabriel to become suspicious of her behavior. In the story, however, Gabriel is not suspicious at all of Gretta's behavior and in fact interprets it as revealing her willingness to be intimate with him. No thoughts of intimacy or desire seem present in the film's Gabriel. What else in the film is different from the book? Think about the scene in which Gretta listens to Bartell D'Arcy singing "The Lass of Aughrim." How is that staged? What changes are there from text screen?

As mentioned above in the question about music, a musical version of "The Dead" called *James Joyce's 'The Dead'* appeared on Broadway at the Belasco Theatre from January-April 2000. It starred Christopher Walken as Gabriel Conroy. Another opportunity for comparison exists if the reader is able to find the score and script for this adaptation.

2. **Gabriel Conroy and the young narrator in "Araby":** How are Gabriel Conroy and the narrator of "Araby" similar? Can we imagine Gabriel as the grown-up version of the boy in "Araby"?

Both Gabriel Conroy and the young, nameless narrator in "Araby" are creatures "driven and derided by vanity" as they are left in the darkness at the end of their stories. As we trace the momentum in their narratives, the situations the two characters place themselves in are quite similar. The young narrator's infatuation with Mangan's sister causes him to make a promise he cannot keep, going to the Araby bazaar and finding himself unable to make the purchase he needs to make. Gabriel Conroy's acute desire for his wife blinds him to

what Gretta is actually feeling and experiencing, thus resulting in his "shameful consciousness of his own person."

To pursue this essay, read both stories closely for clues
about the characteristics of the young narrator and Gabriel.
In "Araby," Joyce subtly foreshadows the conclusion by repeating the word *blind* early on in the story. Do we have any sense
of Gabriel's blindness in "The Dead" at the beginning? Do his
interactions with Lily and Miss Ivors indicate a lack of awareness of women? Do they indicate a lack of awareness of himself? What parallels to the young character in "Araby" can you
draw? What personality traits in the young boy do you see in
Gabriel? You may want to go so far as to consider why Joyce kept
his young narrator in "Araby" nameless: Was it so that readers would make connections between him and Gabriel? Next,
look at the conclusions to the stories. How are their reactions at
the end of their stories similar? Compare their epiphanies and
consider the ways in which they are alike and different. Is there
a dénouement that provides catharsis for the character or the
reader in "Araby"? What about in "The Dead"? What do you see
as the reason for the difference in the endings?

3. **"Spinsters" in "The Dead":** How do the unmarried women in
"The Dead" compare with their counterparts in the other stories in *Dubliners?* Do they face a similar fate, or are they better
off?

The Misses Morkan—the sisters Julia and Kate and their niece
Mary Jane—in "The Dead" are all unmarried women who live
together, teach music (thus making a living for themselves), and
enjoy an annual gathering where they treat their guests to the
best of food and drink. They do not seem to be unhappy, but are
there clues in the reading that might point to a perceived lack
in their lives? How do they compare with the other unmarried
women or "spinsters" in *Dubliners?* Think of all the spinsters
Joyce presents to us: Miss Ivors in "The Dead," Father Flynn's
sisters in "The Sisters," Maria in "Clay," and, the reader might
predict, Eveline in the story by the same name. How do the situations of these women contrast, and how are they similar?

To discuss the fate or plight of unmarried women in *Dubliners*, you must first consider the significance of their presence in the stories in the first place. Why are there so many unmarried women in these tales, and what bigger picture of Ireland at the turn-of-the-century do we get as a result? Is Joyce making a critique of Irish society here? What forces in Ireland might cause so many women to remain unmarried? Think about the size of many Irish Catholic families of the time and the ability of those families to offer dowries and pay for the weddings of their daughters. As a result of this, many young women could not marry, and their options were quite limited. They could teach, enter the convent, or work as caretakers for their family or for another family. Once you have done some background research, move back to the stories and the unmarried women in them. Look closely at their situations in life, and compare and contrast the characters. Do they seem happy or unhappy? Do you get the sense that something is missing in their lives? What makes the difference for the ones who are satisfied and the ones who are not?

Bibliography and Online Resources for "The Dead"

Attridge, Derek, ed. *The Cambridge Companion to James Joyce.* Cambridge: Cambridge University Press, 1990. Print.

Balsamo, Gian. "The Necropolitan Journey: Dante's Negative Politics in James Joyce's 'The Dead'." *James Joyce Quarterly.* 40.4 (2003): 763–81. Print.

Benstock, Bernard. *Narrative Con/Texts in Dubliners.* Urbana: University of Illinois Press, 1994. Print.

Bloom, Harold. *James Joyce's Dubliners.* New York: Chelsea House, 1998. Print.

Blumberg, Roger B. and Wallace Gray. "World Wide *Dubliners*." Web. <http://www.mendele.com/WWD/home.html>

Bosinelli Bollettieri, Rosa Maria and Harold Frederick Mosher, eds. *Rejoycing: New Readings of Dubliners.* Lexington: University Press of Kentucky, 1998. Print.

An Chomhairle Leabharlanna. [The Library Council.] "Ask about Ireland." Web. <http://askaboutireland.ie/>

Ellmann, Richard. *James Joyce.* New York: Oxford University Press, 1982. Print.

Hobby, Blake. "Alienation in James Joyce's *Dubliners*." *Alienation.* New York: Bloom's Literary Criticism, 2009. 61–69. Print.

Joyce, James. *Dubliners. The Portable James Joyce.* New York: Penguin Books, 1967. Print.

Mejlac, Eric Paul. "Dead Silence: James Joyce's 'The Dead' and John Huston's Adaptation as Aesthetic Rivals." *Literature Film Quarterly.* 37.4 (2009): 295–304. Print.

Nash, John. *James Joyce and the Act of Reception: Reading, Ireland, Modernism.* Cambridge: Cambridge University Press, 2006. Print.

Norris, Margot, ed. *Dubliners: Authoritative Text, Contexts, Criticism.* New York: Norton, 2006. Print.

Richardson, Brian. "A Theory of Narrative Beginnings and the Beginnings of 'The Dead' and *Molloy.*" *Narrative Beginnings: Theories and Practices.* Lincoln: University of Nebraska Press, 2008. 113–26. Print.

Schwarz, Daniel, ed. *James Joyce: The Dead.* Boston: Bedford, 1994. Print.

Thacker, Andrew, ed. *Dubliners: James Joyce.* New York: Palgrave MacMillan, 2006. Print.

Winston, Greg C. "Militarism and 'The Dead'." *A New and Complex Sensation: Essays on Joyce's Dubliners.* Dublin: Lilliput, 2004. 122–32. Print.

A PORTRAIT OF
THE ARTIST AS
A YOUNG MAN

READING TO WRITE

A Portrait of *the Artist as a Young Man* was first published serially (in chapters) in the literary magazine *The Egoist* from 1914 to 1915. It was later published in novel form by W. B. Huebsch in New York after several failed attempts with other publishers and thanks to the dedication of the writer Ezra Pound and Harriet Shaw Weaver, Joyce's benefactress. Joyce faced the same types of challenges in publishing *Portrait* as he did with *Dubliners,* namely the charge that the novel was lewd and inappropriate. Eventually, though, a publisher in London was found as well, and the novel was translated into French almost immediately upon Joyce's arrival in Paris.

Portrait, in the Joycean trajectory, is a middle ground stylistically between *Dubliners* and *Ulysses.* Indeed, some of the action begun in *Portrait* continues in *Ulysses,* and we see the further development of Stephen the artist in the latter. A novel rather than short stories, *Portrait*'s length lends itself to a more in-depth view of characters, even those who play supporting roles, and the time span of the novel is years rather than hours or days as we have in *Dubliners.*

Many of the themes presented in *Dubliners*—paralysis, despair, epiphany—are also found in *Portrait,* and Joyce examines with the same critical scrutiny the roles of the Roman Catholic Church and Ireland as forces that impact the characters in the novel. In *Portrait,* however, we also find new themes to take up in our writing, including how Joyce pays homage to his literary predecessors, notions of art and creativity, and coming of age. Joyce, through his protagonist Stephen Dedalus, philosophizes on the meaning and purpose of art and the responsibility of the artist in its creation. We frequently see Joyce's own artistic development through his character, which tempts us to view *Portrait* as autobiographical fiction, and in many instances it is.

As you read *A Portrait of the Artist as a Young Man,* consider focusing on one chapter of the book to find a topic to develop. Because each chapter is stylistically and thematically different, this is a great place to start. Once you settle on a chapter and paper topic, investigate how that topic relates to other chapters and to the different stages of Stephen's development. This can offer an excellent point of contrast in your writing, for as the chapters progress through the novel, Stephen's thoughts and ideas become more complex and sophisticated. Tracking these changes through close reading will offer increasingly nuanced insights into the work.

In the following passage, we witness an extended conversation between Stephen and the dean of studies, an English Jesuit priest. They begin by debating what beauty is and then branch out to discuss the abstract idea of the lamp of knowledge, which in turn gets conflated with a concrete, physical lamp. We join the conversation in progress with the dean speaking first:

—To return to the lamp, he said, the feeding of it is also a nice problem. You must choose the pure oil and you must be careful when you pour it in not to overflow it, not to pour in more than the funnel can hold.

—What funnel? asked Stephen.

—The funnel through which you pour the oil into your lamp.

—That? said Stephen. Is that called a funnel? Is it not a tundish?

—What is a tundish?

—That. The . . . funnel.

—Is that called a tundish in Ireland? asked the dean. I never heard the word in my life.

—It is called a tundish in Lower Drumcondra, said Stephen, laughing, where they speak the best English.

—A tundish, said the dean reflectively. That is a most interesting word. I must look that word up. On my word I must.

His courtesy of manner rang a little false and Stephen looked at the English convert with the same eyes as the elder brother in the parable may have turned on the prodigal. A humble follower in the wake of clamorous conversions, a poor Englishman in Ireland, he seemed to have entered on the stage of jesuit [sic] history when that strange play of intrigue and suffering and envy and struggle and indignity had been all but given through—a late-comer, a tardy spirit. From what had he set out? Perhaps he had been born and bred among serious dissenters, seeing salvation in Jesus only and abhorring the vain pomps of the establishment. Had he felt the need of an implicit faith amid the welter of sectarianism and the jargon of its turbulent schisms, six principle men, peculiar people, seed and snake baptists, [sic] supralapsarian dogmatists? Had he found the true church all of a sudden in winding up to the end like a reel of cotton some fine-spun line of reasoning on insufflation on the imposition of hands or the procession of the Holy Ghost? Or had Lord Christ touched him and bidden him follow, like that disciple who had sat at the receipt of custom, as he sat by the door of some zinc-roofed chapel, yawning and telling over his church pence?

The dean repeated the word yet again.

—Tundish! Well now, that is interesting!

—The question you asked me a moment ago seems to me more interesting. What is that beauty which the artist struggles to express from lumps of earth, said Stephen coldly.

The little word seemed to have turned a rapier point of his sensitiveness against this courteous and vigilant foe. He felt with a smart of dejection that the man to whom he was speaking was a countryman of Ben Jonson. He thought:

—The language in which we are speaking is his before it is mine. How different are the words *home, Christ, ale, master,* on his lips and on mine! I cannot speak or write these words without unrest of spirit. His language, so familiar and so foreign, will always be for me an acquired speech. I have not made or accepted its words. My voice holds them at bay. My soul frets in the shadow of his language.

There is much to discuss in this passage. First, we see great development in Stephen's personality, confidence, and intellect in his thoughtful and thought-provoking conversation with the dean, yet he still feels uncomfortable in the English language, recognizing it as foreign to him because he is Irish. Elsewhere in *Portrait*, however, Stephen distances himself from the Irish language and culture. He is not at home in either language, placing him in a "no man's land" somewhere in between the two languages and cultures. This state of never being accepted or comfortable in a country or language is something Joyce himself struggled with, eventually leading to his own self-imposed exile (much like Stephen's at the end of this work). There is also a differentiation made between what is Irish and what is English, with the dean second-guessing Stephen, telling him he never heard what he assumes to be the Irish word for funnel, *tundish*, in all his life. In return, Stephen feels defensive about his Irishness and assures the English priest that the word is used in Upper Dromcondra where they "speak the best English." The priest then proclaims the word *tundish* "interesting" and one he will have to look up. (In fact, Stephen does look it up later in the novel only to learn that it is an English and not an Irish word after all.) Stephen feels that his "courtesy of manner rang a little false" and begins to make assumptions about the man's motives and background. The conversation ends stiffly, and Stephen seems to regret his jab at the priest. Stephen is sharp with his words, and his mastery of the English language, which in his mind is an acquired speech, is a tool he frequently uses to assert himself and wound others. This passage comes at the beginning of chapter 5, the final one in the novel, and it is the first scene in this chapter in which we see Stephen use his intelligence and ability to articulate his thoughts against an opponent. It is not, however, the last. This scene sets the tone of the chapter and prepares us for future theoretical and philosophical conversations Stephen tries to have with other characters in the novel. He is clearly working through his notions of art, beauty, and poetry, as well as trying to understand exactly who he is as an individual being pulled in many opposite directions—morality and the flesh, duty to family and duty to self, Ireland and exile.

TOPICS AND STRATEGIES

In this section, we will develop some of the ideas and themes presented above in order to help you to plan for essays on *A Portrait of the Artist as a Young Man.* The following writing prompts should give you a good starting point from which you can begin to flesh out your paper.

Themes

There is no lack of themes to explore in *Portrait:* progression from childhood to adulthood and the narrative changes that mark this progression, the development of the artist and his aesthetics, and the distinctions between and among the classes of people in the novel, which Stephen feels quite keenly as he and his family move down the rungs of the class ladder. You could also investigate how some of the themes present in *Dubliners* also play out here, including ideas of epiphany, paralysis, and desperation.

Sample Topics:

1. **Development of the artist:** How do we witness the development of Stephen Dedalus the artist? What changes in his artistic aesthetic do we see along the way?

   Portrait opens with a story that Stephen remembered from his childhood, as well as some songs and rhymes, revealing to the reader the importance early on of language in this individual's life. The seeds of the artist are germinating from the first lines. At school he is bullied by his classmates for proclaiming Byron the best poet, telling the boys, who prefer Tennyson and say that Byron was a "bad man," that they do not know a thing about poetry. He is summarily beaten as a result. As he matures, we see his tastes develop more fully and he is better able to explain his aesthetic to his peers, who may tease him about his loftiness but no longer beat him for his ideas. As a university student, Stephen insists that proper art does not excite desire, and that "beauty expressed by the artist cannot awaken in us an emotion which is kinetic or a sensation which is purely physical. It awakens, or ought to awaken, or induces, or ought to induce, an esthetic stasis, in ideal pity or an ideal terror, a stasis called forth prolonged and at last dissolved by what I call the rhythm of beauty." How does this aesthetic ideal play out in the novel? Does Joyce apply Stephen's ideal? What does Joyce want us to think about Stephen's notion of aesthetic stasis? How does Stephen's philosophy of art develop and mature along with him through the novel? At what other points in the text do you see this maturation process?

2. **Writer as creator:** How does Joyce present, through Stephen Dedalus, the notion that the artist is the ultimate creator? How does he elevate art to a divine status?

Stephen, as he grows into his role of artist, comes to make the connection between his last name, Dedalus, and the mythological Greek architect Daedalus who constructed the labyrinth to house the minotaur. The architect/artist of his future self is one of the primary focus points for this text, and Stephen sees him as a "hawklike man flying sunwards above the sea, a prophecy of the end he had been born to serve and had been following though the mists of childhood and boyhood, a symbol of the artist forging anew in his workshop out of the sluggish matter of the earth a new soaring impalpable imperishable being." At several points in the novel, Stephen speaks of art in general terms and literature, specifically, as "the highest and most spiritual art," and at nearly every point where art is discussed, he equates the artist to a god who is entrusted with creating the beautiful. He shares with Lynch midway through chapter 5 that "The personality of the artist passes into the narration itself, flowing round and round the persons and the action like the vital sea." The qualities of the artist are life-giving and "vital," and he emphasizes his point less subtly as he continues his analogy: "The artist, like the God of the creation, remains within or behind or beyond or above his handiworks, invisible, refined out of existence, indifferent, paring his fingernails." Stephen returns once more to the image of the artist at the end of the novel, when he sets off to "encounter for the millionth time the reality of experience and to forge in the smithy of my soul the uncreated conscience of my race."

As you consider this theme of the artist as creator, certainly the previously cited passages would be useful in detailing Stephen's notion and definition of artist, but look elsewhere in the text for clues as to how he imagines himself a creator/god. Is Joyce presenting his own ideas through Stephen? How do Stephen's colleagues react to his assertion? How do we react to it? Are we to take him seriously or understand him as a young, rather arrogant man who is still testing his theories about art and aesthetics? How does Stephen's philosophy of art and the artist mesh with current literary theory?

3. **Childhood and memory:** How does Joyce use the memories of childhood as a theme that runs throughout *Portrait?* What is the significance of childhood memory in the novel?

At least one-third of *Portrait* is dedicated to Stephen's youth and the memories of that time in his life. All of chapter 1 is devoted to childhood memory, and nearly all of chapter 2 is as well, until the scene where Stephen becomes aware of his coming-of-age on the trip to Cork with his father. Until that point, the memories are somewhat foggy, especially at the beginning when we have only snippets from stories, songs, and memories. Joyce's use of "Once on a time" to begin his novel is also an interesting device used to place the reader in the child's mind, and the bits and pieces provided over the next several pages are clearly memories from early childhood. The young writer's understanding of his surroundings is simple and childlike: "When you wet the bed first it is warm then it gets cold. His mother put on the oilsheet. That had the queer smell." (Note: an oilsheet is a specially treated piece of fabric that can be wiped clean, and in this context it is clear why Stephen's mother uses it after he has wet the bed.) Young Stephen's identification of Dante Riordan with her two brushes is also typical of childhood memory and the association of a person with his or her interesting possessions. He also recalls having done something wrong (he does not tell what, but because it happens right after he mentions his neighbor Eileen Vance, the reader might safely assume it had to do with the little girl) and a poem in which he is terrified into apologizing for the offense: *"Pull out his eyes,*

Apologise, Apologise, Pull out his eyes." His interactions with his classmates when he goes off to school tell a great deal about young Stephen's personality and give early glimpses into the person he will become. His confusion about his father's profession and uncertainty about whether is it appropriate to kiss his mother play out in his later life. Much of the person Stephen is to become is revealed in these early pages.

As you prepare to write an essay on this topic, read these first two chapters closely and critically, looking for elements of foreshadowing and hints about Stephen's future self. Consider also the reliability of the narrator. Certainly these chapters are being written retrospectively by the Stephen at the end of the novel. Does Joyce capture a child's voice in the early pages of *Portrait?* Is the childhood Stephen believable? Why or why not? What scenes support your claim? Consider the pivotal episodes in the first two chapters: when Stephen is teased about kissing his mother, what Stephen writes on the flyleaf of his geography book, his understanding of the argument over Parnell at Christmas dinner, and the pandying incident with Father Dolan. All of these episodes play a formative role in Stephen's life. Why does Joyce write them retrospectively through the eyes of the young Stephen? What impact does this technique have?

4. **Class differences:** How are class and the differences among the classes in Dublin society presented to the reader in *Portrait?* What do these class distinctions, and the progression down the rungs of the class ladder by the Dedalus family, do to impact Stephen?

Stephen Dedalus's class and family situation mirrored Joyce's in many ways. Both the author and his protagonist had fathers who were "gentlemen" but who could not manage to keep a job or keep their families financially stable as a result. As a young boy, Stephen seems a bit confused about what his father "is" when asked by his classmate Nasty Roche, but is nonetheless keenly aware of the class distinctions between one boy and another, and him and those of a different class. In the chapel, a few scenes later, Stephen notices a "cold night smell" that was a "holy smell" and "not like the smell of the old peasants who knelt at the back of the chapel at Sunday mass." He recognizes the class difference here in a sensory way but remembers to add that the peasants were "very holy" and imagines their village and how it would be "lovely to sleep for one night in that cottage before the fire of the smoking turf, in the dark lit by the fire, in the warm dark, breathing the smell of the peasants, air and rain and turf and corduroy." His romantic notion of rural poverty tells the reader that clearly Stephen has no idea of the true situation of the peasants who sit at the back of his chapel. Later, after an exchange with his classmate Athy in the infirmary, Stephen feels sorry for his father because he is not a magistrate and wonders why he is at Clongowes with these sons of magistrates. He then recalls that his father told him his "granduncle presented an address to the liberator [Daniel O'Connell] there fifty years before." Connections, Stephen has learned, sometimes count as much as finances. Stephen realizes when September comes and he does not return to the expensive Clongowes that his father is in trouble, and from that point on we witness the family having to move to increasingly more modest dwellings with less and less furniture and belongings.

Some questions to consider as you plan out this essay would include: What is Joyce trying to convey about class distinctions in turn-of-the-century Ireland? How does class impact Stephen? How does his understanding and perception of class change throughout the novel? Does Stephen change along with his class? What is the importance of the class distinctions Joyce, through Stephen, makes? Track the family's decline over the course of the novel and chart Stephen's attitude toward class with each subsequent move toward poverty that the Dedaluses make.

Character

Portrait offers some excellent opportunities for in-depth character analysis. Certainly, if you are writing a long paper, you could choose to examine Stephen's character, but for a shorter paper, it is probably better (and much more manageable) to study one of the more minor individuals. The supporting characters Dante Riordan, Davin, and Simon Dedalus, Stephen's father, are just three of many great choices for an essay on character.

Sample Topics:

1. **Dante Riordan:** What role does Mrs. Dante Riordan play in the novel? How does Joyce want us to react to this character?

We meet Dante for the first time on the first page of *Portrait*, and she is an important figure in Stephen's life during his early years. We learn that Dante is older than Stephen's parents but younger than his Uncle Charles, and it is unclear to readers exactly what function this woman fulfills in the household. Certainly she holds some authority and influence in the family, as seen in her role in Stephen being chastised in the scene that introduces the poem that would terrify a young child: *"Pull out his eyes, Apologise."* We know that Dante has two brushes, one backed in green velvet for Charles Stewart Parnell and one backed in maroon velvet for Michael Davitt. From this we can gather that she is in favor of Home Rule, at least at the beginning of the novel, since both of these men were Irish politicians who supported that cause. We later discover, however, that religion was more important to her than Irish freedom, since she ripped the green velvet off the brush when Parnell's affair came to light. Davitt also split with Parnell, so Dante keeps the maroon brush intact. Stephen tells us that Dante is a "clever woman and a wellread woman" who tutors Stephen in geography.

Although we learn about Dante in a piecemeal fashion in the early pages of the story, we get a much fuller picture of her true nature at the Dedalus Christmas dinner. Although earlier in the novel she simply seemed stern, at the dinner she is cold and thoroughly unpleasant, traits unearthed, to be sure, by the conversation revolving around religion and politics and the figure in which those two delicate topics clashed: Parnell. What does this exchange reveal about Dante Riordan? How do we explain her zeal and hatred? Is it in character? What does her reaction suggest about the bigger picture of Irish politics during the day? How does Joyce want us to view Dante?

2. **Davin:** What do we make of Stephen's friend Davin? Does Joyce present a sympathetic character in this young man?

Stephen is prompted to think of his college friend Davin as he spies the statue of the national poet of Ireland, Thomas Moore, on the grounds of Trinity College (Stephen and his friends go to University College, Dublin). Much of Moore's work had a pastoral Irish feel and was quite popular during his lifetime and remains well-liked today. It is probably as much the physical appearance of Moore ("a Firbolg in the borrowed cloak of a Milesian" recalls old Irish mythology; the Firbolgs were a relatively simple race while the Milesians were more enlightened) as his love of country that reminds Stephen of Davin. Davin, we are told, is a peasant who "worshipped the sorrowful legend of Ireland." He speaks Irish and stands "armed against" anything that comes to him "from England or by way of English culture." As he is walking with Stephen, Davin shares a story from his past in which a young married woman alone in her home (her husband was out of town) invited him in to spend the night. Davin recounts the story and how he resisted the temptation and walked away. We next encounter Davin at a hurling match (an Irish sporting event), and he and Stephen discuss nationalism. Davin wonders aloud whether Stephen, with his name and his ideas, is "Irish at all?" Davin encourages "Stevie" to "try to be one of us," telling him "In your heart you are an Irishman but your pride is too powerful." Stephen counters, "When the soul of a man is born in this country there are nets flung at it to hold it back from flight. You talk to me of nationality, language, religion. I shall try to fly by those nets." Moments later comes Stephen's infamous proclamation that "Ireland is the sow that eats her farrow." Rather than argue with Stephen further, Davin walks away sadly shaking his head.

What overall impression do we have of Davin? Does Joyce present a sympathetic character? Is Davin really as simple as he seems? He says himself that he is a simple man, and Stephen sees him as simple, but is there something more there? If Joyce gives us Davin as an exemplar of the Irish nationalist movement, what can we surmise about its members? How is Davin a foil to Stephen? What does Stephen think of Davin?

3. **Simon Dedalus:** What is Stephen's relationship with his father? Why does Joyce present such a problematic image of fatherhood?

We first encounter Simon Dedalus on the opening page of *Portrait* through the eyes of the child, Stephen, who listens to him tell a story. A few scenes later, when his parents leave him at Clongowes, Stephen is given some money and advice by his father: write home for anything he needs and "never to peach on a fellow" (in other words, he must not be a tattletale). We see in the Christmas dinner scene that Simon Dedalus is a devoted Parnellite, and his passion for his "dead king," matched by Dante's passion for her religion, utterly ruins the meal, which ends in harsh words, slamming doors, and tears. Another pivotal scene in which we learn much about Simon Dedalus is when he and Stephen travel to Cork to sell a property. Originally from that city, Simon returns to his old neighborhood and visits the pubs he used to frequent. He introduces his son as "only a Dublin jackeen," a thoroughly pejorative term suggesting that he is, as Miss Ivors in "The Dead" would put it, a "West Briton." Add to the mix the long-standing rivalry between Cork and Dublin, Simon has done his son quite a disservice. He says Stephen is a "levelheaded thinking boy," the very opposite of himself, "the boldest flirt in the city of Cork in his day." Waxing nostalgic, feeling competitive, and uninhibited by the alcohol, Simon asserts himself against his son, claiming, "There's that son of mine there not half my age and I'm a better man than he is any day of the week." Returning to the places of his youth and meeting with the people from his past who have also aged, Simon is forced to recognize the passage of time head-on, and his insecurity about growing old causes him to lash out against his son, whose youth and promise he envies. The next scenes where we encounter

Simon Dedalus directly are ones in which we see the family, because of Simon's inability to manage finances well, moving to increasingly less respectable homes and neighborhoods. Finally, Stephen discusses his father with his friend Cranly. When asked what his father was, Stephen answers: "A medical student, an oarsman, a tenor, an amateur actor, a shouting politician, a small landlord, a small investor, a drinker, a good fellow, a storyteller, somebody's secretary, something in a distillery, a tax-gatherer, a bankrupt and at present a praiser of his own past."

How do these various passages create a portrait of Simon Dedalus for the reader? What does Joyce want us to think about this man? Do we sympathize with him? Do we hold him fully accountable? Is he a victim? If so, of what? Is Stephen fair in his assessment of his father? Why does Joyce present this model of fatherhood for us? How has Stephen been impacted by his father? What is the importance of Simon Dedalus to the momentum of the story?

History and Context

Joyce expects that his readers bring a great deal of peripheral knowledge to the novel. Set in Dublin in the final years of the 1800s and beginning of the 1900s, *Portrait* features multiple references to contemporary events and authors who heavily influenced Joyce's (and, by extension, Stephen's) writing. A fuller appreciation of the novel comes with a deeper understanding of the history and context in which the action takes place.

Sample Topics:

1. **Charles Stewart Parnell:** What is the significance of the heated discussion about Parnell over Christmas dinner at the Dedalus home? What impact does this have on Stephen?

   The Christmas dinner scene in *Portrait* is among the most famous in the novel. The tension created by Joyce in this episode is so precise and compelling that the reader feels present at the meal. The taboo topics of religion and politics mix at the dinner table, and the mood goes from uncomfortable and awkward to confrontational as the holiday feast comes to an abrupt end as Dante leaves and the men sit mourning their "dead king" Parnell. Although the reader can get a sense of what is going on without knowing the full historical context of the argument, doing some investigation into the Parnell case makes this scene all the more vivid.

Charles Stewart Parnell (1846–91) was the Irish patriot who fought for Irish Home Rule and wanted British involvement in Ireland to end. He was a member of Parliament and the founder of the Irish Parliamentary Party. A Protestant, Parnell was popular with both Catholics and Protestants, and many considered him Ireland's uncrowned king. However, his political career suffered when his affair with Katherine (Kitty) O'Shea, the estranged wife of Captain William O'Shea, came to light. Captain O'Shea and his wife had been separated for some time, and he knew of the affair but was waiting for her to come into an inheritance before he divorced her. Captain O'Shea named Parnell as the cause for the divorce, however, marking him as an adulterer, which forced many priests to condemn him for his sin. Following the lead of their priests, numerous Irish Catholics withdrew their support from Parnell, which in turn meant the withdrawal of their support for the Home Rule movement, which he led. Parnell married Kitty O'Shea, but the attacks and criticism he faced because of the affair essentially ruined him politically, while also affecting him emotionally and physically. Parnell died on October 6, 1891, at age 45, less than two years after the scandal surfaced.

Because of the rawness of the emotions expressed in the Christmas dinner scene, it is quite likely to be Christmas 1891, a little more than two months after Parnell's death. The proximity of the event explains the passion behind the discussion. What is the significance of this scene in the context of the novel? What does it tell us about the characters? What can the reader surmise about the political environment in Ireland at this time? Consider the most striking elements of the argument: the story about the "very famous spit," the notion of Ireland being an "unfortunate priestridden race," and the final proclamation by Mr. Casey of "no God for Ireland!" How do these elements stand out in the overall narrative and shape

Stephen as he matures? How does this holiday gathering impact Stephen as an adult?

2. **Irish nationalism:** What impression do we have of Irish nationalism, or the Home Rule movement? How do Joyce's characters shape our opinion? How does he want us to view turn-of-the-century Irish politics?

Before beginning this essay, review the preceding topic discussion about Parnell to familiarize yourself with one of the main players in the Irish nationalist movement. Two other important elements in this movement were the Gaelic League and the Gaelic Athletic Association, in which Stephen's friend Davin participated. Certainly Stephen's father, Simon Dedalus, was a nationalist and so was Mr. Casey, as evidenced in their zealous defense of Parnell at the Christmas dinner. The Irish nationalist or Home Rule movement began in the early 1800s, nearly immediately after the Act of Union established Ireland as under the sovereignty of the United Kingdom of Great Britain. There were several degrees of nationalism, from those who believed in complete separation from England to those who recognized some advantages to being linked to the United Kingdom for international purposes but preferred to manage their domestic politics themselves. Part of the nationalist movement included the return to speaking Irish Gaelic (Gaelige) and playing Irish sports such as hurling and Irish football. Where on the continuum of nationalism do we find the characters in *Portrait?* Responding to this question is in many ways a combination of some of the questions already addressed here, including looking closely at the Christmas dinner scene and the characters Dante, Davin, and Simon Dedalus. It would also be useful to explore the character of Stephen and his reaction to nationalism and how his views change over the course of the novel. One of the final statements Stephen makes with regard to his homeland is that "Ireland is the old sow that eats her farrow." Are we to understand Stephen as a filter for Joyce's own thoughts and beliefs, and if so, to what assessment of Irish politics is Joyce leading us? Is the reader allied with Stephen in forming an impression of Irish nationalism? Why or why not? Make references to characters and passages to support your position.

3. **Literary homage:** What is the effect of the many references to other writers in *Portrait*? How do these allusions provide insight into Stephen's character?

From the first pages of the novel, we have the immediate impression that Stephen, even when he is a young child, has an ear for language. He has a lyrical bent, and he enjoys the sounds of words. It is no surprise, then, that he has strong opinions about writers and openly shares them, getting himself in trouble with his schoolmates. When asked who the greatest writer is, Stephen makes the distinction between prose (Cardinal Newman) and poetry (Byron, not Tennyson, who is merely a "rhymester"). Later in the same chapter, Stephen fixates on Shelley's fragment "Art Thou Pale for Weariness" and in the scene that follows goes to collect the monetary prize he was awarded for an essay he wrote, marking the beginning of his career as an artist. His thoughts at the end of chapter 4 are poetic, echoing and blending Yeats and Shelley in the line "A day of dappled seaborne clouds." Indeed, the poem "The Villanelle of the Temptress" serves to showcase Stephen's budding talent but also some of his French and Italian influences as the form was relatively new to English poetry.

How do these literary influences play out in Stephen's character, philosophies, thoughts, and writing? What roles do these writers play? Do we detect echoes of Ibsen, Yeats, Byron, Shelley, and Aquinas in the young writer? Are there other writers who have impacted Stephen? Consider researching Joyce's influences as you undertake this essay, as the author and his fictitious young artist have similar tastes. This essay requires a good deal of research into these writers but would be an interesting avenue to explore more fully.

Philosophy and Ideas

Portrait can be seen as being more overtly philosophical than any other work by Joyce. Although *Ulysses* and *Finnegans Wake* both reveal Joycean philosophy through their technique, *Portrait* is much more explicit, and Stephen explains his artistic and aesthetic vision to his classmates and, by extension, to us. Even as a child, Stephen is a critical thinker and looks at his world much differently than his peers do. Built into this philosophy of art is a gradual turning away from religion, which Stephen sees as one of the forces imprisoning him.

Sample Topics:

1. **"Everything and everywhere"**: How do Stephen's early musings about the world around him develop into his aesthetic vision? What signs early in the novel do we have to suggest that this young boy is already on the way to becoming an artist?

   Not far into the first chapter of *Portrait,* we find Stephen reflecting on the vastness of the universe and his small place in it. He wonders: "What was after the universe? Nothing . . . It was very big to think about everything and everywhere. Only God could do that." It frustrates the young Stephen to think about these things because he cannot fully comprehend them. It makes him tired and pains him that he "did not know where the universe ended. He felt small and weak." Later, he decides that "[b]y thinking of things you could understand them." He is much more inquisitive about his world than his classmates, and critically analyzes his situations and surroundings in ways his peers do not. He is sensitive to the world around him and the nuances of human emotion at a very young age. When his classmates discuss the impending flogging one of the boys is about to get, Athy recites a poem: "It can't be helped; / It must be done. / So down with your breeches / And out with your bum." The boys laugh, but Stephen notices that underneath the bravado they are "a little afraid."

   How does Stephen's acute sensitivity to his world as a child develop into his aesthetic vision as an adult artist? Where else in the early chapters do we find similar indications of a budding artist in Stephen? Does Stephen recognize these differences in himself at this stage in his development? Do his peers see him as different? How do the adults in his life react to Stephen's questioning and academic nature? Limit yourself to the first two chapters of the novel for this question, and concentrate on the ways in which the young Stephen's personality foreshadows the man and artist he will become.

2. **Aesthetics and art:** What is Stephen's philosophy of art or aesthetics? How does Stephen (and perhaps, by extension, Joyce) put this philosophy into practice?

Much of chapter 5 is devoted to Stephen expressing his aesthetics, his philosophy of art. He discusses the concepts of beauty, both with the dean of studies and with his classmates at the university, many of whom seem bested by the intelligence of our protagonist. Stephen is scholarly and critical, and his philosophy of art is well-developed. He insists that art "must not excite desire," and that the aesthetic emotion is "static." Art, he asserts, "is a human disposition of sensible or intelligible matter for an esthetic end." He goes on to apply the philosophies of St. Thomas Aquinas, Aristotle, and Plato in explaining art and beauty to Lynch, who teases Stephen because he is having a difficult time grasping the concepts. He especially draws on Aquinas's notion that *"Three things are needed for beauty, wholeness, harmony and radiance."* His emphasis on these three elements is seen in the discussion of the basket and the "scholastic *quidditas,* the *whatness* of a thing." His aesthetics culminate in the profession of the artist as the "God of the creation . . . refined out of existence."

How does Stephen apply the aesthetics of the philosophers to whom he refers? How do Plato, Aristotle, and Aquinas work their way into Stephen's philosophy of art? Does Joyce seem to hold the same aesthetics as Stephen? Is Joyce simply using Stephen in these passages as a ventriloquist's dummy in order to make his own aesthetics known? How do these scenes fit into the rest of the novel? What is their importance to the whole? Is the philosophy of art as presented in this chapter carried out in practice in the novel?

3. **Religion:** How is religion, particularly Roman Catholicism, presented in *Portrait?* What are the key moments in the novel that impact Stephen's gradual progression away from Catholicism?

The young Stephen seems relatively comfortable with his religion, because he is able to maintain a simplistic view of it—he recites memorized prayers, goes to Mass with his classmates, and obeys the rules of the priests even when they do not make much sense to him. He does not fully understand the implications of the argument about religion and politics at the Christmas dinner table between Dante and his father and Mr. Casey. Yet he still recognizes that something horrible has happened and that religion played a part. In the famous scene where Stephen is flogged by Father Dolan, the prefect of studies, for losing his glasses, the young boy begins to recognize the incongruities within the church, and this marks the beginning of his disenchantment with Catholicism. He breaks with his faith and frequents prostitutes for a while but returns to religion after the fire and brimstone sermons during the retreat in honor of Saint Francis Xavier. He makes a confession and considers the possibility of entering the priesthood as a vocation, noting that he has "often seen himself as a priest wielding calmly and humbly the awful power of which angels and saints stood in reverence!" He sees the priest as a type of artist and, for this reason, can imagine himself in that role, but comes also to recognize that the church is one of the institutions holding him back from reaching his full potential. The adult Stephen's position on religion is fully elucidated in his discussion with Cranly in chapter 5. The two men talk about Stephen's mother's request that he make his Easter duty, which Stephen refuses. He explains that he no longer believes in the Eucharist and that he does not wish to overcome his doubts about religion. Cranly asks him why he fears a "bit of bread," to which Stephen replies that he fears the "chemical action which would be set up in my soul by a false homage to a symbol behind which are massed twenty centuries of authority and veneration."

How does Joyce present Roman Catholicism in the novel? Is it an entirely unfavorable depiction? If not, what scenes are sympathetic toward the religion? We find some balance in the character Cranly with regard to religion—are there other characters like him? How does the assertion by Stephen that he "shall try to fly by" the net of religion play out in *Portrait?* Is he successful in his flight? Why or why not? Support your answer with scenes from the novel.

Form and Genre

In *Portrait,* Joyce begins to experiment more with form and genre than he had with *Dubliners,* laying the groundwork for *Ulysses* and *Finnegans Wake.* Essays addressing these topics consider how the novel is semiautobiographical or, in a similar vein, how it is a *roman à clef.* Another option would be to study the narrative innovations employed by Joyce and how they meld with the aesthetics presented by his protagonist Stephen Dedalus.

Sample Topics:

1. *Portrait* **as semiautobiographical:** How autobiographical is *Portrait?* How closely related are Stephen Dedalus and James Joyce?

Although there are many similarities between Joyce and Stephen, be careful not to conflate the artist and his creation. Nonetheless, looking for clues about the ways in which the two are alike can be compelling for those of us who like to try to solve literary puzzles. For this essay, concentrate only on Stephen's character, and save the supporting characters in the novel for the next question on *roman à clef.* Look at the specifics of Stephen's background: He was born into a relatively well-off family with a governess, went to Clongowes and then Belvedere, watched as his father's decisions drove the family to financial ruin, took a trip to Cork with his father, went to University College, and eventually fled Ireland. Joyce did all of those things as well. Both were urged to consider priesthood and refused the vocation, and both enlisted the services of a prostitute in their teens.

Precisely how autobiographical is *Portrait?* The one-to-one comparison between Joyce and Stephen can be extremely compelling, but at the same time is also extremely risky. As you prepare to write this essay, you will need to consult Richard Ellmann's biography of Joyce for evidence to support the connections you make. You might also want to have a look at the novel *Stephen Hero,* which was the prototype for *Portrait* and was published posthumously. It is much more autobiographical than what Joyce intended for publication. What is the relationship between author and creation? How is the border between the two blurred in *Portrait?* Are there places in the novel where we can say there is a clear distinction between Stephen and Joyce?

2. *Portrait* as *roman à clef:* How does Joyce use the *roman à clef* technique in *Portrait?* Is the approach he adopts effective? Does having the "key" provide the reader with deeper understanding of the characters and events?

This essay, similar to the preceding topic discussion, would require a bit of research on the part of the writer but would be an ideal paper to write if you enjoy historical criticism. The *roman à clef* technique (French for "novel with a key") was a literary style that came into fashion in France in the 17th century. A writer using this technique presents characters and plotlines that are fictional equivalents of actual people and events, providing the people with pseudonyms and sometimes changing the setting. The technique fell out of fashion for several decades because of the fear of libel, but writers in the 1900s, including Joyce, began to popularize it again.

The first topic discussion in this section focuses on the ways in which *Portrait* is autobiographical, making the link between Stephen and Joyce, but many of the supporting characters in the novel are also stand-ins for actual people in Joyce's life. Dante Riordan, Stephen's governess, is the fictional parallel for Dante

Hearn Conway, who also had two brushes, one for Parnell and one for Davitt. And just as Dante in *Portrait* turned her back on Parnell when his adultery came to light, so did Dante Hearn Conway. Both women were extreme with regard to their religion, and both were feared by their charges. The similarities between Simon Dedalus and John Joyce, James Joyce's father, cannot be denied either. The two men are nearly interchangeable. Additionally, the characters of Cranly, Davin, and Lynch have cognates in Joyce's own life. Investigative work in Ellmann's biography will allow you to make the connections between fiction and real life. Is the use of the *roman à clef* technique in *Portrait* effective? Does the reader need to have the "key" to fully appreciate the novel? Why does Joyce use this technique? Why does he change the names of his characters when they are so thinly veiled?

3. **Narrative innovations in *Portrait*:** How does Joyce use narrative in *Portrait*? How would we describe the narrative styles in the novel? How do the various styles fit the stages of development of the artist?

The narrative style changes subtly and gradually over the course of *Portrait.* The novel begins in a child's narrative voice and style with our protagonist recalling the foggiest snippets of early memory: a fragment of a bedtime story, a few lines in a song, and the sensory experience of wetting the bed. Then over the course of the next few pages, the recollections become a bit clearer and Stephen's understanding of the world around him becomes more sophisticated. He recognizes that the boys in the schoolyard are not "nice" boys and that his mother advised him to stay away from them. His imagination is vivid, and his mind is already showing signs of great creativity. As Stephen matures, so does the narrative style from childlike and simple, clouded by the fogginess of memory and the innocence of youth, to complex and layered, complicated by the pressures of the "nets" of religion and politics and the experiences of adulthood.

As you plan for this essay, look for places in the novel where the narrative shifts less subtly than elsewhere throughout. Although for the most part the progression from child to adult is subtle, a few instances reveal a dramatic change. Think about the final pages of chapter 2, as Stephen and his father travel to Cork. We find: "The memory of his childhood suddenly grew dim. He tried to call forth some of its vivid moments but could not." The coming-of-age Stephen looks back on his childhood and realizes it is growing fainter and fainter, and not long after this passage is the scene in which Stephen loses his virginity to a prostitute. Look also at the narrative style of chapter 3, much of which is spent in the retreat, with Stephen hearing about his impending eternal damnation if he continues down the path he has started. The narration is external, emphasizing the external forces acting on Stephen at this point in his life and causing him to make a dramatic change. The feel of chapter 4 is quite mystical and poetic, and Stephen, who has returned to Catholicism, is funneling all his creative energy and urges into religion: "Each of his senses was brought under a rigorous discipline." But this comes to a close when he encounters the girl on the beach, whose beauty becomes the evidence for Stephen that there is indeed a God. Chapter 5 features Stephen's explanation of his aesthetics, and the narration is characterized by a great deal of dialogue at the beginning and middle, while at the end it shifts to a diary or epistolary style. What is the significance of the changes in narrative? What impact do they have on the reader? How do the different styles mark Stephen's maturation process? Why does Joyce end his novel with a diary or epistolary style?

Language, Symbols, and Imagery

An essay on Joyce's use of language and symbolism in *Portrait* offers a multitude of possibilities because of the writer's skill with words and images. Stephen, even at a young age but certainly as an adult, recognizes the impact of language and the power and symbolism behind words.

Sample Topics:

1. **Mothers:** How does Joyce use motherhood and mothers as a symbol in the novel? What impression do we have of mothers thanks to Joyce's imagery and language in describing and depicting them?

The novel opens with Stephen recalling some warm memories of his mother, namely that she had "a nicer smell than his father," that she played the piano, and that she was a "nice mother." At the Christmas dinner, Mrs. Dedalus tries to keep the peace, reminding her husband, Mr. Casey, and Dante that it is a holiday. We do not see much of her again until toward the end of the novel, when she scrubs Stephen's neck, ears, and nose before he goes off to university. As he departs, she tells him that he has been changed by the university, and we are to understand that it is not for the better. We learn a bit more about Mrs. Dedalus and Stephen's relationship with her in Stephen's conversation with Cranly near the end of the novel. Stephen confides in his friend about "an unpleasant quarrel" he had with his mother about religion. She asked Stephen to make his Easter duty and he refused, to his mother's great disappointment. Cranly asks if Stephen loves his mother, to which Stephen replies, "I do not know what your words mean." The conversation turns to whether Stephen's mother has had a happy life, and due to the "nine or ten" children she has had and the family's financial circumstances as a result of Simon Dedalus's folly, Cranly concludes that she must have "gone through a great deal of suffering." Cranly advises Stephen to make his Easter duty, as it would mean a great deal for his mother and cost Stephen little. Stephen still cannot.

The other image we have of motherhood in *Portrait* is that of a sow eating her farrow. Ireland here is portrayed as a cannibalistic mother, at least in Stephen's eyes. She holds her children back from achieving their full potential, casting nets over them and imprisoning them. Ironically, the W. B. Yeats play *The Countess Cathleen,* the play at the National

Theatre alluded to in chapter 5 that Stephen's classmates are petitioning, provides a symbol of a sacrificial mother, as the Countess (Mother Ireland) sells her soul to the devil so that her tenants (the Irish peasantry) may eat. God sees this act of ultimate sacrifice and restores her soul to her, and she ascends to heaven. Many Irish at the time saw this as blasphemous, but Stephen does not. Based on what we know of Stephen and his mother, how would we qualify their relationship? What is Joyce telling us about motherhood, or at least Irish motherhood? We do not know much about Mrs. Dedalus except indirectly. We rarely hear her speak and know very little about who she is as an individual. What does the reader take away from these descriptions and depictions of motherhood? Why is the mother so sacrificial in this novel?

2. **Sexuality:** Discuss Joyce's use of sexual imagery in the novel. How does he present Stephen's coming of age and budding sexuality? What does Stephen's experience with sexuality tell the reader about Irish attitudes toward sex? What do we make of Davin's encounter?

In an Irish Roman Catholic society at the turn of the century, the setting for *Portrait,* sexuality is repressed and feelings about sex are tainted with guilt. We see this in the beginning of the novel, with the boys in Stephen's class teasing him for kissing his mother before bed, and then for not kissing his mother before bed. Stephen is confused about which of the two choices is appropriate. He then begins to wonder about the word *kiss* itself, the sound it makes, and why "people do that with their two faces." In Joyce's treatment of sexuality, particularly Stephen's early thoughts on it, language and image blend. This happens also in the word *suck*. As Stephen gets older, his thoughts about sexuality shift from his mother to Eileen Vance, the Protestant girl next door whose "long thin cool white hands . . . were like ivory; only soft." She put her hand in Stephen's pocket and ran away with her blonde hair streaming "out behind her like gold in the sun."

He brings in images borrowed from Catholicism, specifically the litany of the Blessed Virgin Mary, with *"Tower of Ivory. House of Gold,"* blending his worship of Eileen's beauty with the worship of the Blessed Mother. At the end of chapter 2, Stephen's loss of his virginity to a prostitute tells us a great deal about his attitude toward sexuality. He cries tears of joy and wants to be held by the woman but does not want to kiss her. He feels "strong and fearless and sure of himself. But his lips would not bend to kiss her." As a foil to Stephen, we have Davin's chaste tale in chapter 5 in which he describes walking home one evening and being invited to stay at the house of a woman whose husband was away. She clearly wants him to spend the night with her, but being a gentleman, he refuses and continues walking.

What do we make of Joyce's treatment of Stephen's budding sexuality? Why does Stephen approach his sexuality in the way he does? What influences contribute to his views of sex? How does Stephen's sexuality further develop after his experience with the prostitute? Where does Davin fit into this? Although the presentation of sexuality in *Portrait* seems quite tame by today's standards, it was highly controversial in Joyce's time and nearly meant not getting the novel published. Why does Joyce take this risk? What is his purpose in presenting sexuality in this way?

3. **Bird imagery:** What is the significance or purpose of all the bird imagery in *Portrait?* Do the birds serve as symbols? If so, of what?

The bird imagery in *Portrait* is pervasive. First, the naming of the protagonist is symbolic, of course: Daedalus was the architect who created the labyrinth that housed the minotaur in Greek mythology. The king, not wanting Daedalus to share his knowledge of architecture with anyone else, imprisoned Daedalus and his son, Icarus, in a tower and forbade them from leaving. With all possible traditional methods of escaping prevented, Daedalus decided to create wings for himself and his son using bird feathers and wax. He warned Icarus against flying too closely to the sun, and the two began their escape. Icarus did not heed his father's warning, the wax melted, and the boy fell into the sea and drowned. Daedalus survived and began life in a new country. Certainly the bird images are present in this background story, but Joyce does not stop there. We find in the first few pages images of eagles plucking out eyes, and then in chapter 2 we meet a classmate of Stephen's named Vincent Heron whose face was "beaked like a bird's." Stephen goes on to describe the birdlike qualities of the boy who has a "bird's face as well as a bird's name." In chapter 4, Stephen muses about mythology and his name and the artist Daedalus soaring above the sea, and these thoughts are immediately followed by his encounter with the seabird-girl on the beach. The bird imagery Joyce uses to describe this young woman who stirs in Stephen all the desire and long-ing that he had been stifling with religious devotion is obvi-ous. Her legs are "delicate as a crane's," and the "white fringes of her drawers were like featherings of soft white down." In chapter 5, Stephen's thoughts are occupied for several pages with a flock of birds he sees while on the steps of the library. He wonders what kind of birds they are as he watches their flights and listens to their cries, returning again to thoughts about his name and his mythological father.

What is the significance of the bird imagery? What do the birds symbolize for Stephen? What do they symbolize for Joyce? Do the different species of birds—eagles, herons, cranes—represent different things for Joyce and Stephen? Remember, nothing in Joyce is accidental. Why is there such an emphasis on bird imagery and symbolism? What do these animals represent?

Compare and Contrast Essays

Portrait offers a wealth of opportunities for compare and contrast essays. You could focus on two characters in the novel (for example, Stephen and one of his classmates), or you could look at a character in *Portrait* compared with a character from another one of Joyce's works. Because there is a film version of the novel, that is another possible choice for a compare and contrast essay.

Sample Topics:

1. **Stephen and his classmates:** How does Stephen compare with his classmates? In what ways is he different? What do the differences tell us about him? Why does Joyce not give Stephen someone more like himself to befriend?

   Stephen Dedalus is different from his classmates, first at Clongowes, then at Belvedere, and finally at University College, Dublin in more ways than he is similar to them. He is keenly aware of these differences as well, and although he does not seem to lament the lack of genuine friends, the reader certainly recognizes that something is missing in his life. As you prepare to write this essay, you could take one of several approaches. You could look closely at one specific acquaintance of Stephen's and then do an in-depth comparison of the two individuals. This would probably work best with a character whom Joyce develops a bit more substantially, for instance, Cranly or Davin. Look at how the men interact and how they serve as foils to Stephen. Cranly advises him to make a small sacrifice to please his mother, which reveals how different he is from Stephen with regard to compromising his ideals for the happiness of another person. Davin contrasts with Stephen in both his political views and patriotism but also in his morality, choosing to walk away from the invitation to adultery. The other approach you could take in this essay would be to look at all the acquaintances who enter Stephen's life and how they highlight the young artist as different, even in his childhood. Look at Nasty Roche, Wells, and Athy at Clongowes and how these boys differ substantially from Stephen. Then at Belvedere, consider the characters of Heron and Boland. Finally, look at Cranly, Davin, and Lynch at University College, Dublin. How do these characters compare with Stephen? What does Stephen think about his companions? What differences does he recognize? What do the differences tell us about our protagonist? What purpose do these characters serve in the novel? Why does Joyce not provide Stephen with a true friend in *Portrait?*

2. **Stephen and the male characters in *Dubliners:*** In what ways does Stephen compare with the male characters in *Dubliners?* How is Stephen similar to the young narrators in "Araby" and "An Encounter"? What qualities does Stephen share with Gabriel Conroy in "The Dead"?

The unnamed narrators in "Araby" and "An Encounter" have character traits that are similar to those of the young Stephen in *Portrait.* They are each obsessed with literature, are thoughtful and intellectual, and see themselves as different from their friends. They think about the world in much more sophisticated ways than their peers, similar to Stephen. In what ways do Stephen and the narrators in *Dubliners* see the world and react to it similarly? If the boys switched places in their respective stories, would you expect the same results and reactions? Would Stephen go to the Araby bazaar and come away empty-handed? Would he have the same uneasy reaction to the old man in the meadow? Looking at the adult Stephen, how does he compare with Gabriel Conroy? What characteristics do they have in common? Although Gabriel is older than Stephen, the two men have many similarities. Both are educated and quite confident in their intellect, both have little interest in Irish politics, and both are highly judgmental. In what ways are they different? How do the conversations Gabriel has at the dinner party with Lily and Miss Ivors and then later at the hotel with his wife, Gretta, compare with conversations Stephen has with his supporting characters? Does Gabriel have favorable outcomes in his conversations? Does Stephen? Do the supporting characters serve to present Gabriel and Stephen in a positive light?

3. **Text with film:** How does the 1977 film version of *Portrait* compare with the text? What decisions made by the director of the film change the reader/viewer's understanding and appreciation of *Portrait?*

Joseph Strick, the director of the film adaptation of *Ulysses* (1967) undertook Joyce's *Portrait* a decade later (and used T. P. McKenna, his Boylan in *Ulysses,* to play Simon Dedalus in *Portrait*). The film is set in the late 1800s and early 1900s of Dublin Ireland and its environs. Bosco Hogan, who plays the adult Stephen, and Luke Johnston, who plays the young Stephen, do an excellent job capturing the depth of Joyce's protagonist. The pivotal Christmas dinner scene is acted brilliantly, and the three critical conversations Stephen has with Davin, Lynch, and Cranly are adapted nicely to the screen despite their heady, philosophical nature. However, the screenplay has some holes, and there are scenes in the film that do not exist in the book. For example, after the Christmas dinner scene, in the book we are left to interpret what happened to Dante, understanding that she did not remain in the Dedalus household. However, the film makes this explicit, with the next scene after the dinner showing Dante's trunk being put onto a carriage and her leaving the home, saying one final prayer with Stephen, who peeks at her out of the corner of his eye. Detail is also added to the confession scene. In the book, Joyce spares us the specifics of Stephen's sins, but in the film, we are privy to this information, getting all the facts along with the priest. The final main difference between the book and the film is the importance given to the scene on the beach where Stephen encounters the young woman. In the book, this is the turning point for our protagonist, who recognizes that he is not being called to the priesthood but to the life of the artist. The entire scene, the birdlike grace and beauty of the girl who is part of nature, the ocean, the seaweed, and the clouds blend to create Stephen's epiphany. The book devotes several pages to this experience, while the film gives it less than a minute:

Stephen sees the girl, whose low-cut blouse is revealing (unlike the "soft and slight" breasts of the girl in the original), and tears up the vocation card.

As you plan this essay, study the scenes mentioned in comparison with the novel, and look for others that match or differ greatly from the book. What decisions did Strick make that might differ from our interpretation of the text? Is this a faithful adaptation of the novel? Why or why not? What would you, if you were directing a film version of *Portrait,* do differently?

Bibliography and Online Resources for *"A Portrait of the Artist as a Young Man"*

Attridge, Derek, ed. *The Cambridge Companion to James Joyce.* Cambridge: Cambridge University Press, 1990. Print.

Bloom, Harold. *James Joyce's A Portrait of the Artist as a Young Man.* New York: Chelsea House, 1988. Print.

Brady, Philip and James F. Carens, eds. *Critical Essays on James Joyce's A Portrait of the Artist as a Young Man.* New York: G.K. Hall, 1998. Print.

An Chomhairle Leabharlanna. [The Library Council.] "Ask about Ireland." Web. <http://askaboutireland.ie/>

Clissold, Bradley. "Heredity and Disinheritance in Joyce's *Portrait.*" *Troubled Legacies: Narrative and Inheritance.* Toronto: University of Toronto Press, 2007. 191–218. Print.

Doherty, Gerald. *Pathologies of Desire: The Vicissitudes of the Self in James Joyce's A Portrait of the Artist as a Young Man.* New York: Peter Lang, 2008. Print.

Ellmann, Richard. *James Joyce.* New York: Oxford University Press, 1982. Print.

Fargnoli, A. Nicholas. *Critical Companion to James Joyce: A Literary Companion to His Life and Works.* New York: Facts on File, 2006. Print.

Henke, Suzette. "Stephen Dedalus and Women: A Feminist Reading of *Portrait.*" *A Portrait of the Artist as a Young Man.* Boston: Bedford/St. Martin's, 2006. 317–36. Print.

Hwant, Jung Suk. "Place and Displacement in *A Portrait of the Artist as a Young Man.*" *James Joyce Journal.* 14.2 (2008): 133–50. Print.

Joyce, James. *A Portrait of the Artist as a Young Man. The Portable James Joyce.* New York: Penguin Books, 1967. Print.

O'Malley, Patrick R. "Confessing Stephen: The Nostalgic Erotics of Catholicism in *A Portrait of the Artist as a Young Man.*" *Catholic Figures, Queer Narratives.* New York: Palgrave MacMillan, 2007. 69–84. Print.

Seidel, Michael. *James Joyce: A Short Introduction.* Malden, Mass.: Blackwell Publishers, 2002. Print.

Spinks, Lee. *James Joyce: A Critical Guide.* Edinburgh: Edinburgh University Press, 2009. Print.

Valente, Joseph. "'An Iridescence Difficult to Account for': Sexual Initiation in Joyce's Fiction of Development." *English Literary History.* 76.2 (2009): 523–45. Print.

ULYSSES,
PART 1:
THE TELEMACHIAD

READING TO WRITE

Because *Ulysses* is so grand in scope, three separate chapters will be dedicated to it, dividing the novel into three parts, the ones Joyce imposed on the work structurally: "The Telemachiad," which is comprised of the first three episodes of the novel, "The Wanderings of Ulysses," the largest section of the novel, composed of the middle 12 episodes, and finally "The Homecoming," the final three episodes. (Note: In Joyce's *Ulysses*, following the author's lead, the chapters of the novel are referred to as episodes.) This chapter will focus solely on "The Telemachiad," but before specifically discussing that section of the novel, we must first begin with some background information.

Ulysses, which was number one in Modern Library's list of the 100 best novels written since 1900, is perhaps one of the most discussed (though perhaps not the most widely read) works in English-language literature. Heavily influenced and heavily influential, it is one of the most important modernist novels and is considered to be Joyce's masterpiece. It is famous for being difficult to understand and purposely obtuse, but the reader, armed with some background knowledge, will feel slightly less intimidated approaching this weighty volume. One piece of advice: Make use of Don Gifford's invaluable reference guide *Ulysses Annotated: Notes for James Joyce's Ulysses.* Gifford's book provides explanations for nearly all of the references in the novel that are lost on non-Dubliners who live in the 21st century. *Ulysses Annotated* should be used as a reference guide only, however, and the reader must not get bogged down in looking up everything to discern some hidden meaning in the text.

First, it is important to address the title of the novel. Ulysses, the Roman name for Odysseus, the protagonist of Homer's *Odyssey,* is the source for Leopold Bloom, the protagonist of Joyce's work. Odysseus's epic journey lasts 20 years, ten fighting the Trojan War and then ten more trying to make his way home, while Bloom's lasts only one day, but both characters face similar distractions, diversions, and foes along the way. Joyce clearly intended the connections to be made, from the title of his work to the section breaks to the episode titles that correspond with those of the *Odyssey.* How to interpret these connections is left to the reader, but there is no question about whether they exist or not: Joyce, in his correspondence with his patrons and friends, referred to the episodes by their parallel *Odyssey* titles. A caveat, however—do not rely solely on the parallels as a way to understand *Ulysses.* It is its own work in its own right and can be fully appreciated without elucidating the constant references to Homer's epic. A thoughtful and insightful interpretation can be arrived at without ever having read Homer's *Odyssey.* Do not fall into the trap of making too much of the connection between the two works.

Next, the importance of the date on which the events of the novel take place cannot be understated. June 16, 1904, was the date on which Joyce walked with Nora Barnacle, the woman who would run away to continental Europe with him and eventually become his wife. Setting the novel on this date, Richard Ellmann suggests, "was Joyce's most eloquent if indirect tribute to Nora, a recognition of the determining effect on his life of his attachment to her. . . . June 16 was the sacred day that divided Stephen Dedalus, the insurgent youth, from Leopold Bloom, the complaisant husband" (156). Joyceans around the world commemorate *Ulysses* on that day, celebrating Joyce with readings from the novel, dressing in period costume, and, in Dublin, walking the paths and visiting the establishments the protagonists did.

Joyce provided several schemas for friends as he was writing his novel. These schemas offer insights into how the author developed each episode and how it connected to Homer's *Odyssey.* One set of correspondences was given to Jacques Benoîst-Méchin and was used and published by Stuart Gilbert; the other was sent to Carlo Linati. The two schemas differ slightly with regard to the timing of the episodes but overall give the reader some added insight into the symbolism and intent behind each episode. The schemas are provided by Gifford in *Ulysses Annotated*. Again, any desire or attempt to try to "solve the puzzle" must be resisted. The schemas can help in understanding the novel, but they are not a magic key to unlock hidden meaning.

Another important element to consider as you read *Ulysses* is its intertextuality. The novel is part of a progression in the Joycean canon that begins with the stories in *Dubliners*, moves on to *A Portrait of the Artist as a Young Man*, then to *Ulysses*, and finally to *Finnegans Wake*. The first three works of fiction are closely interrelated. The protagonist of *Portrait*, Stephen Dedalus, is the main character in the Telemachiad and is also featured in the final five episodes with Bloom. Other characters from *Portrait* also appear or are mentioned, including Simon Dedalus and Stephen's friend Cranly. Characters from *Dubliners* are also present, including Bob Dolan from "The Boarding House" and the men from "Grace" who convince Mr. Kernan to attend a retreat with them. Yet the intertextuality does not end with characters. The themes Joyce began to explore in his earlier works find their way into *Ulysses* as well, including the treatment of religion, "Irishness," isolation, decay, and frustration. In many ways, *Ulysses* is a continuation of the process and progress Joyce began with *Dubliners*. (For a brief history of the publication troubles surrounding *Ulysses*, see the "Reading to Write" section in the next chapter on "The Wanderings of Ulysses"; for more on the critical reception of the novel, see the "Reading to Write" section of the chapter on "The Homecoming.")

Now that we have a general background for the novel, we can speak more specifically about "The Telemachiad," the first part of *Ulysses*, which is made up of the first three episodes, "Telemachus," "Nestor" and "Proteus." The novel begins at the Martello Tower at Sandycove Beach, on the southeast outskirts of Dublin in Dublin Bay, with Buck Mulligan and Stephen Dedalus beginning their day. It is eight o'clock in the morning on Thursday, June 16, 1904. The plot of "Telemachus" progresses through their morning activities, and over the course of those two hours, Joyce more fully develops the character of Stephen Dedalus who has returned from his exile abroad due to his mother's death. The next episode in "The Telemachiad" is "Nestor," which takes place in Mr. Deasy's private boy's school in Dalkey, south of the Martello Tower where Stephen lives. Stephen is a teacher at the school, and the hour he spends there is split between working with the boys and speaking with the headmaster, Mr. Deasy. We then follow Stephen to Sandymount Strand for the "Proteus" episode, where we meet once again the Stephen of chapter 5 of *Portrait,* the philosopher and philologist. The prose adopts a stream-of-consciousness style, which Joyce will use to varying degrees throughout the rest of the novel.

As you read "The Telemachiad," look for the ways in which the writing and style have progressed from that of *Portrait.* How has Stephen changed? What has caused the change? Does Stephen seem more comfortable with himself than he did in *Portrait?* Has he matured? In what ways is he the same? Study the following passage for clues to his character in *Ulysses:*

> Buck Mulligan frowned at the lather on his razorblade. He hopped down from his perch and began to search his trouser pockets hastily.
>
> —Scutter, he cried thickly.
>
> He came over to the gunrest and, thrusting a hand into Stephen's upper pocket, said:
>
> —Lend us a loan of your noserag to wipe my razor.
>
> Stephen suffered him to pull out and hold up on show by its corner a dirty crumpled handkerchief. Buck Mulligan wiped the razorblade neatly. Then, gazing over the handkerchief, he said:
>
> —The bard's noserag. A new art colour for our Irish poets: snotgreen. You can almost taste it, can't you?
>
> He mounted to the parapet again and gazed out over Dublin bay, his fair oakpale hair stirring slightly.
>
> —God, he said quietly. Isn't the sea what Algy calls it: a grey sweet mother? The snotgreen sea. The scrotumtightening sea. *Epi oinopa ponton.* Ah, Dedalus, the Greeks. I must teach you. You must read them in the original. *Thalatta! Thalatta!* She is our great sweet mother. Come and look.
>
> Stephen stood up and went over to the parapet. Leaning on it he looked down on the water and on the mailboat clearing the harbour mouth of Kingstown.
>
> —Our mighty mother, Buck Mulligan said.
>
> He turned abruptly his great searching eyes from the sea to Stephen's face.

—The aunt thinks you killed your mother, he said. That's why she won't let me have anything to do with you.

—Someone killed her, Stephen said gloomily.

—You could have knelt down, damn it, Kinch, when your dying mother asked you, Buck Mulligan said. I'm hyperborean as much as you. But to think of your mother begging you with her last breath to kneel down and pray for her. And you refused. There is something sinister in you.

He broke off and lathered again lightly his farther cheek. A tolerant smile curled his lips.

—But a lovely mummer, he murmured to himself. Kinch, the loveliest mummer of them all.

He shaved evenly and with care, in silence, seriously.

Stephen, an elbow rested on the jagged granite, leaned his palm against his brow and gazed at the fraying edge of his shiny black coat-sleeve. Pain, that was not yet the pain of love, fretted his heart. Silently, in a dream she had come to him after her death, her wasted body within its loose brown grave-clothes giving off an odour of wax and rosewood, her breath, that had bent on him, mute, reproachful, a faint odour of wetted ashes. Across the threadbare cuffedge he saw the sea hailed as a great sweet mother by the well-fed voice beside him. The ring of bay and skyline held a dull green mass of liquid. A bowl of white china had stood beside her deathbed holding the green sluggish bile which she had torn up from her rotting liver by fits of loud groaning vomiting.

This scene works to establish Stephen Dedalus as a slightly more mature version of the individual we got to know in *Portrait*. He still has the same philosophical approach to life and is still confident about his decisions (namely, when he would not kneel to pray at his mother's deathbed). His interaction with Buck Mulligan is reminiscent of the conversations he had in *Portrait* with Lynch, Cranly, and Davin. But the omniscient narration that puts us inside Stephen's head at the end of the quoted passage allows the reader to see a slightly more introspective and sensitive side to his character than was evident in *Portrait*. He feels "pain, that was not yet the pain of love," on the death of his mother. Not quite as detached as he was in *Portrait*, Stephen recognizes his loss and allows himself to experience this emotion. His poverty, however, is something that has not changed much, and if anything, it has only gotten worse.

To write about the preceding passage, one potentially strong approach could be to compare and contrast this conversation with the one Stephen had with Cranly in *Portrait* about making his Easter duty. How do Buck Mulligan and Cranly react to Stephen's attitude about religion and his sense of duty to his mother? How are the two similar? How are they different? Both Cranly and Mulligan are deeply critical of Stephen and advise him that sacrificing his personal religious views to make his mother happy would hurt him little but would offer his mother a great deal of comfort. However, Stephen's two friends differ greatly in their personalities. Mulligan is crass and irreverent while Cranly is reserved and thoughtful. Another approach is to consider Stephen's maturation as an artist. Look at the language in the passage and compare it to the language in the final scenes in *Portrait.* What progression has occurred in the space between Stephen leaving Ireland at the end of *Portrait* and his return at the beginning of *Ulysses*? The span of time is relatively short, probably about a year or so, but the change in Stephen is fairly substantial. He has returned a different person, and certainly the death of his mother has added a new dimension to his character.

TOPICS AND STRATEGIES

The following topic suggestions should give you a good starting point from which you can begin to flesh out your paper. (Note: The paper topics below focus on "The Telemachiad," but there are certainly essays that you could develop based on the novel as a whole which have their origins in these episodes. For example, you could look at the character of Buck Mulligan who reappears in several episodes in "The Wanderings of Ulysses," or you could follow a theme such as religion or motherhood through the entire novel. For a short essay, however, the writer is probably better off focusing on a more narrow topic.)

Themes

Many of the themes Joyce has already explored in *Dubliners* and *Portrait* are taken up again in *Ulysses*. Religion is a theme that is central to all of Joyce's works, and "The Telemachiad" is no exception. Motherhood and

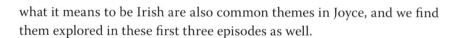

what it means to be Irish are also common themes in Joyce, and we find them explored in these first three episodes as well.

Sample Topics:

1. **Motherhood:** How is motherhood portrayed in "The Telema-chiad"? What mothers, literal and figurative, are discussed? What are the views expressed by the characters about mothers?

We know that Stephen has returned to Ireland from con-tinental Europe because of his mother's death and that he wears black to show that he is in mourning, but the reader wonders if the outward signs of grief indicate inner grieving. As Stephen and Buck Mulligan stand on top of the Martello Tower, they look out to the sea and Mulligan refers to it as "our great sweet mother." This reference triggers the con-nection to Stephen's literal, dead mother and brings him to chastise his friend for not kneeling to pray at her deathbed, a decision that is in line with what we already know about Stephen from *Portrait*, which is that he will not compromise his agnosticism to please his mother. Over the course of the three episodes in "The Telemachiad," we see Stephen working hard to come to terms with her death, feeling a "[p]ain, that was not yet the pain of love" fretting his heart. His thoughts as he makes his way through the morning frequently return to his literal mother who seems to haunt him.

In addition to Stephen's literal mother, we find several figu-rative mothers, as well as another literal mother about whom Stephen muses when speaking to his student Cyril Sargent. The sea, as noted above, is likened to a mother because of its life-giving power. Ireland is also a mother but not one for whom Stephen has much affection. The old milkwoman is symbolic of motherhood, seen as Stephen watches her "pour into the measure and then into the jug rich white milk, hot hers, Old shrunken paps." Then, at school, Stephen wonders about the mother of Cyril Sargent, the boy with "tangled hair . . . scraggy neck . . . weak eyes" and "dull and bloodless" cheeks. Stephen sees Sargent as "[u]gly and futile" but then quickly remembers that "someone had loved him, borne him in her arms and in her heart." He recalls Cranly's assertion in *Portrait* about the only true thing in life: a mother's love. Does Stephen believe this? Can we understand from his attitude toward his own mother and from the figurative mothers in these three episodes that he believes this to be true? Why or why not? Use passages from the text to support your claim.

2. **Religion:** What role does religion play in "The Telemachiad"? What representation of religion do we find in these episodes?

Ulysses opens with Buck Mulligan performing a parody of the Roman Catholic Mass, holding his shaving supplies—a bowl of lather, a mirror, and razor—as though they are the chalice to hold the altar wine (which Catholics believe turns into Christ's blood when the priest prays over it) and paten to hold the wafers for Holy Communion (which become Christ's body). Mulligan's parody of the Mass balances Stephen's refusal to kneel at his dying mother's bedside to pray, and although the first is offensive (especially to Catholics), the latter has the potential to offend everyone. Mulligan continues with his religious parody throughout the whole of the "Telemachus" episode, blessing the meal jokingly and singing the "Ballad of Joking Jesus" on their way to the bath. Haines, the Englishman who shares the Martello Tower with Mulligan and Stephen, laughs "guardedly" at Mulligan, recognizes the blasphemy of the song, admits to not being a believer, and justifies his laughter, saying that Mulligan's "gaiety takes the harm out of it somehow." Haines asks Stephen if he is a believer in the "narrow sense of the word," and Stephen replies, "There is only one sense of the word, it seems to me," meaning you either believe or you do not. For Stephen, there is nothing broad or narrow about it.

We find another representation of religion in the "Nestor" episode in the conversation with Mr. Deasy, the headmaster at the school where Stephen teaches. Deasy is Protestant, and staunchly so, as seen in his *"For Ulster will fight / And Ulster will be right."* This is an anti-Catholic, anti–Home Rule sentiment. Deasy does not stop at Catholicism, however, and expresses anti-Semitic thoughts as well, telling Stephen that

"England is in the hands of the jews [sic]. In all the highest places: her finance, her press. And they are the signs of a nation's decay. Wherever they gather they eat up the nation's vital strength." He then chases Stephen down after he has left the classroom to share that Ireland "has the honour of being the only country which never persecuted the jews [sic]." Stephen smiles at this, perhaps feeling a bit of national pride, but Deasy quickly offers the prejudicial (and historically inaccurate) punch line: "Because she never let them in." How do Deasy's opinions about and Mulligan's parodies of religion set the tone of the novel with regard to religion? Where does Stephen, an agnostic but one who cannot seem to shake the residue of Catholicism, fit into this? What is Joyce trying to communicate to the reader?

3. **Irishness:** If *Ulysses* is an Irish epic, how do the first three episodes establish this? What role do nationalism and patriotism play in the novel? What does being Irish mean?

The images of Ireland in the opening pages of *Ulysses* are overwhelmingly negative, from the "snotgreen sea" of Dublin Bay to the "cracked lookingglass of a servant" as the symbol of Irish art to the milkwoman not speaking Irish while the Englishman Haines does. Then, turning to the "Nestor" episode, we find Stephen teaching Roman and Greek history instead of Irish history to a room of schoolboys. Deasy's conversation with Stephen highlights the challenges inherent to defining Irishness. Deasy is, as Miss Ivors from "The Dead" would put it, a "West Briton" and a Protestant who is in favor of English rule in Ireland. He upholds the "orange" or Ulster Protestant element of Irish history and accuses "you fenians," a group to which he incorrectly imagines includes the apolitical Stephen belongs, of forgetting "some things." Yet it is Deasy who gets quite a bit wrong, and certainly his arrogance and anti-Semitism are offensive. The next episode, "Proteus," reveals to us that Stephen, despite Deasy's assumption, does know his Irish history and mythology. His stream-of-consciousness narrative makes connections between himself and elements of Irish history but also recognizes the complicated nature of what it means to be Irish. He thinks about the "wild geese," Irish expatriates who left to avoid English rule. Although not technically a "wild goose" because his reasons for exiling himself were more complicated than simply politics, Stephen understands the position of being not quite Irish. Certainly when we meet Bloom in the next episode, we have yet another impression of what Irish means. How is Joyce beginning to develop his definition? How is *Ulysses* an Irish epic? Does it only have to do with the setting of the novel? What so far is quintessentially Irish about it? What image or impression does Joyce give us of Irishness?

Character

The characters presented in "The Telemachiad" present strong opportunities for essay discussion. Buck Mulligan is colorful and irreverent, Mr. Deasy is an arrogant anti-Semite, and Cyril Sargent elicits pity and protective instincts. These three characters also give us a chance to see Stephen Dedalus in a slightly different light.

Sample Topics:

1. **Buck Mulligan:** How would we describe Buck Mulligan? Who is he, really? What is his purpose in the novel?

   Buck Mulligan stands in stark contrast to his housemate Stephen. He is brash, outspoken, irreverent, and jovial (but not always in a pleasant way). He is the first character we meet in *Ulysses,* parodying a priest celebrating a Roman Catholic Mass. He teases Stephen, whom he calls Kinch, but turns momentarily sober to chastise him for not kneeling at his mother's deathbed. Over the course of this episode, Mulligan seems quite manic, moving rapidly between jokes and gags and serious, thoughtful insights. We learn that he is a medical student but wonder, based on his personality, how well he can be doing and what kind of doctor he would make.

   What portrait of Buck Mulligan can we develop based on this first episode? Are the jokes and games a defense mechanism? If so, what do the glimpses of Mulligan's other, more sensitive side tell us about his character? Who is the real Buck Mulligan? A writer might be interested in investigating the actual person in Joyce's life on whom Mulligan is based, Oliver St. John Gogarty. Richard Ellmann's biography of Joyce offers suggestions about the ways in which Gogarty morphed into Mulligan, which may provide additional insight into the character. What is Mulligan's purpose in the novel? Certainly he is a foil to Stephen in terms of his personality, but what else does he bring to the text?

2. **Mr. Deasy:** What does Mr. Deasy represent? Is he one of the nets by which Stephen hopes to fly? What is Deasy's purpose in the novel? How would we describe his relationship with Stephen?

Mr. Deasy is the headmaster at a private school for boys in Dalkey, on the outskirts of Dublin. Stephen is working there temporarily, and we get the impression early on that he will not hold this position for much longer. When Deasy pays Stephen his wages, he takes on a fatherly role, offering advice about managing his money, which the reader knows is certainly not something Stephen has heard from his biological father. Yet the manner in which Deasy offers guidance reveals not only his frugality but also his personal biases. He uses it as an opportunity to show how the English are superior to the Irish because they *"owe nothing,"* but completely misunderstands the Shakespeare he is using as his basis for this assertion. Deasy certainly has pro-British sentiments and tries to defend his opinions by telling Stephen he "remember[s] the famine," but Stephen (and the reader who knows a little about Irish history) recognizes that it was British lack of action that exacerbated the Great Famine, causing a population loss of nearly two million Irish due to death or emigration. Deasy is an Ulsterman through and through but recognizes that his is an unpopular position in Dublin. He is supremely confident in his opinions, not just about the superiority of British ways and religion, but also of his ability to cure an outbreak of foot and mouth disease and his belief in the "destruction" brought about by the Jews.

Stephen's inner monologue as he converses with Deasy is more telling than the conversation itself. An astute judge of character, Stephen tells us how we are to see Deasy, and the impression is not a favorable one. Without Stephen's guidance, would our assessment of Deasy be any different? Do we need Stephen to make up our minds about this character? What does Deasy represent? Is he a father figure? How would we describe his relationship with Stephen and vice versa?

3. **Cyril Sargent:** What is the purpose of Cyril Sargent? What do we know about him, and what function does he serve in "Nestor"? How do we learn more about Stephen through this character?

Although the scene is very short, less than two full pages in total, the interaction between Stephen Dedalus and his student Cyril Sargent is memorable and reveals a side of Stephen the reader has not yet encountered, even in *Portrait.* It is Stephen's omniscient narration that provides us this image of Cyril: "Sargent who alone had lingered came forward slowly, showing an open copybook. His tangled hair and scraggy neck gave witness of unreadiness and through his misty glasses weak eyes looked up pleading. On his cheek, dull and bloodless, a soft stain of ink lay, dateshaped, recent and damp as a snail's bed." Stephen sees Sargent as "[u]gly and futile," but his description of him, even as he evokes the "gracelessness" of this child, reveals a softness and sympathy for the boy. Stephen sees himself in this child, who provokes feelings of pity and nostalgia.

Does Cyril Sargent serve any purpose other than to reveal Stephen's softer side to the reader? He is gentle with the boy and works to help him understand, unlike the headmaster, Deasy, who seems simply to have given him the punishment of doing his work over without an explanation of how to get it right. What characteristics of Sargent are reminiscent of the young Stephen we met in *Portrait?* The child's scruffiness is likely an indication of financial troubles similar to those Stephen experienced, and this scene recalls the one in which Stephen, at Clongowes, visits the headmaster after Father Dolan gave him a pandying for losing his glasses. How does Stephen react in his role as teacher? What more do we learn about Stephen in this scene thanks to Sargent?

History and Context

Joyce expects his readers to understand the history and context for his novel, and the fact that he was a walking encyclopedia does not make matters any easier. Thankfully, there are many great resources to help you with this task, including Ellmann's biography and Gifford's *Ulysses Annotated,* as well as the An Chomhairle Leabharlanna (the Irish Library Council) Web site where you can explore Ireland during different time periods.

1. **Ireland in 1904:** How do we describe the setting for *Ulysses?* What was it like in Dublin, Ireland, on June 16, 1904? What can we say about the political, social, and economic environment?

   To write this essay, you will need to do some research into Irish history. A good resource is T. W. Moody and F. X. Martin's *The Course of Irish History* or Edmund Curtis's *A History of Ireland,* but any general Irish history text will do. General background research will give you a better sense of the setting Joyce describes and will enhance your understanding of the plot and circumstances of the characters in the novel.

   By June 1904, Parnell had been dead for more than 13 years, but Home Rule and nationalism were still in full force, though perhaps not necessarily with as strong a leadership as before. The Easter Rising of 1916 was still years away. The time between Parnell's death and the Easter Rising was one of relative stability and prosperity, though Ireland was still suffering the aftermath of the Great Famine with regard to population. The middle class was beginning to grow, as we see in the Bloom household, but poverty was still quite widespread, as evidenced in the Dedalus one. Society was very much governed and guided by the rules and laws of the Catholic Church, yet the sex trade was flourishing as ever (the red-light district in Dublin, Monto, is featured in a later episode).

There was nothing particularly notable or important about the year 1904, with the obvious exception that for Joyce it marked the year he met the woman with whom he would spend the rest of his life. Aside from that personal significance, why did Joyce choose this year to set his novel? Why not choose a more historically critical year, for example 1891 (when Parnell died) or 1916 (the Easter Rising)? What does the everyday quality of June 16, 1904, lend to the novel?

2. **Homer's *Odyssey:*** What parallels can the reader make at this point in the novel to Homer's *Odyssey?* What are the implications of these parallels? What does an understanding of the *Odyssey* add to a reader's appreciation of *Ulysses?*

Joyce, in giving the schemas to Linati and Gilbert, established for readers from that point on the connection between each episode in his novel and the parallel episode in Homer's *Odyssey*. Although he removed the episode names before *Ulysses* was published, the schemas were already being circulated and used, and Joyceans agree to refer to the episodes by their Homeric parallels. However, without Joyce's schemas and without the episode titles, the links to the *Odyssey* are still quite apparent. The novel in its entirety shows a kinship with the Greek epic, and the characters and episodes reveal similarities as well.

Thinking specifically about "The Telemachiad," Stephen clearly corresponds to Telemachus, the son of Odysseus who has been away 20 years. Telemachus is searching for his father and trying to make his way in the world without him. Stephen similarly searches for a positive male role model, as his biological father does not provide this for him (nor does Mr. Deasy, who, standing in for Nestor in the *Odyssey*, offers advice but no real assistance). Proteus the shape-shifter corresponds to the changing nature of the sea and "primal matter," according to the schema published by Gilbert. Consider the parallels and correspondences Joyce makes in his schemas, and then move to the text itself to find how these connections play out in the first three episodes. In what ways is Stephen like Telemachus? Deasy like Nestor? Do we see Stephen searching for his father? How is "Proteus" in *Ulysses* similar to "Proteus" in the *Odyssey?*

3. **Yeats, Swinburne, and Blake:** How does Joyce use Yeats, Swinburne, and Blake in his work? What does their presence in "The Telemachiad" reveal about Stephen Dedalus? About Joyce?

We find the first reference to W. B. Yeats when Buck Mulligan's "drone" of a voice "boomed out of the stairhead":

> *And no more turn aside and brood*
> *On love's bitter mystery*
> *For Fergus rules the brazen cars.*

Stephen reflects on these lines from the poem/song "Who Goes with Fergus," remembering having sung them at his mother's deathbed. Stephen recalls: "Fergus' song: I sang it along in the house, holding down the long chords. Her door was open: she wanted to hear my music. Silent with awe and pity I went to her bedside. She was crying in her wretched bed. For those words, Stephen: love's bitter mystery." He reflects on it again later in "Proteus" as he walks along the beach, his stream-of-consciousness thoughts circling back to his mother throughout the episode. Fergus, we should note, was a king of Ireland who surrendered his crown to become a poet.

Buck Mulligan also recites lines from the poetry of Algernon Charles Swinburne, a decadent poet with connections to the Pre-Raphaelites whose work was controversial during his time because of the overt sexuality in much of his verse. The poem quoted by Mulligan is "The Oblation," which begins:

> *Ask nothing more of me, sweet;*
> *All I can give you I give.*
> *Heart of my heart, were it more*
> *More would be laid at your feet—*
> *Love that should help you to live,*
> *Song that should spur you to soar.*

It is not coincidental that Mulligan only recites the first four lines of this poem, and certainly Stephen would have known the final two in this stanza, which remind him of what he did not give his mother to help her soul to soar.

William Blake is first referenced when Mr. Deasy quotes two lines from "Auguries of Innocence," a poem that shows the contrasts between innocence and experience/evil. The word *augury* means omen or sign, and the poem is a series of signs pointing to the decay of England. Deasy, speaking of the decline of England that he links to Jewish hands, recites: *"The harlot's cry from street to street / Shall weave old England's winding sheet."* Stephen certainly recognizes the poem and follows Deasy's argument but disagrees with his line of thinking, arguing back that everyone is guilty of sinning against the light. We find reference to Blake again on the beach in "Proteus" with Stephen contemplating "Los," from the poet's "Book of Los." Los is the creator in Blakean mythology, and Stephen blends this character with the life-giving power of the sea, with the image of woman as mother/creator, and with the Judeo-Christian God in the book of Genesis, as seen in his "Creation from nothing."

What is the significance of Joyce's use of these three authors? What does their presence in the text indicate about the characters who quote them? What does it indicate about Joyce? How do these particular verses and references shape our understanding of these episodes? How would our reading change if we did not recognize these references?

Philosophy and Ideas

Joyce was a voracious reader and incorporated much of what he read into his own work. This is, in part, what makes reading Joyce feel like such an undertaking. It is best, especially for beginning Joyceans, to work with what is apparent in *Ulysses,* and certainly the following three essay topics are obvious choices.

Sample Topics:

1. **Transubstantiation:** What is transubstantiation, and what role does it play in *Ulysses,* specifically "The Telemachiad"? How

does Roman Catholicism shape the philosophy and ideas of Stephen Dedalus? Of James Joyce?

Transubstantiation is the term used to describe the process through which the bread and wine of the Communion rite are transformed into the body and blood of Christ in the Roman Catholic tradition. The outward appearance of the bread and wine does not change, but the elemental substance does. Catholics receive the Eucharist as a way of accepting Christ into their lives in a physical way, commemorating the Last Supper. Protestant denominations generally do not accept the notion of transubstantiation, and this is one of the fundamental differences between these two branches of Christianity. Although Joyce and his protagonist Stephen Dedalus stopped practicing Roman Catholicism in their late teens or early twenties, the influence of Church teachings always remained, as is evident in all of Joyce's works.

Transubstantiation is referenced in "The Telemachiad" on the first page, when Buck Mulligan performs his parody of the Mass, stating, in a "preacher's tone": "—For this, O dearly beloved, is the genuine Christine: body and soul and blood and ouns. Slow music, please. Shut your eyes, gents. One moment. A little trouble about those white corpuscles. Silence, all." Christine is Christ, obviously, and the white corpuscles are the blood cells that seem to challenge Mulligan's "priest." This one reference sets the tone for future, more veiled references to this holy mystery, including much of "Proteus" in which Stephen contemplates changes but cannot always truly understand them. While "Telemachus" begins with a parody of transubstantiation, "Proteus" begins with "Ineluctable modality of the visible," or the inescapable sensation of the visual. Earlier, in *Portrait*, Stephen admits that the reason why he does not want to make his Easter duty and receive the sacrament of Eucharist is because he does not believe in it. Yet, when Cranly presses him on the point, Stephen confesses that it frightens him to make a sacrilegious communion and pay "false homage to a symbol behind which are massed twenty centuries of authority and veneration." The visual can be detected, but it is the invisible mystery that frightens Stephen. In "Proteus," he closes his eyes and wonders if things will vanish. Discuss the ways in which Stephen, in this shape-shifting episode, plays with notions of the real/visible and the mysterious/invisible. How does the theological notion of transubstantiation factor into such considerations?

2. ***Omphalos:*** Why is the *omphalos* central to "The Telemachiad"? What layers of meaning does it bring to the text?

First, before tackling the use of the term in "The Telemachiad," we must look at the meanings of it. *Omphalos* is the Greek word for navel, but it can also be used to describe the central point of a thing. The third definition for the word is from Greek antiquity, and it refers to the stone in the Temple of Apollo at Delphi, which marks the center or navel of the Earth. Additionally, as Gifford shares in his note on the term, "Some late-nineteenth-century Theosophists contemplated the omphalos variously as the place of the 'astral soul of man,' the center of self-consciousness and the source of poetic and prophetic inspiration" (17). With this background knowledge, the reader can move on to studying how the term is used in the text.

In "The Telemachiad," we find the first reference to *omphalos* in Stephen's thoughts in "Telemachus": "To ourselves . . . new paganism . . . omphalos." He is considering his possibilities as an artist hoping to create a new artistic movement in the same way that political revivalists formed Sinn Fein ("To ourselves"), and "new paganism" presented opportunities in the spiritual realm. If the *omphalos* is indeed the source of poetic inspiration, Stephen may be able to claim it for his literary movement. The next reference comes from Buck Mulligan, who suggests that the Martello Tower in which they live is the *omphalos,* making an obvious correlation to the Delphic oracle and, knowing his arrogance, likely suggesting himself as the presiding voice of wisdom. The final mention comes as Stephen contemplates creation and birth, with "Gaze in your omphalos."

This reference is multilayered, and in this context, questions origins, as Stephen notes that Eve had a "[b]elly without blemish." It also brings him back to his notions of a literary movement, as the contemplation of the navel was seen as a means of inspiration. How do these three citations work together to form a central theme or philosophy that underpins these first three episodes in *Ulysses?* What layers of meaning do they bring to the text? How is *omphalos* central to "The Telemachiad" and the rest of the novel?

3. **Friedrich Nietzsche:** How does the nineteenth-century German philosopher play a role in *Ulysses?* How does Buck Mulligan interpret Nietzsche? Why does Joyce incorporate Nietzsche?

Friedrich Nietzsche was a nineteenth-century German philosopher whose works were not as widely read during his lifetime (1844–1900) as they were posthumously. His popularity in Ireland grew in the early 1900s, and Joyce discovered him in 1903, and as his biographer Richard Ellmann suggests, "it was probably on Nietzsche that Joyce drew when he expounded to his friends a neo-paganism that glorified selfishness, licentiousness, and pitilessness, and denounced gratitude and 'other domestic virtues'" (142). Oliver St. John Gogarty, the model for Buck Mulligan, was also a convert to Nietzsche's philosophical views (Ellmann 172).

In "Telemachus," Buck Mulligan makes reference to Nietzsche, exclaiming "—My twelfth rib is gone. . . . I'm the *Uebermensch.*" This concept of the *übermensch* is central to the work *Thus Spoke Zarathustra,* written by Nietzsche in 1883 and published in English translation in 1896. The *übermensch,* or superman, lives in this world and is not encumbered by otherworldly promises, such as the ones made by Christianity. Without the need to live for another world, the *übermensch* lives as he wishes, which Joyce and Gogarty may have interpreted as carte blanche for immorality. This is certainly how Mulligan uses Nietzsche. Does Stephen put stock in this philosophy? Does Joyce? Where in the text do you find evidence of Nietzsche's influence?

Form and Genre

Joyce is famous for playing with narrative form and for mixing genres, and *Ulysses* is perhaps the best example of this. While the more truly experimental narrative comes in later episodes, Joyce uses stream-of-consciousness prose, riddles, puns, and wordplay in "The Telemachiad" to break with the more traditional forms of narrative writing.

Sample Topics:

1. **Riddles and wordplay:** What is the function of the riddles, jokes, puns, and wordplay in the first three episodes? How would we describe Joyce's use of humor in "The Telemachiad"?

    Most of the humor in "Telemachus" comes from Buck Mulligan, and Joyce uses this character to reveal an irreverent and brashly confident foil to Stephen's pensive and understated personality. Nothing is off-limits to Mulligan, who parodies the Catholic Mass, refers to Stephen's mother as "beastly dead," mocks the milkwoman (though she does not understand), and then sings the blasphemous "Ballad of Joking Jesus." Mulligan's sense of humor and comic play serve not only to expose his personality, but also to set the tone of this episode and stand as one of 18 narrative forms in the novel. Joyce, in the schema published by Gilbert, gives "Narrative (young)" as the technique he employed in writing "Telemachus." Certainly the narrative style, at least the one used for Buck Mulligan, is very sophomoric.

    A different style of humor is used in "Nestor" and "Proteus." As we move away from traditional narrative and increasingly into the perspective of Stephen Dedalus, we encounter his modes of joking, punning, and playing on words. Unlike Mulligan's humor, which is immature and irreverent, Stephen's wit is more sophisticated, more insightful, and more ironic. He jokes with his students at school, offering them a riddle that cannot be solved unless the answer is already known. They ask him for a "hard one," and he gives them the impossible. Stephen sees the irony in Mr. Deasy's use of Iago in Shakespeare's *Othello* as an example of how to manage money and how the English can be proud to say *"I paid my way."* In "Proteus," he is able to laugh at his own expense, and his self-deprecating humor is a stark contrast to Buck Mulligan's. Stephen thinks: "Cousin Stephen, you will never be a saint. Isle of Saints. You were awfully holy, weren't you? You prayed to the Blessed Virgin that you might not have a red nose. You prayed to the devil in Serpentine avenue that the fusby widow in front might lift her clothes still more from the wet street." He calls Ireland a "Paradise of pretenders," and recognizes that he fits into that continuum of "kings' sons." What does Stephen's sense of humor tell us about him? How does it contrast with Buck Mulligan's? What is the purpose of humor in these first three episodes? What does it add to the narrative?

2. **Stream-of-consciousness prose:** What impact does Joyce's stream-of-consciousness prose narration have on the reader? Does it bring the reader into the text or create a distance from it? How effective is this narrative technique?

Although Joyce certainly was not the first to use stream-of-consciousness prose, his work with that style of narrative prose stands as one of the best examples of it. In "The Telemachiad," the prose style moves from omniscient narration in the first episode, interspersed with Stephen's inner monologues, to fully stream-of-consciousness, first-person narration in "Proteus," with "Nestor" providing the transition between the two, fitting somewhere in between with regard to narrative style. The stream-of-consciousness prose, also known as inner monologue, puts the reader inside the narrator's head, allowing him or her to see and what the narrator sees and have access to what the narrator thinks.

When we are in Stephen's head during his moments of stream of consciousness interspersed in the prose of "Telemachus" and "Nestor" and for the entirety of "Proteus," what more do we learn about this character? As you plan to write this essay, select several important passages on which to focus. Perhaps you will choose a common theme among the three episodes, for instance, some element about religion or the death of his mother. Or, perhaps you will choose to look at all of Stephen's inner monologues during an exchange with another character, for example, Haines or Cyril Sargent. Look at his spoken words and how they differ from his private thoughts. What do these differences and Stephen's unspoken thoughts tell us about his personality? Does the stream-of-consciousness narrative help the reader to feel closer to Stephen? Does it advance our connection to the text or create a distance for the reader?

3. **Evolution of the novel in the Joycean canon:** Where does "The Telemachiad" fit into the Joycean canon? How does it provide a transition from *Portrait* to the rest of *Ulysses* and eventually *Finnegans Wake?*

Sequentially and chronologically, "The Telemachiad" provides a transition between *A Portrait of the Artist as a Young Man* and the rest of *Ulysses.* We pick up with Stephen Dedalus almost where we left off in *Portrait,* as about two years have elapsed. He has matured a bit, his aesthetics have become more honed thanks to some much-needed time away from Ireland and her nets, and he is becoming the artist we might have predicted. In terms of the character development of Stephen Dedalus, "The Telemachiad" follows the trajectory of *Portrait.*

Stylistically it also provides a segue into the gradually more challenging narrative styles of *Ulysses.* "Telemachus" is about as straightforward a narrative as the style found at the end of *Portrait,* and even though Stephen's inner monologues grow increasingly more regular in that episode and "Nestor," the slow and steady pace at which this happens acclimates the reader to the new technique. There is nothing jarring stylistically for the reader until "Proteus," but she has been prepared for it in the earlier two episodes. Can we see "The Telemachiad" as a transition section of the novel? Why did Joyce keep his textual experimentation relatively minimal? Was he thinking of audience, or is it more in line with the characters themselves to follow this narrative style?

Language, Symbols, and Imagery

That Joyce was a talented linguist is evident in his prose. He is comfortable incorporating multiple foreign languages into his text, and expects the reader to keep up. He is also fond of symbolism and uses ocean imagery as well as symbols and images relating to birth and death to reinforce the cyclical nature of life.

Sample Topics:

1. **Foreign languages:** Why does Joyce use so many different foreign languages in "The Telemachiad"? What effect does this have on the reader? What purpose do these words and phrases serve?

   In addition to English, Joyce was fluent in Italian, French, German, Greek, and Latin, studied Irish and Russian, and enjoyed casually investigating other languages for use in his texts (especially *Finnegans Wake*). In "The Telemachiad" alone, Joyce uses all of the above with the exception of Russian, and some of them he uses several times. Few readers today are as fluent as Joyce was in as many different languages, so we need either multiple dictionaries or Gifford's companion text *Ulysses Annotated* to make sense of this linguistic puzzle.

   To write an essay on Joyce and his foreign language use, choose a passage in the text where foreign language comes into play. Probably "Proteus" would offer you the greatest possibility. Then do your research, consulting dictionaries and Gifford for translations. Some of the foreign language passages are songs, parts of the Catholic Mass or Catholic prayers, works from other pieces of literature (for example, the *Odyssey*) or common colloquialisms. What purpose do these foreign language words or phrases serve in the text? Is it Joyce or his character simply showing off his erudition? If so, what do we make of foreign language in an inner monologue when nobody is there to be impressed? Do the words and phrases create an unnecessary distance between reader and text or reader and character? What does the foreign language tell us about the character who speaks it? For example, why does Haines, an Englishman, speak

Irish when the other characters, including the old milkwoman, do not? Consider the cultural and social implications of foreign language in "The Telemachiad."

2. **Ocean imagery:** What is the significance of the ocean imagery in the first three episodes? What is the importance of setting for the plot so far?

"The Telemachiad" occurs at or near the ocean. The Martello Tower in which Stephen, Buck Mulligan, and Haines live is situated right on the shore, and Stephen and Mulligan stand on the open top of the tower, at the parapet, looking out to the sea. Mulligan says the sea is a "grey sweet mother . . . The snotgreen sea. The scrotumtightening sea. *Epi oinopa ponton.*" Then several moments later, Stephen thinks: "Inshore and farther out the mirror of water whitened, spurned by lightshod hurrying feet . . . A cloud began to cover the sun slowly, shadowing the bay in deeper green. It lay behind him, a bowl of bitter waters." He makes the leap from the sea before him to his mother's deathbed, mingling seas and waters and motherhood all in one. Later, in "Proteus," the ocean figures largely in the plot, with its "seaspawn and seawrack, the nearing tide." He returns to the notion that the sea is life-giving, thinking of a midwife and childbirth, then back to the watery womb.

What is the significance of the ocean imagery in "The Telemachiad"? How does the imagery work with the symbolism and themes present in these first three episodes? What does the sea symbolize for Mulligan, Stephen, and Joyce? Look at the ways in which the sea is described and how motherhood and creation are depicted in the various passages. Think, too, about the shores and natural and man-made surroundings such as the Martello Tower and Sandymount Strand. Is the tower a symbol? What symbols do we find as Stephen walks along the shore in "Proteus"?

3. **Birth and death:** What images does Joyce use to reinforce the themes of birth and death? Why does Stephen imagine

these with such vividness? What does the realistic description achieve?

This essay uses some of the sea images from the preceding topic discussion and then expands them to specifically address birth and death. Look closely at Stephen's inner monologue in which involuntary memory is evoked by his surroundings. Certainly the sea is one of those images, as seen in "Telemachus" when he recalls her death and the gruesomely vivid images: "Silently, in a dream she had come to him after her death, her wasted body within its loose brown grave-clothes giving off an odour of wax and rosewood, her breath, that had bent on him, mute, reproachful, a faint odour of wetted ashes." He remembers his mother in her final days or as a corpse and is haunted by those memories rather than being comforted by earlier memories of happier times. When motherhood is evoked in these episodes, whether by the image of the sea or by Cyril Sargent, it leads Stephen to grisly images of birth and then death, all stemming from memories of his mother and his preoccupation with motherhood in general. What does the dog in "Proteus" represent? What do Stephen's realistically graphic stream-of-consciousness thoughts achieve in the narrative? What do these images do for the reader? Why is Stephen so fixated on such ghastly imagery?

Compare and Contrast Essays

"The Telemachiad" offers many points for comparison, with other Joycean texts and with other parts or episodes in *Ulysses*. Because this first part of the novel focuses on Stephen Dedalus, perhaps the most obvious comparisons are with elements of *A Portrait of the Artist as a Young Man*.

Sample Topics:

1. **Stephen, *Portrait* to *Ulysses*:** How has Stephen matured in the relatively short time between leaving Ireland at the end of *Portrait* and his return at the beginning of *Ulysses?* What differences do we see in his character? In what ways is he the same?

Stephen Dedalus, at the end of *A Portrait of the Artist as a Young Man,* leaves Ireland to explore the world and find his voice as an artist. The final journal entry is dated April 27 but does not give a year. The next we encounter him is the morning of June 16, 1904. More than two years has gone by, he has experienced life outside the confines of Ireland, and his mother has died. Those are the obvious differences, but what are the more subtle differences between the Stephen from *Portrait* and the character we meet again in *Ulysses*? There are several different approaches to writing this essay. You could compare Stephen and his relationship with his mother from one novel to the next. Or, you can look at Stephen and his interactions with his peers from one to the next. A final compare and contrast essay could be to look at his development as an artist.

Once you have chosen an area on which you will focus, then select passages from the text that highlight the similarities and differences between *Portrait* Stephen and *Ulysses* Stephen. Look primarily at the journal entries that close *Portrait.* What do they tell us about the character? How would we describe his attitude and interactions with his family and friends? Then think about Stephen in "The Telemachiad." What can we say about him? In what ways is Stephen different? In what ways is he the same?

2. **Stephen's companions,** *Portrait* **to** *Ulysses:* What comparisons can we make between Stephen's companions in *Portrait* and the ones he spends time with in "The Telemachiad"? Why does Joyce continue to surround Stephen with people who are so different from him in character and personality?

This essay is similar to the one outlined above, and the approach to writing it is the same, but the focus is slightly different. Use the same sections of the novels, chapter 5 of *Portrait* and "The Telemachiad" and, specifically, "Telemachus," to discuss the men with whom Stephen spends a great deal of time: Cranly, Lynch, Davin, Buck Mulligan, and, to a lesser degree, Haines. How are these companions different? How are they similar? What do they bring to their relationship with Stephen? What does Stephen get from each of these men? Compare and contrast them with one another as well as with Stephen. They are all very different from one another, and all very different from Stephen. Why does Joyce always surround Stephen with such dissimilar people? What is their purpose with regard to Stephen's character development?

3. **Mr. Deasy and Haines:** How do these two men compare? What traits do they have in common? How are they different? What is Stephen's opinion of them?

Although we do not know a great deal about Mr. Deasy, the headmaster at the school where Stephen teaches, and Haines, the temporary tenant at the Martello Tower where Stephen and Buck Mulligan reside, they share enough in common to warrant a study.

Haines, whose first name we never learn, is an English scholar from Oxford who is taking up temporary residence in Ireland. Stephen does not like Haines very much, and Mulligan tells Stephen that Haines "can't make you out." Haines is, as Mulligan suggests, "a woful lunatic," who talks in his sleep about "shooting a black panther." When we meet him shortly after this exchange, he complains that the tea Mulligan has made is too strong. Haines is apparently writing a book on the folk legends of Ireland, and when the milkwoman arrives, he tries to speak Irish with her. Buck Mulligan make a slight jab at Haines's expense, telling the milkwoman: "He's English . . . and he thinks we ought to speak Irish in Ireland." He is sympathetic for what he imagines (and what Stephen reinforces) to be the plight of the Irish—being servant to the two masters of the "imperial British state . . . and the holy Roman catholic and apostolic church [sic]." Haines shares: "We feel in England that we have treated you rather unfairly. It seems history is to blame." He goes on to profess some anti-Semitic views about not wanting England to "fall into the hands of German jews [sic]." In brief, Haines is an anti-Semitic Englishman who feels a bond with Ireland. He is likely based on Samuel Chevenix Trench who briefly lived with Joyce and Gogarty in the Martello Tower (Ellmann 172–73).

Mr. Deasy is modeled on Francis Irwin, headmaster of the Clifton School in Dalkey where Joyce taught for a few weeks, and Henry Blackwood Price, an Ulsterman Joyce met in Trieste who was interested in hoof and mouth disease (Ellmann 153). Deasy is an Ulsterman, an Irish Protestant whose politics are in line with British policies in Ireland. He is pro-England, citing that country as an example for Ireland with regard to money. He, like Haines, is also anti-Semitic, fearing what will happen to England at the hands of the Jews. He is confident of his intelligence and his opinions, but Stephen (and the astute reader) sees how Deasy misunderstands the character Iago in Shakespeare's *Othello.* How are these two men similar? How are they different? What does their relationship with Stephen and their attitude toward him tell the reader about them? What do Stephen's thoughts tell us about these two characters? Are they stereotypes? What do they offer to "The Telemachiad"?

Bibliography and Online Resources for "*Ulysses,* Part 1: The Telemachiad"

Arnold, Bruce. *The Scandal of Ulysses: The Life and Afterlife of a Twentieth Century Masterpiece.* Dublin: Liffey Press, 2004. Print.

Attridge, Derek, ed. *The Cambridge Companion to James Joyce.* Cambridge: Cambridge University Press, 1990. Print.

Brown, Richard, ed. *A Companion to James Joyce.* Malden, Mass.: Blackwell, 2008. Print.

Burgess, Anthony. *Re Joyce.* New York: W.W. Norton, 2000. Print.

An Chomhairle Leabharlanna. [The Library Council.] "Ask about Ireland." Web. <http://askaboutireland.ie/>

Edmunson, Melissa. "'Love's Bitter Mystery': Stephen Dedalus, Drowning, and the Burden of Guilt in *Ulysses.*" *English Studies.* 90.5 (2009): 545–56. Print.

Ellmann, Richard. *James Joyce.* New York: Oxford University Press, 1982. Print.

———. *Ulysses on the Liffey.* New York: Oxford University Press, 1972. Print.

Fargnoli, A. Nicholas. *Critical Companion to James Joyce: A Literary Companion to His Life and Works.* New York: Facts on File, 2006. Print.

Gifford, Don and Robert J. Seidman. *Ulysses Annotated: Notes for James Joyce's Ulysses.* Berkeley: University of California Press, 1988. Print.

Gilbert, Stuart. *James Joyce's Ulysses: A Study.* New York: Vintage Books, 1955. Print.

Gillespie, Michael Patrick and A. Nicholas Fargnoli, eds. *Ulysses in Critical Perspective.* Gainesville: University Press of Florida, 2006. Print.

Joyce, James. *A Portrait of the Artist as a Young Man. The Portable James Joyce.* New York: Penguin Books, 1967. Print.

——. *Ulysses.* New York: Vintage Books, 1990. Print.

Kenner, Hugh. *Joyce's Voices.* Urbana-Champaign, Ill.: Dalkey Archive Press, 2007. Print.

Kiberd, Declan. "Joyce's Homer, Homer's Joyce." *A Companion to James Joyce.* Malden, Mass.: Blackwell, 2008. 241–53. Print.

McCourt, John, ed. *James Joyce in Context.* Cambridge: Cambridge University Press, 2009. Print.

McDonald, Russell. "Who Speaks for Fergus? Silence, Homophobia, and the Anxiety of Yeatsian Influence in Joyce." *Twentieth Century Literature.* 51.4 (2005): 391–413. Print.

Murphy, Niall. *A Bloomsday Postcard.* Dublin: Lilliput Press, 2004. Print.

Nash, John. *James Joyce and the Act of Reception: Reading, Ireland, Modernism.* Cambridge: Cambridge University Press, 2006. Print.

Norris, Margot, ed. *A Companion to James Joyce's Ulysses.* Boston: Bedford Books, 1998. Print.

Ruggieri, Franca, John McCourt, Enrico Terrinoni, and Derek Attridge, eds. *Joyce in Progress.* Newcastle on Tyne: Cambridge Scholars, 2009. Print.

Seidel, Michael. *James Joyce: A Short Introduction.* Malden, Mass.: Blackwell Publishers, 2002. Print.

Spinks, Lee. *James Joyce: A Critical Guide.* Edinburgh: Edinburgh University Press, 2009. Print.

Staley, Thomas F. and Bernard Benstock, eds. *Approaches to Ulysses: Ten Essays.* Pittsburgh: University of Pittsburgh Press, 1970. Print.

Tymoczko, Maria. *The Irish Ulysses.* Berkeley: University of California Press, 1994. Print.

Vichnar, David, ed. "Hypermedia Joyce Studies: An Electronic Journal of James Joyce Scholarship." Web. <http://hjs.ff.cuni.cz/main/hjs.php?page=index_page>

ULYSSES, PART 2: THE WANDERINGS OF ULYSSES

READING TO WRITE

(Note: A great deal of general background information for Ulysses *is provided in the previous chapter of this book in which strategies for writing about "The Telemachiad" are discussed. You will find a discussion of the critical reception of* Ulysses *in the next chapter on "The Homecoming." In this chapter, you will learn a bit about the history behind the publication of the novel.)*

JAMES JOYCE began writing *Ulysses* almost immediately after finishing *A Portrait of the Artist as a Young Man,* but he had been planning the novel in his mind for several years before putting pen to paper. He began work formally on the novel in 1914 while living in Trieste, Italy. He moved with his family to neutral Zurich, Switzerland, when World War I broke out and continued writing the novel. He completed *Ulysses* in Paris, France, in 1921. The novel began serial publication in 1918 in *The Little Review,* an American literary magazine, thanks in part to Ezra Pound who advocated for Joyce. There was still the question, however, of finding someone willing to publish it in its entirety, and because of the scandals surrounding its serialization in *The Little Review* (the United States Post Office confiscated and burned copies of the magazine featuring episodes from *Ulysses*), few publishers were willing to consider it.

Joyce was fortunate to be surrounded by people who not only revered him and his work but also had the right connections to help make things happen for the writer. While Pound worked on the American audiences and Harriet Shaw Weaver tried to make headway in England, it was Sylvia Beach, an American expatriate in Paris who owned the bookshop Shakespeare and Company, and Adrienne Monnier, a Parisian literary tastemaker whose shop, La Maison des Amis des Livres, was across the street from Beach's, who brought Joyce his fame in France. They were also instrumental in getting *Ulysses* published. Beach and Monnier found a printer willing to take the job. Shakespeare and Company would be the official publisher, and Maurice Darantière, "an intellectual printer in Dijon," would do the typesetting and pressing (Ellmann 504). They agreed on a first run of 1,000 copies, paid for by as many advance copies as possible, for which Joyce would receive 66 percent of the profits (504). The first copy of *Ulysses* was in Joyce's hands on his fortieth birthday, February 2, 1922. The novel was later published in England and the United States, though not without additional difficulty; there was even a ban on *Ulysses* in the United States, which was lifted 1933 by Judge John Woolsey. It was translated into French, German, and Danish during Joyce's lifetime and multiple languages since.

"The Wanderings of Ulysses" is made up of the middle 12 episodes of the novel, each one increasingly more challenging with regard to narrative technique than the one before. Joyce's intention was to reflect in the novel's style the gradual change from day into night, and the increasing difficulty of understanding what happens in the darkness. This part of the novel begins simultaneously in time as "The Telemachiad," at eight o'clock on the morning of Thursday, June 16, 1904. We meet here for the first time Leopold Bloom and his wife, Molly, at their home at 7 Eccles Street in Dublin. We follow Bloom as he makes his way through the city, making purchases, taking a bath, attending a funeral, going to work, going to the library, stopping in at several bars, visiting a maternity hospital, and finally ending up in a brothel. Bloom is preoccupied with thoughts about his son, Rudy, who lived only 11 days, his daughter, Milly, who is 15, and his wife, Molly, and her newly begun affair with Blazes Boylan.

As you read these episodes in preparation to write an essay, be aware of Bloom's perception of the world around him. He is observant and insightful, despite how others may characterize, misunderstand, and abuse him, as seen in the following passage in "Calypso" in which Bloom returns home after running a few morning errands:

Two letters and a card lay on the hallfloor. He stopped and gathered them. Mrs. Marion Bloom.

His quick heart slowed at once. Bold hand. Mrs. Marion.

—Poldy!

Entering the bedroom he halfclosed his eyes and walked through warm yellow twilight toward her tousled head.

—Who are the letters for?

He looked at them. Mullingar. Milly.

—A letter for me from Milly, he said carefully, and a card to you. And a letter for you.

He laid her card and letter on the twill bedspread near the curve of her knees.

—Do you want the blind up?

Letting the blind up by gentle tugs halfway his backward eye saw her glance at the letter and tuck it under her pillow.

—That do? he asked, turning.

She was reading the card, propped on her elbow.

—She got the things, she said.

He waited till she had laid the card aside and curled herself back slowly with a snug sigh.

—Hurry up with that tea, she said. I'm parched.

—The kettle is boiling, he said.

But he delayed to clear the chair: her striped petticoat, tossed soiled linen: and lifted all in an armful on to the foot of the bed.

As he went down the kitchen stairs she called:

—Poldy!

—What?

—Scald the teapot.

On the boil sure enough: a plume of steam from the spout. He scalded and rinsed out the teapot and put in four full spoons of tea, tilting the kettle then to let water flow in. Having set it to draw, he took off the kettle and crushed the pan flat on the live coals and watched the lump of butter slide and melt. While he unwrapped the kidney the cat mewed hungrily against him. Give her too much meat she won't mouse. Say they won't eat pork. Kosher. Here. He let the bloodsmeared paper fall to her and dropped the kidney amid the sizzling butter sauce. Pepper. He sprinkled it through his fingers, ringwise, from the chipped eggcup.

Then he slit open his letter, glancing down the page and over. Thanks: new tam: Mr. Coghlan: lough Owel picnic: young student: Blazes Boylan's seaside girls.

The tea was drawn. He filled his own moustachecup, sham crown Derby, smiling. Silly Milly's birthday gift. Only five she was then. No wait: four. I gave her the amberoid necklace she broke. Putting pieces of folded brown paper in the letterbox for her. He smiled, pouring.

> *O Milly Bloom, you are my darling.*
> *You are my looking glass from night to morning.*
> *I'd rather have you without a farthing*
> *Than Katey Keogh with her ass and garden.*

Poor old professor Goodwin. Dreadful old case. Still he was a courteous old chap. Oldfashioned way he used to bow Molly off the platform. And the little mirror in his silk hat. The night Milly brought it into the parlour. O, look what I found in professor Goodwin's hat! All we laughed. Sex breaking out even then. Pert little piece she was.

He prodded a fork into the kidney and slapped it over: then fitted the teapot on the tray. Its hump bumped as he took it up. Everything on it? Bread and butter, four, sugar, spoon, her cream. Yes. He carried it upstairs, his thumb hooked in the teapot handle.

Nudging the door open with his knee he carried the tray in and set it on the chair by the bedhead.

—What a time you were, she said.

She set the brasses jingling as she raised herself briskly, an elbow on the pillow. He looked calmly down on her bulk and between her large soft bubs, sloping within her nightdress like a shegoat's udder. The warmth of her couched body rose on the air, mingling with the fragrance of the tea she poured.

A strip of torn envelope peeped from under the dimpled pillow. In the act of going he stayed to straighten the bedspread.

—Who was the letter from? he asked.

Bold hand. Marion.
—O, Boylan, she said. He's bringing the programme.
—What are you singing?
—*La ci darem with J. C. Doyle, she said, and Love's Old Sweet Song.*

This passage does so much in such a small space. It establishes a first impression of two main characters and two important supporting characters: Leopold (Poldy) Bloom; his wife, Marion (Molly); their daughter, Millicent (Milly); and Molly's lover, Blazes Boylan. From this scene and the scenes before, we begin to understand the dynamics of the Bloom marriage. He brings her breakfast in bed, and she orders him around and complains that he takes too long. He knows that the letter is from Blazes Boylan and that she is having an affair with him, and she is trying to be secretive about it. He is domestic and is devoted to his daughter, Milly. He also seems quite fond of his cat. Molly gives the impression of being spoiled, staying in bed and having her breakfast brought to her. As Bloom makes up the tray, he double checks that he has everything on it, and the reader understands that Molly would likely chastise him for getting it wrong if something was missing. In this scene, Bloom is the domestic drudge, pampering Molly who lingers in bed making demands.

We also get a sense of the characters of Blazes Boylan, Molly's lover, and Milly Bloom, Molly and Leopold's daughter who never physically appears in the book but is in her parents' thoughts throughout the day. When Bloom picks up the letter for his wife, he notices it is addressed to "Mrs. Marion Bloom," which goes against the etiquette of the time. A married woman should have been addressed by her husband's first name instead of her own, and so the envelope should have read "Mrs. Leopold Bloom." Bloom recognizes both the misstep with regard to propriety as well as the "bold hand" as belonging to Boylan. The fact that Molly hides the letter under her pillow only confirms for Bloom the contents of this correspondence. Molly admits that Boylan, a concert promoter, will be stopping by later that afternoon with the program for the show she will be giving. Bloom knows there is more to the visit than business.

Milly Bloom is also presented in this selection, though it is not the first time she has been mentioned in the book. She is introduced in "Telemachus" when Buck Mulligan talks about his friend Alec Bannon in Westmeath who has "found a sweet young thing down there. Photo girl he calls her." When we learn in "Calypso" that Milly has been sent to study photography in Westmeath and has written home to her father about a "young student," we make the connection and realize that Bloom's daughter is the photo girl. Bloom clearly loves Milly, who seems to take after her mother, expressing great interest in the mirror she finds in Professor Goodwin's hat. Bloom muses: "Pert little piece she was." He appreciates the bold liveliness in his daughter's personality, but the reader wonders whether Milly is just a younger version of Molly and whether those traits are to be admired or frowned upon.

Finally, the reader gets insights into how Bloom's mind works and how Joyce continues to use stream-of-consciousness narrative style or inner monologue in the novel. Bloom's voice is very different from Stephen's, and although we hear the musings and preoccupations of both men via stream of consciousness, their thought patterns and modes of expression are different. Their minds circle back to the same ideas, but their language and turns of phrase are different. Stephen is erudite and cold, he is detached from the world of emotion and identifies with the world of knowledge. He is rational and prefers not to acknowledge his feelings. Bloom, on the other hand, is sentimental. He is intelligent, like Stephen, but does not allow his intellect to smother his softer side. Another difference between the two men's narratives is that Stephen's is confident while Bloom's is insecure and at various points, defeated. He recognizes his place in the world and in relation to his wife, and although he is not happy with it, seems resigned to it.

TOPICS AND STRATEGIES

In this section, we will consider some ideas for essay topics for "The Wanderings of Ulysses" section of the novel. The following prompts and suggestions should give you a good starting point from which you can begin to flesh out your paper. (Note: The paper topics focus on "The Wanderings of Ulysses," but there are certainly essays you could develop based on the novel as a whole that have their origins in these episodes. For example, the theme of fatherhood carries through to the end of the novel when Bloom takes care of Stephen, his surrogate son. Lust is also certainly present in "The Homecoming" section, particularly in the "Penelope" episode. For a short essay, however, the writer is probably better off focusing on a more narrowed topic.)

Themes

The three themes presented in the chapter on "The Telemachiad," motherhood, religion, and Irishness, are developed throughout "The Wanderings of Ulysses." A writer could study those, but some new themes appear in this part of the novel that also warrant investigation: fatherhood, lust, and death.

Sample Topics:

1. **Fatherhood:** What does it mean to Leopold Bloom to be a father? How is fatherhood presented in these episodes? What images of fathers do we have?

   Bloom muses on his role as a father beginning in "Calypso," continuing in the subsequent episodes, and culminating in "Circe" with his phantasmal vision of his dead son, Rudy. Bloom also takes on a fatherly role with Stephen Dedalus, tracking him down at the maternity hospital, following him to the brothel, and eventually bringing him home and offering him a place to stay the night. We first see his joy in being a father when he reads the letter from Milly in "Calypso," recalling her gift to him when she was small and thinking what a "Pert little piece she was." She turned 15 the day before, June 15, 1904, and Bloom had missed her first birthday being away from home. He reads the letter twice and feels melancholy about Milly growing up and becoming a woman. He is reassured that she "knows how to mind herself" but also recognizes that she is vain, like her mother. It is also in this episode that we learn there had been a son, Rudy, who died in infancy, and that he would be 11 now had he survived. Bloom thinks about Rudy again in "Hades" on the way to the funeral, jealous of Simon Dedalus for having a son who is alive and well. He recalls the morning Rudy was conceived and imagines what life would be like if he were still alive. He remembers his son's funeral: "Our. Little. Beggar. Baby. Meant nothing. Mistake of nature. If it's healthy it's from the mother. If not the man. Better luck next time." But for Bloom and Molly there would never be a next time; he fears intercourse with her because he cannot face losing another child.

Where else in "The Wanderings of Ulysses" do we find evidence of Bloom's preoccupation with fatherhood and paternity? What does he say about these two concepts? How does he feel about being a father? What comparison does Joyce, through Bloom, make between motherhood and fatherhood? In "Circe," Bloom wants to be a mother and gives birth as the "new womanly man." What does all of this convey about parenting?

2. **Lust:** What does "The Wanderings of Ulysses" tell us about lust? What does Joyce communicate about chastity and marital fidelity?

Lust is a central theme to many of the episodes in "The Wanderings of Ulysses." Certainly we know about Molly's affair with Blazes Boylan, but we frequently forget that Bloom is not being completely faithful in his marriage vows, either. He has been carrying on a correspondence with a woman named Martha Clifford under the pseudonym Henry Flower, Esq. Their letters back and forth are quite tame by today's standards but hint at the prospect of a sexual relationship should the two ever arrange to meet Mrs. Josie Breen, in person. In "Laestrygonians," Bloom meets with a woman, Mrs. Josie Breen, who had been interested in him when he was courting Molly and whose husband has received an anonymous postcard with the potentially libelous but unclear note "U.P.: up" on it. Later, in "The Sirens," the barmaids Miss Douce and Miss Kennedy tease the men at the Ormond Hotel, and the episode is filled with sexual tension and frustration. It is during this episode that Molly and Boylan meet for their tryst, and though we do not witness it, we know, as does Bloom, that it is happening. More evidence of lust and sexuality is seen in "Nausicaa" in which Bloom masturbates in reaction to seeing Gerty MacDowell's undergarments. Gerty is not innocent in this, as she is aware of his gaze and leans back purposely to reveal herself to him. The lustiness of the characters in *Ulysses* is the centerpiece of "Circe," the surrealist play that closes "The Wanderings of Ulysses." "Circe" takes place in a brothel, and while no sexual intercourse occurs, many of

Bloom's fetishes are brought to the fore, including being abused physically and verbally by Bella Cohen, the madam, and watching Boylan have sex with Molly.

How are lust and sexuality portrayed in "The Wanderings of Ulysses"? Does Joyce present the reader with a "normal" or "healthy" attitude toward sexuality? What does he say about marriage? This theme will appear again in "Penelope," but in that episode we learn Molly's thoughts about sex, sexuality, and marriage. In these episodes, we are made privy to Bloom's feelings. What do we learn about this man? What do we learn about Joyce? Does the sexuality presented in "The Wanderings of Ulysses" still cause offense today?

3. **Death:** How does the theme of death weave through these episodes? What are the characters' attitudes about death? How does Joyce present it?

The "Hades" episode during which Bloom and his companions attend the funeral of Paddy Dignam is the obvious one to turn to when discussing the theme of death in "The Wanderings of Ulysses," but Bloom's thoughts turn to death several times before and after, specifically when he remembers his son, Rudy, and his father, Rudolph Virag Bloom, who committed suicide. Although Bloom is usually able to force negative thoughts from his mind, he keeps returning to memories of his father and son. He is aware that he is the last in the male line of his family and is remorseful about it. The fact that Bloom is wearing black, which is immediately understood by all those with whom he speaks as a marker of mourning, results in his constantly having to explain that it is Paddy Dignam's funeral he is attending, not a family member's. But the questioning of his interlocutors forces Bloom to recall Rudy and his father's deaths all over again.

To write this essay, look to the text for places, both in "Hades" and in the other episodes, where death is treated as a topic or theme. We know Stephen is still in mourning clothes for his mother. Simon Dedalus, though he does not mention his wife's death in the cab ride to Glasnevin Cemetery where

Dignam is to be buried, breaks down when they arrive, saying, "Let Him take me whenever He likes." When the discussion in the cab turns to suicide, Martin Cunningham takes a "charitable view of it," telling the men "It is not for us to judge," knowing Bloom's family circumstances. At the cemetery, Bloom recognizes the reality of death and questions the existence of an afterlife while his companions wonder about Parnell's return, suggesting that his coffin is filled with stones. What do these different views of death offer to the reader? Why do Bloom's companions romanticize death? Why is Bloom so realistic? What do these presentations about death tell the reader?

Character

An excellent essay could be written on Leopold Bloom, Molly Bloom, or Stephen Dedalus, but since there are so many interesting supporting characters in "The Wanderings of Ulysses," make the most of the opportunity and do an in-depth study on one of them.

Sample Topics:

1. **Milly Bloom:** How do we characterize Milly Bloom? What can we say about her? What impact does she have on the story overall?

   Although she is not a character we actually meet in *Ulysses*, Milly Bloom has a presence in the novel through the thoughts and recollections of her father. Bloom's thoughts throughout the day frequently cycle back to fatherhood and his children. As he walks home, before he even sees that he has a letter from his daughter, he imagines her running to him: "she runs to meet me, a girl with gold hair on the wind." From this we gather that she loves her father very much, and Milly's letter confirms this: She is sweet and tender, addressing him with "Dearest Papli." From Bloom's recollections, we come to understand her as a smaller version of her mother, vain and drawn to mirrors. Bloom calls her a "pert little piece," and the lively tone of her letter is in line with this. She is affectionate in her expression but is distracted by the piano and admits to being in a hurry. Bloom recognizes that Milly is "coming out of her shell" and then worries about her being taken advantage of by Bannon. She is "[v]ain: very," emphasized by Bloom having caught her "pinching her cheeks to make them red." Later, in "Hades," Bloom recognizes the similarities between his wife and daughter: "Molly. Milly. Same thing watered down. Her tomboy oaths. O jumping Jupiter! Ye gods and little fishes! Still, she's a dear girl. Soon be a woman."

What character sketch can we develop for Milly Bloom based on her father's thoughts and memories? What can we add to that sketch based on Mulligan's statements about her in "Telemachus"? If she is spending time with one of Mulligan's friends, what might we be able to assume about her? If she sends her best regards to Blazes Boylan, what does that tell us? She seems devoted to her father, certainly, but what else can we say about this young woman? How important is she to the overall story? What does her presence through her absence tell us about her and about Bloom?

2. **Blazes Boylan:** What type of individual does Joyce present in the character of Hugh "Blazes" Boylan? How does Bloom see him? How do Bloom's companions see him?

We get a more complete sketch of Boylan from Molly Bloom later on in the novel in the "Penelope" episode, but the opinions of the men in "The Wanderings of Ulysses" help to give a preliminary view of him. Since we are in Bloom's head for most of this part of the novel, the natural instinct is to sympathize with him and despise Boylan, yet Joyce praises him through the other characters with whom Bloom interacts. In the carriage on the way to the cemetery, Martin Cunningham, Mr. Power, and Simon Dedalus notice Boylan walking along the road. The men seem to fall over one another to get to the window to salute him and are upset when they think he cannot see them. Bloom wonders what everyone sees in "the worst man in Dublin." After his lunch in Davy Byrne's pub, Bloom spots Boylan's straw hat, tan shoes, and "turnedup trousers" and hides from him, hoping not to be seen. He again watches

Boylan flirting in the bar at the Ormond Hotel in "Sirens" with the barmaids Miss Douce and Miss Kennedy and having a drink before going off to see Molly. The women primp and preen for the men, teasing them, but especially Boylan who is the focus of their games. Boylan appreciates this greatly and does not avert his gaze. Molly is not the only woman in Dublin whom Boylan hopes to possess. He also ogles the salesgirl in Thornton's shop in the "Wandering Rocks" episode. He goes into the store to purchase a basket of wine and fruit to send ahead of his visit, asking the "blond girl" to have the basket sent at once, since it is "for an invalid." He watches her "slim fingers" as they "reckoned the fruits." He twice looks into the "cut of her blouse," appreciating her young body and calling her, degradingly, a "young pullet."

How would we describe Boylan based on the little we have learned about him so far in the novel? Why do the men seem to revere him? Is he what we would call a "man's man"? Is it only Bloom's jealousy and sadness that prevent him from seeing the positive side of Boylan? Does Boylan have a positive side? Is he a stereotype? For a more complete character analysis of Boylan, the writer might choose to incorporate Molly's assessment of him in the "Penelope" episode, but this is not entirely necessary. An engaging essay can be developed by looking closely at the character of Boylan as portrayed in "The Wanderings of Ulysses."

3. **Gerty MacDowell:** What does the reader make of Gerty MacDowell? Is Gerty a sympathetic character? How does she embody Nausicaa?

The "Nausicaa" episode features the overly sentimental and romantic Gerty MacDowell on the beach at sunset, eight o'clock in the evening, with her friends Cissy Caffrey and Edy Boardman. They have come to watch fireworks. Gerty spies Bloom watching her, admiring her "winsome Irish girlhood," "slight and graceful" figure, "waxen pallor of her face [which] was almost spiritual in its ivorylike purity" and "rosebud mouth . . .

a genuine Cupid's bow, Greekly perfect." The entire episode is written in the style of women's literature of the time, filled with dreamy, sappy language and clichés, and this verbal mode typifies Gerty. She hopes to be swept off her feet by some gentleman who will love her. At the turn of the century, Ireland was still recovering from the Great Famine, and the deaths and emigration caused a serious decline in population, making it uncertain whether a young woman, even one as "winsome" as Gerty, would marry.

Gerty is excited knowing that Bloom is watching her, and she begins to fantasize about him, wondering what makes him seem so sad, and her mind turns to more romantic thoughts of marriage and lovers' passion. She leans back, as if to get a better view of the fireworks but really to give Bloom a better view of her undergarments. She exposes herself to him, aware that he is doing "something not very nice that you could imagine sometimes in the bed." After Bloom masturbates, Gerty glances at him "with a pathetic little glance of piteous protest, of shy reproach under which he coloured like a girl." She forgives him for his brutish behavior, imagines they will meet again, and walks away, revealing to Bloom and to the reader her limp.

How does Gerty MacDowell compare with Nausicaa in the *Odyssey?* Why does Gerty entice Bloom? What is in it for her? Why does she take the risk of exposing herself to him? Does she truly believe they will meet again? How would we characterize this young woman? What does Bloom think of her, both before and after she walks away?

History and Context

As stated in the previous chapter, Joyce was a veritable walking encyclopedia who read almost everything he could get his hands on and retained it as well. Thus, much is required of a reader when working with Joyce's literature. *Ulysses* takes place in a specific time in history, and investigation into that period will yield a deeper understanding of the novel.

Sample Topics:

1. **Judaism in Ireland:** Why is so much made of the fact that Bloom is of Jewish descent? What is the significance of Joyce's protagonist having Jewish roots?

   Anti-Semitism is prevalent throughout the novel, but several episodes in "The Wanderings of Ulysses" highlight this bias. Leopold Bloom is of Hungarian Jewish descent but was born in Ireland, as he points out to the Citizen in the "Cyclops" episode. He is in a conversation with John Wyse about persecution, hatred, and nationalism when he offers: "A nation is the same people living in the same place. . . . Or also living in different places." He is then asked by the citizen what his nation is, and Bloom replies: "Ireland. . . . I was born here. Ireland. . . . And I belong to a race, too . . . that is hated and persecuted. Also now. This very moment. This very instant." Bloom leaves but then returns to more hateful anti-Semitic remarks and defends himself, shouting "Mendelssohn was a jew and Karl Marx and Mercadante and Spinoza. And the Saviour was a jew and his father was a jew. Your God . . . Christ was a jew like me." Bloom's defense of himself and his ancestry results in the Citizen hurling a biscuit box at him as he makes his escape. But the Citizen and the men in Barney Kiernan's pub are certainly not the only ones who mark Bloom as a Jew despite having been born in Dublin and baptized three times. Ironically, nobody seems to identify Molly as Jewish even though her mother was a Spanish Jew.

   Why is there so much made of Bloom's Jewish heritage? Why did Joyce make the hero of his Irish epic a Hungarian Jew? Is the anti-Semitism in the novel a marker of the times in which Joyce was writing (the Dreyfus affair was still very much a part of the news when Joyce was working on *Ulysses*)? In addition, as Richard Ellmann points out, Joyce's return to Ireland in 1903 occurred during one of the "rare manifestations of anti-Semitism" in that country, "a boycott of Jewish merchants in Limerick that was accompanied by some violence" (373). Ellmann continues, sharing that Joyce "was not a propagandist for the better treatment of minorities," but that he was drawn to "two characteristics of Jews which especially interested him . . . their chosen isolation, and the close family ties which were perhaps the result of it" (373). Joyce could have created any character with these traits. Why did Joyce make Bloom Jewish? What is the significance of his Jewish heritage and ancestry?

2. **Wandering with Bloom:** What impression does a reader have of Dublin as he or she wanders with Bloom? Why does Joyce create this impression?

Ulysses reproduces the Dublin landscape and characters of June 16, 1904, but a visitor to the city today could essentially walk the same streets and see many of the same sights. Although exiled from Ireland's capital while he was writing the novel, Joyce never really left Dublin—he carried the sights and sounds and smells with him wherever he went and captured them in his writing. A reader can still walk into Davy Byrne's pub and get a glass of burgundy and a gorgonzola sandwich, just as Bloom did more than 100 years ago. We can follow the progress of the various characters in "Wandering Rocks." The Martello Tower in which Stephen and Buck Mulligan (as well as their real-life counterparts Joyce and Gogarty) lived still stands and is a Joyce museum today. Although Dublin is a living city and there is much new architecture and expansion, the center city area explored by Bloom and his companions remains to a large extent the same.

What impression does Joyce create of Dublin? Is it a positive one? Joyce claimed that he wrote with such fine detail about Dublin that the city could be re-created based solely on his works. Is this the case? An essay on this topic would be an excellent choice for a writer who has visited Dublin and participated in a Joyce walking tour, seeing the same sights that the characters in *Ulysses* saw over the course of their day. How does Joyce use his setting? What do we think of the city and its inhabitants? Is Joyce nostalgic for his city? Does he create a place a reader would like to visit or live in?

3. **Music:** How does music weave itself through these episodes? What is the importance of music to the dramatic action of the novel?

Music plays a central role in *Ulysses,* from the songs being practiced by Molly Bloom for her upcoming concert to the ones running through Bloom's head over the course of the day to the music in the bar at the Ormond Hotel in "Sirens." In some ways, music is as much a character in the work as the human ones we meet. Music was, not surprisingly, a central part of Joyce's life. He had a beautiful tenor voice and briefly considered a singing career. He loved music, and his knowledge of classical music, opera, traditional Irish airs and ballads, and popular music of the time was extensive. Some songs in particular, namely "Love's Old Sweet Song," weave their way through the text, reappearing and serving to remind Bloom of his wife, Molly, and her infidelity with Boylan. Other songs feature prominently in various chapters, for example, music from the opera *Martha* and "The Croppy Boy," a song about the Irish Rebellion of 1798 appear in "Sirens."

To pursue this topic, you will undoubtedly need to use Gifford's *Ulysses Annotated* and should also consider doing some additional research into music in Joyce by reading Zack Bowen's work on the topic. Once you have more background information, including song lyrics, you can then do an in-depth analysis on Joyce's use of music in the novel. Is there an added layer of meaning to the text when music is referenced? What is the purpose and significance of the music in *Ulysses?* Can today's reader recognize these references and understand the added dimension they bring to the text? How does the music in the novel guide the reader to a deeper understanding of the workings of Bloom's mind?

Philosophy and Ideas

In "The Wanderings of Ulysses," Joyce explores some philosophical concepts and ideas which are central to the overall narrative. Molly Bloom asks her husband about metempsychosis in "Calypso," and that concept plays out for the rest of the novel. National identity and defining yourself through that identity are also very important, and Stephen's explanation of Shakespeare's *Hamlet* provides us yet another opportunity to think about paternity and family lineage.

Sample Topics:

1. **Metempsychosis:** What is metempsychosis, and why is it important to the central narrative of *Ulysses?* What role does it play in the novel?

Molly Bloom, early in the morning of June 16, 1904, asks her husband, Leopold, for help in understanding a word she has found in one of her romance novels:

—Here, she said. What does that mean?
He leaned downwards and read near her polished thumbnail.
—Metempsychosis?
—Yes. Who's he when he's at home?
—Metempsychosis, he said, frowning. It's Greek: from the Greek. That means the transmigration of souls.
—O, rocks! she said. Tell us in plain words.

He goes on to explain that metempsychosis is the term the Greeks used to explain reincarnation, "that we go on living in another body after death . . . That we all lived before on the earth thousands of years ago or some other planet. They say we have forgotten it. Some say they remember their past lives." Bloom continues to think about metempsychosis at intervals during the day, especially in the "Oxen of the Sun" episode at the maternity hospital and the "Circe" episode at Bella Cohen's brothel when he is with Stephen and thinking about Rudy. The concept of metempsychosis blends with paternity and fatherhood for Bloom and so is especially evident in those scenes where he remembers his dead father and son.

What is Joyce trying to communicate with this concept of metempsychosis? Reincarnation is not a concept within the theology of Roman Catholicism, but it is present in Judaism. How does this concept fit into the novel? Does Bloom believe in metempsychosis? Why do this term and concept keep reappearing in *Ulysses?*

2. **National identity:** How do the main characters define themselves with regard to nationality? What is Joyce telling us about national identity? What does nationality mean in the modern world?

The three main characters, Leopold Bloom, Molly Bloom, and Stephen Dedalus, all have reason to consider their national identity. Leopold Bloom, an Irish-Hungarian Jew, is an obvious case, and his nationality has been called into question over the course of the novel by himself and others. He emphasizes to anyone who questions his identity (particularly the Citizen in "Cyclops") the fact that he is Irish and was born in Ireland, yet his thoughts over the course of the day frequently cycle back to his Hungarian Jewish heritage. He was baptized Roman Catholic and thus identifies with a vast majority of the Irish population of the time, but he does not practice his religion and reflects more on Judaism when it comes to a religious tradition, particularly in "Circe." Molly and Stephen also have problematic national identities. Molly Bloom was born and grew up in Gibraltar, a British overseas territory, the daughter of the Irish major Tweedy and Lunita Laredo, who was a Spanish Jew. Her Irish identity is only called into question once, in a conversation between Ben Dollard and Simon Dedalus in the Ormond Hotel in "Sirens," when Dollard asks "Irish? I do not know, faith. Is she, Simon?" Dedalus replies "O, she is . . . My Irish Molly, O . . . From the rock of Gibraltar . . . all the way." Later, in "Penelope," Molly recognizes her Irish looks, having "the map of it all" on her face, meaning it is obvious that she is Irish. Nobody besides Bloom seems to recognize that Molly is also half Jewish. Stephen Dedalus, despite his "absurd name," is fully Irish, though he does not identify with his nationality and culture. He sees Ireland and his Irish national identity as a cage that stifles the artist in him. He has exiled himself and, if Stephen is partly Joyce himself, will likely leave again.

In addition to the three main characters, other characters in the novel contribute to the developing theme of national identity. What do we make of Haines, the Englishman who advocates speaking Irish? What can we say about the Citizen whose rabid nationalism is wholly offensive? What about the gentlemen in Glasnevin Cemetery who hope for the return of Parnell? How can we define national identity in an Irish city controlled by the British government? How can we define national identity in a modern world? What does Joyce offer us to deal with these questions?

3. **Shakespeare's *Hamlet:*** What is Stephen's theory about *Hamlet*? How does it fit into the narrative as a whole? What purpose does it serve in *Ulysses*?

In "Telemachus," Buck Mulligan urges Stephen to share his theory about Shakespeare's *Hamlet* with Haines, and Stephen promises to do so later. In "Scyllla and Charybdis," Stephen makes good on this promise, explaining in the National Library that Shakespeare is both the ghost of King Hamlet and Hamlet himself, "the son consubstantial with the father." His theory is greatly informed by the fact that Shakespeare wrote *Hamlet* after the death of his own father, John Shakespeare, and son, Hamnet Shakespeare, and that Shakespeare himself played the role of the dead King Hamlet. Stephen also asserts that Anne Hathaway Shakespeare has cuckolded the bard, leading to the character of Gertrude, and claims that King Hamlet is not just a murdered king but a betrayed husband as well. Certainly, Stephen's own recent experience with death, that of his mother, influences his theory, but Stephen is, like a Shakespearean player, putting on a show for his listeners. Much of what he has posited he does not actually believe. What the reader observes in this theory, that which is unknown to Stephen at the time, is that Bloom is a parallel for Shakespeare: His father is dead, his son is dead, and his wife, Molly, (a parallel for Gertrude) is about to cuckold him.

How does *Hamlet* and Stephen's theory about it help to enrich *Ulysses?* What other parallels between the two works might the reader draw? How does the notion of metempsychosis or reincarnation factor into this? What do we make of the appearance of the ghost of King Hamlet, suffering in purgatory for his own sins until his death is avenged? How does religion come into play here? How does Stephen's dead mother fit in? She haunts him, but does she have a purpose in the same way that Hamlet's dead father does? To produce a strong essay on this topic, you must be fluent in both *Ulysses* and *Hamlet.* Stephen presents a complicated, convoluted theory here, one which he only half believes, and much of it is performance.

Form and Genre

James Joyce breaks all the rules when it comes to conventional narrative forms and style in *Ulysses.* Although the novel begins in a relatively straightforward and traditional way in "Telemachus," the writing and style become more experimental as we move from day to night, progressing through the episodes. Any episode could be singled out for further examination with regard to form and genre, but the following three suggestions offer probably the greatest opportunities when addressing issues of form and genre.

Sample Topics:

1. **"Oxen of the Sun" and the birth of literature:** How does this episode parallel the development of the English language? How does the style represent gestation and progression?

   The archaic style of the prose at the beginning of "Oxen of the Sun" gradually becomes more modern and comprehensible as we move through the episode, ending in an English prose style that would have been standard and commonplace when Joyce was writing, even if it seems dated now. Joyce's technique was to write the episode, which is set in the National Maternity Hospital while Mina Purefoy is in labor, showing gestation and birth as parallels to the development of the English language. There are nine relatively distinct sections of the episode with regard to prose style, just as there are nine months in a human pregnancy. These styles begin with Anglo-Saxon alliteration ("Before born babe bliss had. Within womb won he worship.") moving through Middle English techniques, to the seventeenth-century style of Milton, Pepys, and Swift and into the eighteenth century with Sterne, Goldsmith, and the gothic writers and romantics. He then moves into the nineteenth century, with Dickens and Carlyle, bringing the reader (at least those at the time *Ulysses* was published) and the English language into the present day. By the end of the episode, Mina Purefoy has delivered her child, symbolic of the development and birth pangs of literature in English.

To develop an essay on this topic, the reader/writer must play literary detective, deciphering the various prose styles and watching for the shifts from one style to the next representing the development of the language. Gifford's guidebook is critical here, as it gives all the references needed to trace this progression. But writing this essay is much more than simply solving a puzzle. Once you have the parallels, you must then examine what they represent. You should also study Joyce's choice of styles and writers. He had at his disposal all of English language literature; why did he choose these specific writers, some of whom were scarcely studied in his day, let alone now? What do the writers represent? What were their contributions to language and literature?

2. **"Aeolus" and journalism:** How does the journalistic style in "Aeolus," interspersed with headlines, affect the way we read the episode? What impact does it have on our understanding of the events occurring?

Set in the offices of the newspaper *The Freeman's Journal,* "Aeolus" uses a journalistic writing style with news headlines interspersed throughout the text. Sometimes the headlines introduce a new section of text, but other times they seem randomly placed and may indicate what is happening in Bloom's mind, a sort of inner monologue in headline form. The plot of this episode is rather straightforward: Bloom is trying to place an ad in the paper for Alexander Keyes but is encountering difficulty in doing so, mainly from the editors Nannetti and Crawford. Stephen delivers Mr. Deasy's letter about foot and mouth disease and interacts with the men at the office, seeming more himself with them than he does with his usual companions. Bloom, on the other hand, is alienated in this episode—he is ignored, patronized, and made fun of behind his back. We get all of these events, however, in a stilted fashion, with snippets of information provided as newspaper articles.

As you plan out this essay, think of the *Odyssey* parallel: Aeolus is the "warden of the winds," and in the Gilbert schema, Joyce names Crawford as the Aeolus parallel. He also offers that the organ for this episode is the lung. How do these pieces of information guide your interpretation? How does the style of "Aeolus" impact the reading of the episode? How does it impact our understanding of what is happening? Does it enhance it? Does it distract? Why did Joyce use this form for this episode? How do the style and the theme or plot work together here?

3. **"Nausicaa" and turn-of-the-century women's romance novels:** How would we describe the narrators of "Nausicaa"? Does the style of the narrative match the action in the episode?

Gerty MacDowell, the parallel for Homer's Nausicaa, must certainly have a penchant for the types of romance novels that Molly Bloom enjoys, since the first part of this episode, which she narrates, is entirely in that style of writing. She spends some time on the beach at Sandymount Strand with her friends Cissy Caffrey and Edy Boardman and their young siblings, waiting for the fireworks to begin. She thinks about marriage and feels the loss of her recent breakup with her boyfriend Reggie Wylie. She still fantasizes about what it would be like to be married to him, her fantasies then shifting to Bloom when she sees him watching and admiring her. Gerty's narrative style is syrupy and saccharine, reflecting what Joyce clearly imagined were the preoccupations of a particular female mind. Her narrative finds a logical, rational, realistic response in the second half of the chapter, after Gerty limps away. Bloom's stream-of-consciousness narrative is nearly the opposite of Gerty's stylistically. He has his own little fantasies, however, imagining "Girl friends at school, arms round each other's neck or with ten fingers locked, kissing and whispering secrets about nothing in the convent garden." He criticizes women for being false friends and superficial in general, making the assumption that this is the case for every woman simply because it is the case for his wife, Molly.

What do these narrative styles tell us about Joyce and how he felt about women? Is the episode misogynistic? Is Gerty treated fairly by Bloom? Does she treat herself fairly? Does the style of the narrative match the action taking place? Look at the two halves of the episode—how do the narrator's tone and technique suit what is happening? How is the reader impacted by Gerty's florid style? How is the reader impacted by Bloom's straightforward style? Where do our sympathies lie?

Language, Symbols, and Imagery

"The Wanderings of Ulysses" is filled with symbols and imagery and offers numerous directions to pursue in discussing Joyce's stylistic manipulations.

Sample Topics:

1. **Flower imagery:** How does Joyce use flowers in the text to emphasize symbolically the meaning he hopes to convey? How effective is the flower symbolism and imagery in Ulysses?

    Aside from the obvious symbolism of naming his protagonist Leopold Bloom (and his pseudonym Henry Flower, Esq.), Joyce uses flower imagery and symbolism liberally throughout his novel, especially in "The Lotus-Eaters" and "Circe." Joyce, through Bloom, makes use of the language of flowers, which dates back to Greek and Roman times but was given new life during the Victorian era, just before the time period in which the novel is set. Certain flowers symbolized emotions, feelings, or moral states. The language of flowers, also known as florigraphy or floriography, would have been part of the vernacular during Joyce's lifetime, but today's reader must do a bit of research into the meanings behind the flowers mentioned in *Ulysses*. In "The Lotus-Eaters," Bloom/Henry Flower, Esq. reads Martha's letter, into which she has pressed a "yellow flower with flattened petals." He muses, "I think it's a" but does not finish the sentence. However, he goes on to mention tulips, a symbol of love, cactus, which is a phallic symbol, violets, which are a symbol of modesty and faithfulness, roses, which depending on their color symbolize anything from love to beauty to friendship to jealousy, and anemone, which is symbolic of illness or desolation. He also adds to the list "manflower" and "nightstalk," which along with cactus provide phallic imagery, foreshadowing his "languid floating flower" in the bath at the end of the episode. In "Sirens," Bloom thinks of the flower Martha sent and wonders if it was a daisy: "Was it a daisy? Innocence that is." Later, in the "Cyclops" episode, a series of tree-women are named, each symbolizing yet another emotion or quality. In "Circe," several flowers are mentioned, including the potato flower, the dahlia, and quince. Finally, in "Penelope," Molly thinks about poppies and rhododendrons.

These references are just a few examples of Joyce's use of flowers in this text. To write this essay, you will need to note any mention of flowers and trees and then research their meaning at the turn of the century. How does the language of flowers fit into the language of *Ulysses*? Why does Joyce use flowers so extensively in his work? Is the symbolism lost on the modern reader? Must we know the symbolism behind each individual flower (or, in the case of "Cyclops," tree) mentioned in the novel? What does it add to our understanding and appreciation if we do?

2. **Bloom's lemon soap:** What does the bar of lemon soap Bloom keeps in his pocket symbolize? Is it a talisman for him?

Bloom stops at Sweny the chemist's to purchase face lotion for Molly, and while inside he finds a soap made of "sweet lemony wax," which he proceeds to purchase. He then indulges in a fantasy about lying in the bath, "oiled by scented melting soap, softly laved." Certainly the soap imagery is important to the final few pages of "The Lotus-Eaters," but it crops up again in "Hades," "Aeolus," and "Circe." The bar of lemon soap, like other thoughts that cycle through Bloom's mind on that day, resurfaces as well. In "Hades," he is aware of the soap for the entire carriage ride to the cemetery, sitting down on it when he gets in the cab, thinking "I am sitting on something hard. Ah, that soap in my hip pocket. Better shift it out of that. Wait for an opportunity." He does not get his opportunity, though, until they arrive. He allows his companions to get out of the carriage and changes the soap from his hip pocket to his "inner handkerchief pocket." He spends the entire carriage ride physically uncomfortable, mirroring his emotional discomfort thanks to the conversation: the mention and sighting of Boylan, discussion of his wife's concert (knowing they know that she is having an affair with Boylan), and, finally, talk of a suicide case. Death itself makes Bloom uncomfortable as well, forcing him to recall his son's passing. His mind cycles back to the soap in "Aeolus" after watching the typesetter read backward, reminding him of his father reading his "hagadah book." He walks to the staircase and takes out his handkerchief and wonders why it smells like "citron-lemon" and then remembers the soap. He moves it back to his hip pocket, buttoning it so the soap will not be lost. The soap then becomes a player in the surreal "Circe," becoming a "soapsun" with Sweny's face in the center. The soap recites: "We're a capital couple are Bloom and I; / He brightens the earth, I polish the sky." Finally, in "Ithaca," Bloom uses the "partially consumed tablet of Barrington's lemonflavoured soap" to wash at the sink at the end of the day.

What is the significance of the bar of lemon soap? Why does Bloom keep returning to it through the day? What is happening each time the soap makes an appearance? Is there a connection between the action of the story and Bloom recalling the soap? In the language of flowers, what does lemon symbolize? Does Bloom unconsciously see the soap as a talisman? If so, from what does it protect him?

3. **"Circe" and surrealist images:** What purpose does "Circe" serve? Why did Joyce write this episode as a surrealist play rather than a more straightforward narrative? What effect does "Circe" have on the reader?

At nearly four times the length of any other episode in *Ulysses,* "Circe" can seem long. However, we must take that length as a clue to the importance of the episode. Occurring in Nighttown or Monto, the red-light district in Dublin, and more specifically, in Bella Cohen's brothel, the episode is written as a pseudo-psychological surrealist play. Some of the players are actual people in various incarnations, but some of them are inanimate objects such as the bar of soap, the quoits of the Bloom bed, a crab, and a pianola. Historical figures also appear with speaking parts, as do the ghosts of Bloom and Dedalus family members. Some of the play is imagined in Bloom's mind, while some is in Stephen's. Both men become ensnared in deeply troubling scenes in this play: Bloom is declared "bisexually abnormal," gives birth to eight male white and yellow children, is visited by his grandfather, is emasculated by Bella/Bello, watches Boylan have sex with Molly, and has a vision of his dead son, Rudy. Stephen sees Father Dolan, the priest who flogged him in *Portrait,* the ghost of his mother, and has a run-in with a few British officers. Bloom keeps Stephen safe through much of the episode, pays for the chandelier Stephen broke, and helps him out of the brothel and out of the sticky situation with Privates Compton and Carr.

Why did Joyce use this technique in writing the "Circe" episode? Could he have presented the same ideas in another way? How does the form and genre of the episode match the actions contained within it? What effect does the surrealism of "Circe" have on the reader? How do we cope with a play embedded within a novel when we know that plays are meant to be seen and not read? Taking that into account, you may want to watch the "Circe" episode in the 1967 film *Ulysses* and the 2004 film *Bloom* to have a visual referent or adaptation to match with the text. Could Joyce have gotten his message across any other way? How effective is the style of this episode?

Compare and Contrast Essays

Possibilities abound in this category for excellent, interesting essays. You could compare Bloom or Stephen's character from one episode to the next or a character from *Dubliners* who also makes an appearance in "The Wanderings of Ulysses" (Bob Doran from "The Boarding House" or Ignatius Gallaher from "A Little Cloud," for example). Or, you could use one of the following topic suggestions and compare and contrast characters from *Ulysses* with ones from the *Odyssey,* two characters within *Ulysses* who share similar traits, or the narrative styles of two episodes in "The Wanderings of Ulysses."

Sample Topics:

1. ***Ulysses* characters and their parallels in the *Odyssey:*** How do the characters in *Ulysses* match their *Odyssey* parallels? Do some fit better than others? How does Joyce make use of these cognates?

   In Joyce's Irish epic, the parallels to Homer's *Odyssey* are sometimes obvious and sometimes a bit of a stretch. He offered them in his schemas to Carlos Linati and Jacques Benôist-Méchin (later published by Stuart Gilbert), so access to those would greatly aid the writer who wishes to tackle this essay. These correspondences and hints as to how Joyce uses them are also published in Gifford's *Ulysses Annotated.* In addition, Gifford offers brief synopses of the episodes in the *Odyssey* that Joyce parallels, a great refresher for writers who have not recently read Homer's work. (This essay is not a good choice for the student who has never read the *Odyssey.*) To write an essay on this topic, choose a character in Homer and his or her cognate in Joyce and look at how they are similar and different. While Odysseus/Bloom, Telemachus/Stephen and Penelope/Molly are obvious choices, supporting characters such as Nausicaa/Gerty, the Cyclops/the Citizen, the Sirens/Miss Douce and Miss Kennedy, or Circe/Bella also offer excellent opportunities for comparison. Indeed, depending on the page requirement for your essay, working with the supporting characters might be your best bet.

   If you were to choose Nausicaa and Gerty, for example, first look at the action in the Homeric episode: Odysseus washes ashore where the princess Nausicaa and her companions are doing laundry. Odysseus is naked, but Nausicaa is not afraid of him. He tells her his story, and she listens sympathetically, offering him clothing and helping him to strategize the presentation of his plight to her parents. He does as she advises, and her parents help him on his way home to Ithaca. While in her company, Odysseus praises Nausicaa's beauty, and for her part, Nausicaa expresses an interest in Odysseus, but the two do not become lovers. Gerty MacDowell is quite a close cognate for Nausicaa. She is described as "as fair a specimen of winsome Irish girlhood as one could wish to see." Gerty fantasizes about Bloom, imagining what it would be like to be married to a man like him, and does not run when she notices that he has his hands in his pockets, knowing that he is "working." She notices that he has had a difficult day and offers herself to help ease his pain, deeming him "a sterling man, a man of inflexible honour to his fingertips."

When preparing to write this essay, look in the text for specific details to support your comparison. Find instances in which the characters are similar and ones in which they are different. How do the characters correspond? What changes has Joyce made to suit his work? How has he adapted the characters to twentieth-century Dublin?

2. **The Citizen and Mr. Deasy:** How do the Citizen and Mr. Deasy compare as characters? Is it only their anti-Semitism that unites these two men? Do they share any other attributes?

Mr. Deasy, the headmaster at the school where Stephen temporarily works, is an Ulster Orangeman, a Protestant who, despite having been born in Ireland, feels more of an affinity for the British way of life. He appreciates the presence of British rule in Ireland and, in his conversation with Stephen, praises the best quality of England: the fact that they "paid their way." He is anti-Catholic *("For Ulster will fight / And Ulster will be right.")*, anti-Semitic ("England is in the hands of the jews [sic] . . . As sure as we are standing here the jew [sic] merchants are already at their work of destruction."), and antiwoman ("A woman brought sin into the world. For a woman who was no better than she should be, Helen, the runaway wife of Menelaus, ten years the Greeks made war on Troy. A faithless wife first brought the strangers to our shore here, MacMurrough's wife and her leman O'Rourke, prince of Breffni. A woman too brought Parnell low."). The Citizen also has his fair share of prejudices: he is, unbelievably, more anti-Semitic than Mr. Deasy ("I'm told those Jewies does have a sort of a queer odour off them for dogs about I do not know what all deterrent effect and so forth and so on"), anti-British (*"Sinn fein! . . . Sinn fein amhain!* The friends we love are by our side and the foes we hate before us."), and despises religions other than Roman Catholicism ("Saint Patrick would want to land again at Balykinlar and convert us . . . after allowing things like that to contaminate our shores.").

For this essay, look at the extreme biases of these two men. They share one, hatred of Jews, but are at opposite ends of the spectrum with regard to their feelings toward Great Britain and religion. What about women—do we know how the Citizen feels? Joyce makes of Mr. Deasy a misguided and pompous windbag, just like Nestor in the *Odyssey.* The Citizen, however, is not only hateful but is the perfect cognate for Homer's Cyclops because he metaphorically sees with just one eye. Which character is more despicable? How do they express their hatred? How do these men compare?

3. **The narrative styles of two different episodes:** What similarities can we draw between two episodes in "The Wanderings of Ulysses"? What differences? How do two episodes compare with regard to narrative style?

To begin, you need to choose two episodes in this section of the novel. You might decide to focus on the unreliable narrators in "Cyclops" and "Nausicaa," looking at how our reading and comprehension of the episode are guided by a speaker in whom we cannot place complete trust. Or you could look at the techniques Joyce used in "Aeolus," setting the episode in a journalistic style with news headlines, as compared with "Circe," the surrealist play. Another excellent option would be to study the musical style of "Sirens," with its distracting cacophony, alongside the even more distracting style of "Oxen of the Sun," imitating the development of English language literature. Once you choose your two episodes, look at the way Joyce breaks from the traditional prose narrative form in each one. Focus on sentence structure, tone, language, and narrator. Consider Joyce's purpose in using a particular style for a particular episode: Is it effective? Does it emphasize the action in the episode? Does it give us insight into how we are to read and understand the episode? Think about their Homeric correspondence as well. Does the narrative style in the *Ulysses* episode reveal an even stronger link to the parallel episode in the *Odyssey*? Finally, consider the characters as presented in these two episodes, especially the ones narrating them—what more do we learn about Joyce's Dublin inhabitants as a result of their narratives?

Bibliography and Online Resources for "*Ulysses*, Part 2: The Wanderings of Ulysses"

Arnold, Bruce. *The Scandal of Ulysses: The Life and Afterlife of a Twentieth Century Masterpiece.* Dublin: Liffey Press, 2004. Print.

Attridge, Derek, ed. *The Cambridge Companion to James Joyce.* Cambridge: Cambridge University Press, 1990. Print.

Bowen, Zack. "Joyce, Minstrels and Mimes." *James Joyce Quarterly.* 39.4 (2002): 813–19. Print.

Brown, Richard, ed. *A Companion to James Joyce.* Malden, Mass.: Blackwell, 2008. Print.

Burgess, Anthony. *Re Joyce.* New York: W.W. Norton, 2000. Print.

Cecconi, Elisabetta. "'To Let Him Have the Weight of My Tongue': The I-Narrator's Voice in 'Cyclops'." *Joyce in Progress.* Newcastle on Tyne: Cambridge Scholars, 2009. 59–73. Print.

An Chomhairle Leabharlanna. [The Library Council.] "Ask about Ireland." Web. <http://askaboutireland.ie/>

Dowling, Martin W. "'Thought-Tormented Music': Joyce and the Music of Irish Revival." *James Joyce Quarterly.* 45.3 (2008): 437–58. Print.

Ellmann, Richard. *James Joyce.* New York: Oxford University Press, 1982. Print.

———. *Ulysses on the Liffey.* New York: Oxford University Press, 1972. Print.

Fargnoli, A. Nicholas. *Critical Companion to James Joyce: A Literary Companion to His Life and Works.* New York: Facts on File, 2006. Print.

Fordham, Finn. "'Circe' and the Genesis of Multiple Personality." *James Joyce Quarterly.* 45.3 (2008): 507–20. Print.

Gifford, Don and Robert J. Seidman. *Ulysses Annotated: Notes for James Joyce's Ulysses.* Berkeley: University of California Press, 1988. Print.

Gilbert, Stuart. *James Joyce's Ulysses: A Study.* New York: Vintage Books, 1955. Print.

Gillespie, Michael Patrick and A. Nicholas Fargnoli, eds. *Ulysses in Critical Perspective.* Gainesville: University Press of Florida, 2006. Print.

Jauchen, Michael O. "Prostitution, Incest, and Venereal Disease in *Ulysses'* 'Nausicaa'." *New Hibernia Review.* 12.4 (2008): 84–100. Print.

Joyce, James. *Ulysses.* New York: Vintage Books, 1990. Print.

Kenner, Hugh. *Joyce's Voices.* Urbana-Champaign, Ill.: Dalkey Archive Press, 2007. Print.

McCourt, John, ed. *James Joyce in Context.* Cambridge: Cambridge University Press, 2009. Print.

Murphy, Niall. *A Bloomsday Postcard.* Dublin: Lilliput Press, 2004. Print.

Nash, John. *James Joyce and the Act of Reception: Reading, Ireland, Modernism.* Cambridge: Cambridge University Press, 2006. Print.

Norris, Margot, ed. *A Companion to James Joyce's Ulysses.* Boston: Bedford Books, 1998. Print.

Ordway, Scott J. "A Dominant Boylan: Music, Meaning, and Sonata Form in the 'Sirens' Episode of *Ulysses.*" *James Joyce Quarterly.* 45.1 (2007): 85–96. Print.

Ruggieri, Franca, John McCourt, Enrico Terrinoni, and Derek Attridge, eds. *Joyce in Progress.* Newcastle on Tyne: Cambridge Scholars, 2009. Print.

Seidel, Michael. *James Joyce: A Short Introduction.* Malden, Mass.: Blackwell Publishers, 2002. Print.

Senn, Fritz. "Charting Elsewhereness: Erratic Interlocations." *Joyce's 'Wandering Rocks'.* Amsterdam: Rodolpi: 2002. 155–85. Print.

Spinks, Lee. *James Joyce: A Critical Guide.* Edinburgh: Edinburgh University Press, 2009. Print.

Staley, Thomas F. and Bernard Benstock, eds. *Approaches to Ulysses: Ten Essays.* Pittsburgh: University of Pittsburgh Press, 1970. Print.

Tymoczko, Maria. *The Irish Ulysses.* Berkeley: University of California Press, 1994. Print.

Vichnar, David, ed. "Hypermedia Joyce Studies: An Electronic Journal of James Joyce Scholarship." Web. <http://hjs.ff.cuni.cz/main/hjs.php?page=index_page>

ULYSSES, PART 3: THE HOMECOMING

READING TO WRITE

(Note: A great deal of general background information for Ulysses *is provided in the chapter devoted to "The Telemachiad." In the previous chapter on "The Wanderings of Ulysses," a bit about the history behind the publication of the novel is shared. The critical reception of* Ulysses *is discussed below.)*

THE SERIALIZED publication of the episodes in *Ulysses* caused quite a stir. Margaret Anderson was the first to publish the novel episode by episode in her journal, *The Little Review*. She published the first 14, and it was "Nausicaa" that earned her a trial for obscenity. The judge ruled that *Ulysses* was indeed obscene, and Anderson was fined and had to promise not to print any more copies of the novel (or anything else obscene, for that matter). The final four episodes ("Circe," "Eumaeus," "Ithaca," and "Penelope") were never serialized (Ellmann 503). Certainly if the court had found "Nausicaa" obscene, it would have found "Circe" and "Penelope" even more so. Even Ezra Pound, one of Joyce's earliest advocates, had been warning the author that there would be legal problems on the horizon, but Joyce would not be censored. Pound, when Joyce began writing *Ulysses*, acted as an intermediary for him with publishers and touted him as his latest discovery, but midway through the novel, Pound had begun to disapprove, asking

Joyce if "Bloom . . . could not be relegated to the background and Stephen Telemachus brought forward" (Ellmann 459). Pound also thought the new style for each episode was unnecessary (459). Joyce's fellow Irishman George Bernard Shaw and modernist writer Virginia Woolf both found *Ulysses* disgusting. Others in Joyce's circle also expressed confusion about what he was doing and why, while still others found the novel distasteful, including his own wife, Nora. His brother Stanislaus expressed "qualified admiration," offering that it "lacked serenity and warmth," specifically disliking "Circe" and "Penelope" (531). Others, however, praised Joyce for *Ulysses,* calling it a masterpiece, including Sylvia Beach, Valery Larbaud, Stuart Gilbert, Louis Gillet, and Samuel Beckett. Irrespective of how people felt about the novel, though, it certainly caused a stir when it was published in 1922. In the months following publication, many reviews, both laudatory as well as critical, appeared in international newspapers and magazines. Joyce took these very much to heart. He was also gravely disappointed in the fact that *Ulysses* was banned in the United States, and when the ban was lifted by Judge John Woolsey on December 6, 1933, Joyce was elated. Since 1933, *Ulysses* has been read, studied, adapted, and written about (quite extensively). It has become part of the canon of literature in English and has been translated into a long list of languages.

Part 3 of *Ulysses,* "The Homecoming," consists of the three final episodes: "Eumaeus," "Ithaca," and "Penelope." As Bloom makes his way home with his surrogate son Stephen, the two men bond (and Stephen sobers up) over coffee at the cabman's shelter and talk in the kitchen at the Bloom residence (once they manage to get inside). Stephen leaves, and Bloom gets into bed with his drowsing wife, Molly, with whom he recounts his day, leaving out some details, of course, but not before recounting it in his own head after coming back inside from urinating with Stephen and seeing him off. With the exception of the "Eumaeus" episode in which we meet a few new characters, we have only Bloom, Stephen, and Molly in "The Homecoming." This section takes place in the early hours of the morning of Friday, June 17, 1904. The musings of our three main characters in their final hours before bed are among the most open and honest in the entire novel. We see sides to them that were hidden during the day.

As you read "The Homecoming" with writing an essay in mind, one of the themes to make note of is fatherhood or paternity. Bloom/Odysseus is on his way home with Stephen/Telemachus to Molly/Penelope to reclaim his territory. Joyce sets us up with the Homeric parallels but then frustrates the reader (and his own characters) by separating Stephen/Telemachus from his "parents" (he chooses not to spend the night at the Bloom residence), and not resolving the problems in the marriage of Molly and Bloom. Look at the following passage from "Ithaca" as an example of Joyce's playing with the expectations of the reader:

What parallel courses did Bloom and Stephen follow?

Starting united both at normal walking pace from Beresford place they followed in the order named Lower and Middle Gardiner streets and Mountjoy square, west: then, at reduced pace, each bearing left, Gardiner's place by an inadvertence as far as the farther corner of Temple street, north: then at reduced pace with interruptions of halt, bearing right, Temple street, north, as far as Hardwicke place. Approaching, disparate, at relaxed walking pace they crossed both the circus before George's church diametrically, the chord in any circle being less than the arc which it subtends.

Of what did the duumvirate deliberate during their itinerary?

Music, literature, Ireland, Dublin, Paris, friendship, woman, prostitution, diet, the influence of gaslight or the light of arc and glow-lamps on the growth of adjoining paraheliotropic trees, exposed corporation emergency dustbuckets, the Roman catholic church, ecclesiastical celibacy, the Irish nation, jesuit education, careers, the study of medicine, the past day, the male-cent influence of the presabbath, Stephen's collapse.

Did Bloom discover common factors of similarity between their respective like and unlike reactions to experience?

Both were sensitive to artistic impressions musical in preference to plastic or pictorial. Both preferred a continental to an insular manner of life, a cisatlantic to a transatlantic place of residence. Both indurated by early domestic training and an inherited tenacity of heterodox resistance professed their disbelief in many orthodox religious, national, social and ethical doctrines. Both admitted the alternately stimulating and obtunding influence of heterosexual magnetism.

Were their views on some points divergent?

Stephen dissented openly from Bloom's view on the importance of dietary and civic self help while Bloom dissented tacitly from Stephen's views on the eternal affirmation of the spirit of man in literature. Bloom assented covertly to Stephen's rectification of the anachronism involved in assigning the date of the conversion of the Irish nation to christianity [sic] from druidism by Patrick son of Calpornus, son of Potitus, son of Odyssus, sent by pope Celestine I in the year 432 in the reign of Leary to the year 260 or thereabouts in the reign of Cormac MacArt (266 A.D.) suffocated by imperfect deglutition of aliment at Sletty and interred at Rossnaree. The collapse which Bloom ascribed to gastric inanition and certain chemical compounds of varying degrees of adulteration and alcoholic strength, accelerated by mental exertion and the velocity of rapid circular motion in a relaxing atmosphere, Stephen attributed to the reapparition of a matutinal cloud (perceived by both from two different points of observation, Sandycove and Dublin) at first no bigger than a woman's hand.

Was there one point on which their views were equal and negative?

The influence of gaslight or electric light on the growth of adjoining paraheliotropic trees.

Throughout the novel, Joyce offers themes of parenthood. Stephen is fixated on motherhood because of the death of his mother, which brought him back to Ireland, but he is also, we learn, estranged from his father. In "Scylla and Charybdis," Stephen offers that "A father . . . is a necessary evil. . . . Amor matris, subjective and objective genitive, may be the only true thing in life. Paternity may be a legal fiction. Who is the father of any son that any son should love him or he any son?" Bloom focuses on parenthood in general, and while he enjoys being a father to his daughter, Milly, he deeply misses his son. He seems to agree with Stephen about motherhood, and in "Circe" his imagination allows him to become a mother in a surrealistic scene of wish fulfillment. The events leading up to "The Homecoming" give the reader the impression that Bloom will become Stephen's surrogate father and guide him to make the most of himself. In "Eumaeus," we see the first hints that this will not come to pass. When Bloom appreciates the beauty of the Italian language, Stephen immediately shares with him that the speakers were arguing. Bloom tries to offer Stephen helpful advice but Stephen quickly dismisses it each time. Then, in "Ithaca," as we are provided with the catechism lists of their similarities and differences, we begin to see that this partnership is tenuous and will not last.

Joyce frustrates our expectations for these two men. We hope that Stephen will be able to find an adult male with whom he can connect. He certainly needs some good advice, and Deasy is not the person to give it. Buck Mulligan, as Simon Dedalus correctly points out, is a bad influence on Stephen. When we see the abundant kindness in Bloom and the care he shows for Stephen, we anticipate that he might be the man to help the young artist. But they are too different to make a real connection. The two loners in the novel will likely continue as such.

TOPICS AND STRATEGIES
Themes

Many of the themes offered for essay topics in the other chapters on *Ulysses*, motherhood, fatherhood, religion, and lust, for example, would also work in this chapter. With the exception of homecoming, the themes presented here could work for the two previous sections as well. For a short essay, focus on the theme as it plays out in one of the episodes. For a longer research or term paper, you could look at how the theme develops over the course of the entire novel.

Sample Topics:

1. **Homecoming:** Why is the Joycean homecoming so full of nervous tension and anxiety? Why is it so difficult for Bloom to go home?

   As he plans his way home, Bloom worries that Molly will be upset that he is bringing Stephen along with him, which contributes to his nervousness about returning to 7 Eccles Street, but certainly there is more to it than that. Unlike Odysseus, Bloom does not return home to a room filled with his wife's suitors, he has not been gone 20 years, and he did not spend eight years with another woman. Although he collected a letter from a woman with whom he has been secretly corresponding, visited a brothel, and masturbated after being enticed by Gerty MacDowell, he was not, technically, unfaithful to Molly. She, however, has committed adultery with Blazes Boylan, and this is the central reason why Bloom hesitates to return home: He does not want to have to face the fact that his relationship with Molly has changed dramatically.

What evidence do we have for Bloom's reluctance and stalling in returning home? Is his hesitation unconscious, or is he aware of it? Or is it a bit of both? Look in the text for instances when he thinks about going home and what his attitude is about that return. Focus on finding support in "Eumaeus" and "Ithaca," but look for instances elsewhere in which Bloom considers going home and how he feels about that prospect. We are conditioned to think of homecomings as happy, positive events, but Joyce forces us to shift our perception. Why is the homecoming in *Ulysses* so anxious and difficult? What message is Joyce trying to send?

2. **Isolation and loneliness:** What does Joyce communicate to his readers about human connections? Why are the three main characters so isolated?

The connections that the characters, especially the main ones, establish with others in *Ulysses* are fleeting and insignificant for the most part. Bloom, despite his efforts and natural inclination to be kind and compassionate, fails to truly bond with anyone in the novel. He is an outsider in nearly every way—a Hungarian Jew in "The Heart of the Hibernian Metropolis," the son of a man who committed suicide in a country where suicide is taboo, a man who was baptized but is still considered a Jew. Stephen, though Irish through and through, is also isolated and lonely in Dublin, and his associations with other characters in the novel, especially Buck Mulligan and Bloom, are superficial and self-serving. He is most comfortable and at ease with himself in "Aeolus" with the newspaper men, but he does not spend much time in their company. Molly is also an outsider and alone, and her encounter with Boylan on the afternoon of June 16 was merely a physical one, with no emotional connection or intimacy. She recognizes this and begins to plan how she might make the most of the affair, extorting gifts from Boylan in exchange for her sexual favors. Molly's daughter, Milly, has set out on her own to make a life away from her parents, and we know that Molly's relationship with her husband lacks a real emotional bond, due to Bloom's fear of sex after the death of their son, Rudy.

Why does Joyce present such isolated individuals? Is it something in their personalities that causes them to be so alone, or is it a symptom of the modern world? Or is it a bit of both? Do the supporting characters in the novel seem as lonely as the three main characters? What is Joyce trying to communicate to his readers about human connections? Are genuine connections with other human beings possible?

3. **Hope:** Does the novel give the reader hope? Is *Ulysses* ultimately a life-affirming novel?

This essay looks at the desperation, sadness, decay, depravity, and loneliness of Dublin and its characters and then potentially adds a critical "but." Despite all of these, many critics insist that the novel is hopeful and affirmative. The events of June 16, 1904, may have included a funeral, an act of adultery, visiting a brothel, enduring anti-Semitic hatred, recollections of deceased loved ones, gross intoxication, and surreal humiliation, but the novel ends with a repeated and resounding "Yes." June 17 will be a new day, and we have some hints of what will come. Stephen, we learn in "Eumaeus," will soon be leaving his temporary post at Deasy's school. Bloom, on climbing into bed, kisses Molly's bottom even though he knows she has been with Boylan (whom he knows is only one of the other men Molly has been with besides himself), and asks for breakfast in the morning, asserting his role as man of the house. Molly compares Bloom and Boylan, and her husband comes out the winner ("Poldy has more spunk in him yes thatd [sic] be awfully jolly"). And certainly she gets the final words in the novel, remembering the passionate picnic she had with Bloom on Howth where he proposed to her.

Does the novel promise hopeful new beginnings for the three main characters? Will June 17, 1904, mark a fresh start? If so, where in the text do we find evidence for this? Is *Ulysses* ultimately an optimistic work? Despite all the unpleasantness contained in this novel, do we finish with the promise of better days ahead? Is it life affirming? What is Joyce telling us about the human condition? Knowing the importance of the date June 16, 1904, in Joyce's own life, does the fact that he sets his epic on this day further indicate a glimmer of hope?

Character

While there are a few supporting characters in "The Homecoming" worth a closer look, this section of the novel presents the writer with the opportunity to study the three main characters, Bloom, Stephen, and Molly, in depth. You could focus on the character as seen in this part of the novel or how that individual develops from beginning to end, depending on the length requirement of the assignment.

Sample Topics:

1. **Leopold Bloom:** Is Bloom the best hope for Ireland? What does Joyce want us to think about his hero?

Leopold Bloom is Joyce's "wandering Jew," despite the fact that he has been baptized into Catholicism. He is a foreigner despite having been born in Ireland. He is viewed as an artist despite being a salesman. He is alone even when surrounded by fellow Dubliners. He is ridiculed and mocked, not just in the surreal "Circe" by Bella Cohen and by the Citizen in "Cyclops," but by the men in the cab on the way to Glasnevin Cemetery in "Hades," by Buck Mulligan in "Scylla and Charybdis," and by the newsmen in "Aeolus." He is even treated somewhat harshly by Stephen Dedalus in "Eumaeus," when he is chided for admiring the Italian language and offering sensible advice. His wife cuckolds him and does not have enough respect to hide the evidence. But despite being treated so disrespectfully, Bloom shows genuine kindness. He cares for animals (his cat, for example, gets breakfast before he or Molly does), helps a blind man cross the street, attends a funeral service for Paddy

Dignam even though he knows he will not be welcomed, cares for Stephen by following him to the red-light district, paying for the chandelier he broke, sobering him up, and bringing him home. Although he is envious and jealous of Boylan, he does not take it out on Molly, recognizing that her seeking attention from another is partly his fault for refusing to be intimate with her. In spite of his obvious flaws and quirks, Bloom is generous, sympathetic, and kind.

Does Joyce present Bloom as the best hope for Ireland? How does he measure up against the other men in the novel, particularly those who claim to have Ireland's best interests, such as the Citizen, the newsmen, and the men in the cemetery who lament Parnell's death, hoping that he is actually alive and that his casket is filled with stones? The heroes of the past are dead and gone—who will take their place? How does Joyce suggest that Bloom is the new Irish hero?

2. **Molly Bloom:** Is the reader sympathetic to Molly? Has Joyce written a likeable character? Is Molly believable or realistic? What do we learn about Joyce through this character?

Molly Bloom is a 33-year-old singer who was born in Gibraltar to a major in the Irish military and a Spanish, Jewish mother. We learn about her in bits and pieces throughout the novel from Bloom and other men with whom she has apparently had dalliances and through her morning interaction with her husband. It is not until her monologue "Penelope," however, that we get a fuller picture of this woman. Her thoughts are brutally honest, covering topics ranging from her jealousy of other women, her views of sexuality, and her suspicions about her husband and recognition of his quirkiness. She symbolizes Penelope, the deserted wife, but also Calypso, trapped in her marriage, and even Nausicaa the temptress, at least in relation to Boylan. She is an earth goddess, whose warm, "couched body" Bloom desires, but she is beginning to lose her youthful charms as well as her slim figure, as several men suggest (the Citizen goes as far as referring to her as a "fat heap"). She enjoys the mildly pornographic novels Bloom brings her, and while clearly not highly educated, she has street smarts and knows intuitively how the world of men operates and how to manipulate it.

Knowing what we do of Molly, can we say that Joyce has created a likeable character? Are we sympathetic to her situation? Is her stream-of-consciousness monologue realistic? Is she offensive to women? Is she a feminist? Some critics have attacked Joyce for being misogynistic in creating such a character, while others claim Molly as a true feminist, so there is no wrong answer to this question, but you must support your thesis by referring to specific passages in the text. What do we learn about the other characters in *Ulysses* through Molly's monologue? What do we learn about Joyce?

1. **Stephen Dedalus:** How does the reader feel about Stephen by the end of *Ulysses?* What progression have we witnessed in his character?

Stephen Dedalus, the protagonist of *A Portrait of the Artist as a Young Man,* appears again in *Ulysses,* a few years older and having spent some time abroad in Paris. His return to Ireland was necessitated by his mother's ill health, and he has remained there after her death, taking a temporary position at Mr. Deasy's school for boys. Stephen in *Ulysses* is a bit more mature and less pompous than the young artist in *Portrait,* but he certainly still has some emotional problems to address. He is riddled with guilt for not kneeling at his mother's bedside as she was dying, and he is isolated from everyone in the novel, including Buck Mulligan with whom he shares the Martello Tower, his father and siblings who live in absolute poverty because of Simon's alcoholism, and Bloom who tried to befriend him and offer him fatherly advice. He still pontificates, this time in the National Library, about his theories on Shakespeare's *Hamlet* but is perhaps not quite as confident in his ideas as he had been in *Portrait.* Stephen is a complex and complicated young man who continues to struggle to break free from the nets of Irish society: Roman Catholicism and British rule. He searches for his identity and wastes his time and talent on teaching children in whom he has little interest, companions who use him, and prostitutes who happily take his money but offer him nothing substantial in return. Yet, at the end of this novel, we have hints of promise for Stephen Dedalus. He has given his key to Buck Mulligan, recognizing that he will not return to the tower, and he tells Corley that there will be a job in a day or two at Garrett Deasy's school, suggesting that he plans to leave his current position.

What progression do we see in the character of Stephen Dedalus from *Portrait* to *Ulysses* and within *Ulysses* itself? Has he come into his own as an artist? What are Stephen's most apparent personality traits? Are these traits favorable? Does Joyce present a sympathetic character in Stephen? What does Joyce want us to think and feel about this young artist? Do we have the sense that the young man is about to make a positive change for himself? Why or why not?

History and Context

Contextualizing works of literature greatly aids in the reader's understanding. Learning more about the cabman's shelter and the significance of Gibraltar at the turn of the century will help you to appreciate their importance in the novel. Also, since *Ulysses* has such an obvious connection to the *Odyssey,* reading "The Homecoming" from that perspective tells much about how Joyce used the Greek epic and how he staged his own.

Sample Topics:

1. **Cabman's shelter:** What is the significance of the cabman's shelter? What roles does it play in *Ulysses* and in Irish society in the early 1900s?

   The cabman's shelter under the Loop Line Bridge, near Butt Bridge, not far from the Custom House, is the setting for much of the "Eumaeus" episode. The shelter no longer exists today (there is a monument to James Connolly, one of the heroes of the 1916 Easter Uprising near where the shelter used to stand), but similar ones still remain in London, where the shelters have their origin. Joyce, in "Eumaeus," describes Skin-the-Goat Fitzharris's shelter as "an unpretentious wooden structure." The two men sit at the counter and drink "a boiling swimming cup of a choice concoction labelled [sic] coffee" and eat a "rather antediluvian specimen of a bun, or so it seemed." The refreshments available at this shelter clearly leave much to be desired, and the clientele is also rather questionable.

Historically, as we learn in Norman Beattie's "Bloomsday for Cab Drivers," cabman's shelters were the brainchild of Sir George Armstrong, whose servant on a cold January day in 1875 could not find a cab because all the drivers had left their carriages to warm up in a pub. He began a charity to build shelters where cabbies could purchase food and warm up on cold nights. The shelters began in London, with the structures appearing in Dublin some years later.

What is the significance of setting "Eumaeus" at a cabman's shelter? How does it parallel with Eumaeus the swineherd's dwelling in the *Odyssey?* What correspondence does Joyce make here? How does he portray the cabman's shelter and its clientele? What impact does this setting have on the reader? What hints does it provide for the comprehension of the plot?

2. **Gibraltar:** What do we know about Gibraltar at the beginning of the twentieth century? How much do we learn about it from Molly? Is it significant that she was born and raised there?

The territory of Gibraltar is on the southern tip of the Iberian Peninsula and shares a border with Spain. It lies at the confluence of the Mediterranean Sea and the Atlantic Ocean, and the northern coast of Africa is only about 20 miles away, across the Strait of Gibraltar. It is famous for its rock formation, known as the Rock of Gibraltar, which is the distinguishing characteristic of this small territory. Gibraltar has been inhabited since the earliest times, and a skull dating to the same period as Neanderthal Man was found there in 1848. The Phoenicians settled there and used the port city of Carteia as a stopping point before venturing out into the Atlantic. Gibraltar came under Muslim rule in the eighth century and for the next several centuries went back and forth between Spanish and Muslim rulers. Queen Isabella of Spain, during the Spanish Inquisition, made Gibraltar officially part of Spain in 1501. In 1704, English and Dutch marines invaded and captured Gibraltar, and the territory was ceded to Great Britain in 1713 under the Treaty of Utrecht. Unhappy with this decision, the Spanish, sometimes assisted by the French, led attacks to regain control of Gibraltar. They were unsuccessful, and Gibraltar was declared a British colony in 1830. The possession of Gibraltar has been in question ever since, with Spain continually pursuing the case of ceding it back to them. The population of Gibraltar is made up of a blend of mostly British, Spanish, and Portuguese residents.

We know from the text that Molly was born and raised in Gibraltar, that her father was in the Irish military stationed there and that her mother was a Spanish Jew. In "Nausicaa," Bloom recalls stories about Gibraltar that Molly has told him, and then we learn about Gibraltar directly from her own recollections in "Penelope." What does she share about Gibraltar? What do we learn from Molly about the place where she grew up? What significance does being from Gibraltar have on how we perceive Molly? Why did Joyce choose Gibraltar as the birthplace of his heroine?

3. **"The Homecoming" in the Homeric context:** How does Bloom's homecoming in *Ulysses* parallel with its Homeric counterpart? How do we read *Ulysses* in this context?

In the *Odyssey*, Odysseus must return home in disguise for fear of his life. He cannot simply return home and announce himself, as Penelope's suitors would likely murder him. He visits Eumaeus, a loyal swineherd at his estate, for assistance. It is there that he meets his son Telemachus, and the two venture on to the house. Odysseus, disguised as a beggar, joins the competition to see who can string Odysseus's bow, and only he can. He locks the suitors in the room and murders them while Penelope sleeps. Odysseus slowly reveals himself to Penelope, who is reluctant to accept him as her husband until he correctly responds to a question about their bed to which only they know the answer. They then retire to that bed, lovingly reunited.

How does Bloom's homecoming differ from that of Odysseus? Why does Bloom prolong his return home? Does he overcome the suitors vying for Molly's attention? Does Molly present any "tests" for her husband in order for him to join her in bed? Do the Blooms lovingly reunite? What differences are apparent in these two homecomings? What similarities do we see? How do these similarities and differences impact our reading and understanding of the final three episodes of *Ulysses*?

Philosophy and Ideas

Some of the ideas presented in "The Homecoming" are ones that Joyce has been exploring through his characters throughout the entire novel, such as the notion of Bloom as Everyman and the instinctive nature of human sexuality, but a new one, astrology and astronomy, is also introduced.

Sample Topics:

1. **Astrology and astronomy:** What is the role of astrology and astronomy? Do they add an additional dimension to the narrative? Do they tell us more about the characters?

Although we never get Bloom's exact birth date, we learn those of Molly, Stephen, Milly, and Rudy, which means we also know their astrological signs. Molly, born on September 8, is, ironically, Virgo, the virgin. Stephen's sign (assuming, as many critics do, that he shares a birth date with the author) is Aquarius, the water bearer, ironic also since he hates bathing. Milly is a Gemini, the twins, and she is seen as a sort of twin for her mother, Molly. Rudy was a Capricorn, the mountain goat. Stephen, in "Scylla and Charybdis," thinks about the implications of the positions of the stars and planets when he was born: "Read the skies. . . . Where's your configuration?" In "Oxen of the Sun," we learn that "the equine portent grows again . . . over the house of Virgo," meaning the constellation Pegasus, which Gifford tells us is "symbolic of poetic inspiration," is visible above the horizon (433). We then find astrology and astronomy mentioned extensively in "Ithaca," when Stephen and Bloom go outside to relieve themselves before Stephen departs. Bloom shows the "various constellations" to his companion and explains their significance.

What significance do Bloom's explanations have for the reader? What is their impact on the novel as a whole? What importance do the characters' astrological signs have? Do astrology and astronomy add an additional dimension to the characters and the overall narrative? Do we put much faith in these heavenly symbols? Does Joyce?

2. **Bloom as Everyman:** Is Leopold Bloom a literary reincarnation of Everyman? If so, how? What makes him a universal figure?

The fifteenth-century morality play *The Summoning of Everyman,* frequently referred to simply as *Everyman,* features the original Everyman, an allegorical character who symbolizes all of mankind. The play centers on the conflict between good and evil, and all the characters are symbolic, representing an abstract notion such as beauty, discretion, and good deeds. Writers since that time have used the idea of Everyman in their works, and this character has come to represent someone with whom the reader can identify. Everyman usually finds him- or herself in unusual circumstances, often out of his or her control, and must act or react based on that situation. Many critics have suggested that Joyce's Leopold Bloom is a modern version of this character. He surely finds himself in extraordinary conditions at many points during his long day, and he negotiates them as well as he might. He has his failings, of course, but some of us may also be able to recognize ourselves in those as well. His generosity and kindness in the face of adversity are his overwhelming characteristics, and the reader readily recognizes this.

Is Bloom a modern Everyman? What personality traits does he possess that make him Everyman? Although the modern Everyman need not be a moralizing character, is Bloom? How or how not? Joyce used *Everyman* as one of the styles he imitated in "Oxen of the Sun," so it is not coincidental that Bloom, in "Ithaca," compares himself to "Everyman or Noman" (what Odysseus called himself with the Cyclops in the *Odyssey*). What did Joyce intend with this comparison? Do we see ourselves in this unlikely hero?

3. **Sexuality and human drives:** What does Joyce communicate to his readers about human sexuality? What is his depiction of sexuality?

The longest episode in *Ulysses* takes place in a brothel. Bloom masturbates as Gerty MacDowell reveals herself to him. Molly commits adultery with Blazes Boylan. The barmaids in the Ormond Hotel, Miss Douce and Miss Kennedy, tease and tempt the men who patronize the saloon. The entire novel is brimming with sexuality and sexual imagery, both actual and contemplated or imagined. The presentation of sexuality runs the gamut from Molly's recollection of Bloom's passionate marriage proposal on Howth in "Penelope" to the cataloging of Bloom's fetishes in "Circe." Ironically, Joyce found it inappropriate to discuss sexuality in mixed company, and "any discussion of a phallic symbol was taboo in the presence of ladies" (Ellmann 567). Yet he gave some of the most scandalously sexual thoughts to his heroine Molly and made Bella Cohen into a dominatrix. Extramarital affairs and prostitution seem tame compared with some of the other elements in this novel, including voyeurism, transvestism, and coprophilia (sexual arousal involving feces).

What impression does the reader get of human sexuality as portrayed in *Ulysses?* What do Bloom's fetishes reveal to the reader about his personality? Do we have the impression that perhaps his extreme fantasies are the result of a nonexistent sex life with his wife? We are presented most of the fetishes in "Circe"—do we question their authenticity as a result? What do we make of Joyce's depiction of Molly's sexuality? Is she what we would consider "normal" in the early 1900s? Is she "normal" by today's standards? What is Joyce trying to communicate to the reader in his depiction of sexuality?

Form and Genre

Ezra Pound disapproved of Joyce's experimenting with different forms of the narrative in each new episode of *Ulysses,* but they certainly provide many opportunities for strong essay topics. The final three episodes are no exception.

Sample Topics:

1. **"Eumaeus" and "old narrative":** What is "old narrative"? How does this episode differ from the "young narrative" of "Telemachus" and the "mature narrative" of "Calypso"?

The technique Joyce provides in the schema published by Gilbert for the episode "Eumaeus," which begins part 3, reads: "The Homecoming," is "narrative (old)." This style contrasts with the "narrative (young)" of "Telemachus," which begins part 1, "The Telemachiad," and the "narrative (mature)" of "Calypso," which begins part 2, "The Wanderings of Ulysses." The young, joking, sophomoric style of "Telemachus" develops into the more mature, thoughtful, self-aware style of "Calypso" and then finally into the old, tired, and drawn-out style of "Eumaeus." This progression follows a human's development but also, perhaps, the trajectory of the day. "Eumaeus" takes place at one o'clock in the morning on June 17, at the end of a very long day. Stephen is drunk and tired, and Bloom is simply tired. Add to the mix the sailor W. B. Murphy and his tales of wandering, it makes for a sluggish episode. The sentences are extremely long (though punctuation is still the norm here, unlike in "Penelope"), and some are unfinished, leaving the reader wondering what the narrator or speaker was going to say. The language is also a bit dated, though not nearly as dated as "Oxen of the Sun," and seems appropriate to the technique of old narrative.

Examine closely the narrative technique of "Eumaeus" and look for passages that effectively represent this old style. Look at sentence length, unfinished thoughts, and old-fashioned words, phrases, and idioms that mark this episode as "old." Then, look for the corresponding markers in "Telemachus" and "Calypso" that reveal those narratives to be young and mature, respectively. What differences among the three do you see? Do these techniques help the reader to understand better what is happening in the episode? What additional layer of meaning do they provide for the episode?

2. **"Ithaca" and catechism:** What impact does presenting this episode in the form of a catechism have on the reader? Why did Joyce employ this technique?

Joyce makes use of the "catechism (impersonal)" in the "Ithaca" episode (as contrasted with the "catechism (personal)" in "Nestor," in which Stephen and Mr. Deasy ask questions that can only be answered if the answer is already known). Catechism, simply defined, is the method of testing knowledge, usually religious knowledge, in the form of a series of questions and answers. In the Roman Catholic Church, parents must know the catechism to have their child baptized, and then a young person must know the catechism to be confirmed into the church, usually as a teenager. This is a matter of memorization and rote learning, essentially. There is a standardized question as well as a standardized answer. The catechism is meant to be an objective presentation of the facts about the church and provides an objective way of testing someone's knowledge and preparedness for the sacrament (baptism or confirmation) he or she is about to receive.

The catechism form and technique in "Ithaca" borrows from Roman Catholicism, but the subjects for this series of question and answers are broad and secular for the most part. The language is also academic and formal, keeping in line with the church's catechism. In addition, the omniscient narrator of this episode takes a seemingly objective tone throughout, but it seems quite clear that sympathies lie with Bloom. The technique here, unlike in a religious catechism, is frequently humorous and ironic, while the style generally otherwise adopts a neutral, serious tone.

What impact does Joyce's use of this technique have on the reader of "Ithaca"? How do readers who did not grow up following Roman Catholicism (or a branch of Christianity that uses catechism) understand this episode? Is it purposely distancing, no matter what the reader's religious background? Why does Joyce put the distance between the reader and the text? Is it symbolic? As we make our way through *Ulysses,* one of the hopes we potentially develop is to see Stephen make a meaningful connection with someone (indeed, this is a lingering hope from *Portrait*), and as we progress through "Circe" and "Eumaeus," we begin to expect that he may find this connection with Bloom. Does the impersonal, detached style of "Ithaca" begin to show us that this will not come to pass? What was Joyce's intention in using this seemingly objective, impersonal technique?

3. **"Penelope" and "female monologue":** Does "Penelope" accurately and fairly represent the musings of a woman? What do we learn about Molly? What do we learn about Joyce?

The eight sentences of "Penelope," each marked with the beginning of a new paragraph, are written in a sleepy, stream-of-consciousness narrative in which Molly Bloom leaps from topic to topic through word association. It is the early hours of the morning of June 17, 1904, and although Joyce does not provide a time in his schema, we know it is probably about three o'clock since "Ithaca" takes place at two. Joyce shared that "*Penelope* is the clou of the book. . . . Though probably more obscene than any preceding episode it seems to me to be perfectly sane full amoral fertililisable [sic] untrustworthy engaging shrewd limited prudent indifferent *Weib*" (Ellmann 501–02). If "Penelope" is indeed the critical point of interest or central idea in the book, we must understand that to indicate that the episode is more than the random, and sometimes quite obscene, drowsy musings of Molly Bloom. What makes this the *clou* of the novel?

In "Penelope," Joyce, through Molly, provides us insight not only into her thoughts and feelings but also her perceptions of the world around her. Molly may be relatively simple, but she understands her husband, whom she affectionately calls Poldy, better than anyone else. There is love in her expression, despite her occasional jibes. She reveals her jealousy of other women with whom she compares herself, indicating a lack of self-confidence underneath the bravado. She certainly does not hide her sexuality from the reader, and we get more details about her tryst with Blazes Boylan than we need to know, but she also reveals a good deal of vulnerability when it comes to intimacy. She knows that Boylan will not marry her and resents him for being so rough and familiar with her. She wants romance, which is missing from her life despite this new affair with her manager. The thoughts that finish her soliloquy return to her husband, Bloom, and her overwhelmingly positive memory of his marriage proposal to her, ending the novel on the most affirming word in the English language: "Yes."

Does "Penelope" accurately represent the thought processes of a woman living in Catholic Dublin in 1904? Is the stream-of-consciousness prose comprehensible? Why did Joyce leave out punctuation and apostrophes? Does the narrative capture the drowsy reflections we have before sleep? Why does Joyce apply this narrative technique to Molly? What does it tell the reader about her? What might it tell us about Joyce's opinion about women? Is the narrative fair to women?

Language, Symbols, and Imagery

The symbols and imagery present in "The Homecoming" reinforce the character sketches Joyce had been developing over the course of the novel. Language is used precisely in these episodes, particularly the final word with which Joyce ends his epic.

Sample Topics:

1. **Keys/keylessness:** How does the fact that Bloom and Stephen are both keyless symbolize their situation? What role do keys play in the novel?

In "Telemachus," the first mention of keys comes when "a voice," which we later know is Haines the Englishman, asks "Have you the key?" He and Mulligan want to open the door to let out the smell of burning breakfast (not coincidentally, Bloom also burns his morning meal). The key is in the lock. Then, after breakfast, Mulligan asks Stephen again if he has the key, which he does. Mulligan then requests the same key to "keep my chemise flat" from blowing away in the wind. Stephen later recognizes, "I will not sleep here tonight. Home also I cannot go." From the first episode, he knows that returning to the tower is not an option, and divesting himself of the key cinches that decision. Bloom is also keyless, but by accident. (However, some critics suggest that he has left his keys at home on purpose, as an excuse to either return and surprise the lovers, or to forfeit his right to the home and, consequently, his wife.) He misses his keys at several points during the day, first in "Calypso," when he goes out to get his breakfast, and then in "Aeolus," when he puts the soap back in the back pocket of his trousers and remembers that his keys ought to be there as well. He ponders the possibility of returning home to get them: "I could go home still: tram: something I forgot. Just to see before dressing. No." Then again in "Ithaca," Bloom "inserted his hand mechanically into the back pocket of his trousers to obtain his latchkey," but it was in "the corresponding pocket of the trousers he had worn on the day but one preceding."

What is the significance of Stephen and Bloom's keylessness? Is there a difference in how we perceive their keylessness? Stephen consciously gave his away, while Bloom, because he had to wear black for Paddy Dignam's funeral, put on the wrong trousers, the ones without his key. What does a key symbolize? What does the lack of a key mean for these men? What role do keys play in the novel?

2. **Numbers:** How does Joyce use numbers in *Ulysses?* How are the numbers symbolic?

Numbers appear with great regularity in the last two episodes of *Ulysses,* particularly the numbers three, eight, and nine. In "Ithaca," Bloom notices the "Four polygonal fragments of two lacerated scarlet betting tickets, numbered 8 87, 8 86." The number eight, which symbolizes infinity when on its side or recumbent, is also the number symbolizing perfection, the earth, and prosperity. It is the number Joyce associates with

Molly, who is recumbent at the beginning and end of *Ulysses,* the only times we hear and see her in person, shaped like the recumbent eight, ∞. It is no coincidence that Bloom presents Molly with eight poppies, because her birthday is the eighth of September, or that there are eight sentences in the episode. Threes are also prevalent, as are their square, nines. Three, as Joyce would have known, is central to many world religions, including Christianity, with the Holy Trinity of Father, Son, and Holy Spirit. The shamrock, which legend tells us was used by Saint Patrick, the patron of Ireland, to explain the Trinity, has three leaves. There are three main characters in *Ulysses,* a parody of the Trinity. Bloom was baptized three times, we learn in "Ithaca," and we are also told that in three days, on the summer solstice, the sunrise will occur at "3:33 a.m." Bloom, not to be outsymbolized by Christianity, reminds the reader that Judaism also places importance on the number three, mentioning the "Three seekers of the pure truth, Moses of Egypt, Moses Maimonides, . . . and Moses Mendelssohn."

Where else in "The Homecoming" do we see numbers? Where in the rest of *Ulysses* do we find numbers? How does Joyce use them symbolically? Do these numbers resonate with today's readers? Are they yet another puzzle a reader must try to solve in order to make the most of the novel? How does numerology fit into the Joycean world of symbolism? What role do numbers play in *Ulysses?*

3. **Yes:** Why does Joyce use the most affirmative word in the English language to end his novel? What impact does the final "yes" have on the reader? On the understanding of *Ulysses?*

Molly Bloom begins her monologue with the word *yes.* This word, the most positive in the English language, is found in her soliloquy more than 80 times. She sometimes uses it to affirm her thoughts or assumptions, as seen in the first "yes": "Yes because he never did a thing like that before as ask me to get his breakfast in bed with a couple of eggs." She also uses it to confirm her sexual arousal: "Poldy has more spunk in him yes thatd be awfully jolly." Finally, she uses it to remember the sexual excitement she caused for the men with whom she has been intimate, blending their arousal with her own, as seen when she describes her encounter with Mulvey in Gibraltar: "yes O yes I pulled him off into my handkerchief pretending not to be excited but I opened my legs I wouldnt let him touch me inside my petticoat I had a skirt opening up the side I tortured the life out of him." Finally, her series of yesses at the conclusion of her soliloquy and the novel signal not only sexual arousal but also utter affirmation, as they occur during an intimate moment shared by Molly and Bloom in which they kiss passionately and he proposes marriage. Her "yes" is an acceptance of his offer, but it also indicates arousal and excitement resulting from the memory of that moment.

What is the overall effect of all these affirmatives? Why does Joyce use so many yesses in Molly's monologue? How do they impact the momentum and progression of the narrative? Do they work as punctuation, in a sense? Do they provide transition from one thought to the next? With more than 80 yesses in the episode, this essay requires a writer to be meticulous in tracking Joyce's use of the word and its purpose. Is there a pattern to the yesses? What is the linguistic function of this word in "Penelope"?

Compare and Contrast Essays

A writer has many choices with compare and contrast essays addressing "The Homecoming" episodes. He or she may compare Bloom and Stephen, an episode in this section with one from another section, or the characters in these episodes with their *Odyssey* counterparts. Or you could explore the possibilities presented in the following topic discussions, looking at Bloom and his competition, Molly and hers, or the text and its film adaptations.

Sample Topics:

1. **Molly and Gerty:** How does Molly compare with Gerty? What do they imagine about each other? How does Bloom compare them?

Molly Bloom, Leopold's wife of 16 years, is 33 years old. She is a singer by profession, has one daughter, aged 15, and would have had an 11-year-old son, Rudy, had he not died soon after he was born. She is from Gibraltar but identifies herself as fully Irish. She is described as being voluptuous, and she seems comfortable with her body and her sexuality. She is straightforward and does not mince words in her monologue, or with her husband when they have a conversation in "Calypso": "O rocks! . . . Tell us in plain words!" She can be sharp with Bloom, ordering him around and making demands. Her affair with Blazes Boylan, her concert producer, shows both her desperate need for male attention as well as her lack of respect for her marriage vows.

Gerty MacDowell, who never reveals her exact age but shares that she has the "fluttering hopes and fears of sweet seventeen," is a stereotypical young girl of her day. She is immersed in the dreamy and idealistic notions of a teenager at the turn of the century: fashion, romance, a happy marriage to a "manly man with a strong quiet face." Gerty is described as a "fair specimen of winsome Irish girlhood," whose eyes are "of the bluest of Irish blue" and whose "crowning glory was her wealth of wonderful hair." She is slim, and, we learn halfway through the "Nausicaa" episode when Bloom takes over the narration, physically disabled. When she sees that Bloom is watching her, she imagines that he is sad and lonely and decides to entice him, revealing her upper thigh and undergarments. After he climaxes, she chastises him: "A fair, unsullied soul had called to him and, wretch that he was, how had he answered? An utter cad he had been." She is aware of her sexuality and is already using it as a way of gaining power. In writing an essay on this topic, you will want to look at the ways in which Molly and Gerty are similar—both use their sexuality to control the men in their lives—and the ways they are different—Molly benefits, albeit slightly, from the use of her sexuality, while Gerty does not. Molly understands Bloom for the person he really is, while Gerty has only a fantasy image of him. Both women long for true romance, however, and are unfulfilled. Gerty wants a man who will "take her in his sheltering arms, strain her to him in all the strength of his deep passionate nature and comfort her with a long long kiss. It would be like heaven." Molly wants something similar: "why cant you kiss a man without going and marrying him first you sometimes love to wildly when you feel that way so nice all over you you cant help yourself I wish some man or other would take me sometime when hes there and kiss me in his arms theres nothing like a kiss long and hot down to your soul almost paralyses you." Look at some of the personality traits of these two women and how Bloom compares them. What do they imagine about each other? How does Joyce set up this comparison?

2. **Bloom and Boylan:** What are the similarities and differences between Bloom and his rival Boylan? How do they compare? How does Joyce present them? Are they opposites or near opposites?

Leopold Bloom is sensitive, generous, and kind for the most part. He is a businessman, selling advertisements in the newspaper, and seems to have a great deal of free time on his hands. He is intelligent but is also a bit naïve. He loves his wife, so much that he allows her to bully him, and is aware of the affair she is beginning with Boylan. He chooses not to confront her about this but knows he has every right to divorce her. He misses his daughter, Milly, and deceased son, Rudy. Bloom is Hungarian Jewish by ancestry but Irish by birth and Roman Catholic by baptism, though he is seen as Jewish by his companions. He is an isolated outsider and the unlikely hero of Joyce's novel.

Blazes Boylan is gregarious, well liked, and seems to be a bit of a personality in Dublin. He is a concert producer, singer, and manages a fighter. We do not see enough of Boylan to get a sense of his intellect, but we do get the impression that he is crafty and clever. He is a ladies' man, courting not only Molly but also flirting with the shop girl at Thornton's and the barmaids at the Ormond Hotel. He is admired by men as well, and Bloom's companions on the way to Glasnevin Cemetery go out of their way to say hello and be noticed by him, while Bloom thinks Boylan is the "worst man in Dublin." Even Milly, Bloom's daughter, asks to give Boylan her best regards in the letter she sends her father. But Bloom is not the only one who sees through Boylan's façade; Molly also does, as we learn in "Penelope." She does not like the way he undressed casually in front of her and then slapped her on the bottom as he was leaving. She knows her affair with Boylan will not amount to anything, so she decides to make the most out of it while she can and demand gifts from him.

Joyce sets Bloom and Boylan up as opposites and rivals for Molly's attention, and certainly they are very different, but are there ways in which the two are similar? How does Bloom compare himself with Boylan? Does Boylan ever take Bloom into account as a rival? What impression of the two do we get from Molly? How do they measure up in her eyes?

3. **Text with films:** How do the film adaptations stand up to the text? What differences and similarities are there? Are the adaptations faithful portrayals of the novel?

There are many options with this essay choice. You could compare the 1967 film *Ulysses*—directed by Joseph Strick and starring Milo O'Shea as Bloom, Barbara Jefford as Molly, and Maurice Roeves as Stephen—with the novel. Or, you could compare the 2004 film *Bloom*—starring Stephen Rea as Bloom, Angeline Ball as Molly, and Hugh O'Conor as Stephen—with the novel. Or, you could compare the films to each other. All three options provide excellent possibilities for the writer.

Joseph Strick's 1967 film, *Ulysses,* takes some liberties in adapting Joyce's text to the screen. For starters, it is set in the 1960s instead of 1904, with the characters not in period costumes. There are cars, instead of horse and carriages, and other modern conveniences. Milo O'Shea's version of Bloom is comical, bordering on slapstick. Barbara Jefford's Molly seems even more acerbic than Molly in the novel, and Maurice Roeves plays an ever darker, more brooding Stephen. The director took these characters and further emphasized these aspects of their personalities. He chooses to omit the "Eumaeus" episode and combines "Cyclops" and "The Sirens" into one scene, with the emphasis on Bloom's interaction with the Citizen. "Ithaca" is filmed as a voiceover to what is happening onscreen with Stephen and Bloom, and "Penelope" is also a voiceover, as we see Molly in bed and get glimpses of the things that run through her head, memories of the day she had and days longer ago.

The 2004 film *Bloom*, directed by Sean Walsh, is more faithful to Joyce's original work, setting his film in 1904 and using period costumes and props. One major difference, however, is that Walsh follows a clock order rather than presenting the first three episodes of "The Telemachiad" and then moving into "The Wanderings of Ulysses." Instead, he moves back and forth between Stephen and Bloom, based on the time their morning events occurred. He omits "The Sirens" episode, and although we see some of the action of "Ithaca," there is no voiceover to accompany it. The other major difference in Walsh's adaptation is that he begins and ends with Molly's soliloquy, giving the first part of it to open his film and the second half as the conclusion. Angeline Ball, who plays Molly, speaks much of the monologue into the camera, directly addressing the audience. Ball's Molly is much softer, much more sensitive than Jefford's, though still as matter-of-fact as she is in the novel. Stephen Rea's Bloom, though still comic, is not a jester and is more multidimensional than O'Shea's. O'Conor's Stephen seems nearly perfect—he is still brooding but also has the dry humor of Stephen in the novel.

To write this essay, look closely at the ways in which the two films are similar and how they differ. You might focus on one episode, for example, "Circe." The 1967 film was limited slightly by social norms and notions of acceptability. The 2004 version, however, is very graphic, in line with the episode in the novel, and reveals the extent of Bloom's sado-masochistic vision. Strick's "Circe" seems a bit campy, while Walsh's has a dark side, especially with Bloom's interactions with Bella/Bello. Both directors make the most of elaborate staging and costuming, however, emphasizing the theatrical elements of the episode. As you plan your essay, think about the choices a director is forced to make. Strick and Walsh could not have possibly included all of *Ulysses* in their films. Why did they make the decisions they did? What was the artistic reason for those decisions? Did any decisions detract from the film? What would you, as director of the next film adaptation of *Ulysses,* do differently? Would your cast be different? What would you borrow from these earlier versions?

Bibliography and Online Resources for "*Ulysses,* Part 3: The Homecoming"

Arnold, Bruce. *The Scandal of Ulysses: The Life and Afterlife of a Twentieth Century Masterpiece.* Dublin: Liffey Press, 2004. Print.

Attridge, Derek, ed. *The Cambridge Companion to James Joyce.* Cambridge: Cambridge University Press, 1990. Print.

Beattie, Normal. "Bloomsday for Cab Drivers." Web. <http://www.taxi-library. org/bloomsday/bl1.htm>

Brown, Richard. "Molly's Gibraltar: The Other Location in Joyce's *Ulysses.*" *A Companion to James Joyce.* Malden, Mass.: Blackwell, 2008. 157–73. Print.

Brown, Richard, ed. *A Companion to James Joyce.* Malden, Mass.: Blackwell, 2008. Print.

Burgess, Anthony. *Re Joyce.* New York: W.W. Norton, 2000. Print.

An Chomhairle Leabharlanna. [The Library Council.] "Ask about Ireland." Web. <http://askaboutireland.ie/>

Di Battista, Maria. "*Ulysses's* Unanswered Questions." *Modernism/Modernity.* 15.2 (2008): 265–75. Print.

Ellmann, Richard. *James Joyce.* New York: Oxford University Press, 1982. Print.

———. *Ulysses on the Liffey.* New York: Oxford University Press, 1972. Print.

Fargnoli, A. Nicholas. *Critical Companion to James Joyce: A Literary Companion to His Life and Works.* New York: Facts on File, 2006. Print.

Gifford, Don and Robert J. Seidman. *Ulysses Annotated: Notes for James Joyce's Ulysses.* Berkeley: University of California Press, 1988. Print.

Gilbert, Stuart. *James Joyce's Ulysses: A Study.* New York: Vintage Books, 1955. Print.

Gillespie, Michael Patrick and A. Nicholas Fargnoli, eds. *Ulysses in Critical Perspective.* Gainesville: University Press of Florida, 2006. Print.

Hegglund, John. "Hard Facts and Fluid Spaces: 'Ithaca' and the Imperial Archive." *Joyce, Imperialism, and Postcolonialism.* Syracuse, N.Y., N.Y.: Syracuse, N.Y. University Press, 2008. 58–74. Print.

Joyce, James. *Ulysses.* New York: Vintage Books, 1990. Print.

Kenner, Hugh. *Joyce's Voices.* Urbana-Champaign, Ill.: Dalkey Archive Press, 2007. Print.

McCourt, John, ed. *James Joyce in Context.* Cambridge: Cambridge University Press, 2009. Print.

Murphy, Niall. *A Bloomsday Postcard.* Dublin: Lilliput Press, 2004. Print.

Nash, John. *James Joyce and the Act of Reception: Reading, Ireland, Modernism.* Cambridge: Cambridge University Press, 2006. Print.

Norris, Margot, ed. *A Companion to James Joyce's Ulysses.* Boston: Bedford Books, 1998. Print.

Ruggieri, Franca, John McCourt, Enrico Terrinoni, and Derek Attridge, eds. *Joyce in Progress.* Newcastle on Tyne: Cambridge Scholars, 2009. Print.

Seidel, Michael. *James Joyce: A Short Introduction.* Malden, Mass.: Blackwell Publishers, 2002. Print.

Spinks, Lee. *James Joyce: A Critical Guide.* Edinburgh: Edinburgh University Press, 2009. Print.

Staley, Thomas F. and Bernard Benstock, eds. *Approaches to Ulysses: Ten Essays.* Pittsburgh: University of Pittsburgh Press, 1970. Print.

Tymoczko, Maria. *The Irish Ulysses.* Berkeley: University of California Press, 1994. Print.

Vichnar, David, ed. "Hypermedia Joyce Studies: An Electronic Journal of James Joyce Scholarship." Web. <http://hjs.ff.cuni.cz/main/hjs.php?page=index_page>

INDEX

Characters in literary works are indexed by first name (if any), followed by the name of the work in parentheses.